Writing in the Devil's Tongue

Writing in the Devil's Tongue

A HISTORY OF ENGLISH COMPOSITION IN CHINA

XIAOYE YOU

Southern Illinois University Press
Carbondale

13   12   11   10   4   3   2   1

Publication was supported by a subvention from the
College of the Liberal Arts, Penn State University.

Library of Congress Cataloging-in-Publication Data
You, Xiaoye, 1974–
Writing in the devil's tongue : a history of English
composition in China / Xiaoye You.
      p. cm.
Includes bibliographical references and index.
ISBN-13: 978-0-8093-2930-4 (pbk. : alk. paper)
ISBN-10: 0-8093-2930-1 (pbk. : alk. paper)
1. English language—Study and teaching—Chinese
speakers. 2. English language—Rhetoric—Study
and teaching—China. 3. Report writing—Study and
teaching—China. 4. Language and culture—China.
I. Title.
PE1130.C4Y68 2010
428.0071′0951—dc22   2009016922

In memory of
Lynn Walters, 1966–1993

We will not strive to put before you a model of English writing; our style will often be uncouth and our sentences ungrammatical, but we will try to use the *great* English language to express the thoughts that come into our minds.

—"Greeting," *St. John's Echo*, 1890

CONTENTS

PREFACE

A sense of complacency, if not outright chauvinism, is tangible these days in certain parts of American composition studies. Sensational statements of one kind or another—"Composition Studies Saves the World!"; "Globalizing Composition"; "Transnationalizing/Globalizing Rhetoric and Composition Studies"; and so forth—reveal not only tremendous disciplinary pride but also compositionists' confidence in what the discipline can do: namely, rescue the troubled world at large.[1] And why shouldn't we be confident about what the discipline can achieve? After all, we have gained a better understanding of our students, students of diverse linguistic, cultural, racial, sexual, and class backgrounds who have made such a strong presence in American universities since the 1960s; and we have developed effective pedagogical approaches to address those students' needs. Projecting this national experience to the rest of the globe, we naturally become optimistic. Indeed, the rest of the world is also hopeful now, looking to American composition studies for standards of English writing practices and proven pedagogies.

As the teaching of composition is increasingly connected to global politico-economic dynamics, our disciplinary effort to lift composition out of narrow nation-state bounds is the right direction to go. However, American composition scholars do not seem fully cognizant of the geopolitical differences and stakes involved in the teaching of English writing. For one thing, while English has been taught as the native language, the official language, or a second language in the United States, it is typically taught as a foreign language in the majority of nations in the world. A different name for English entails a different history of the language in a particular country. A different name for English entails a whole different constellation of values and practices in teaching English writing.

I come from China, where English has been long ridiculed as a "foreign devil's tongue." The expression captures at once colonialism, Chinese nationalism, and Occidentalism, all of which characterize the history of English in the country. The language was forced upon the Chinese by Western colonial powers in the nineteenth century, so ever since, the Chinese have drawn a clear line between native Chinese and Western languages by calling the latter "foreign devils' tongues." They did this even though they used the devils' tongues unapologetically to advance their own nationalist and personal agendas. In fact, this derogatory, racialized expression was a time-honored Chinese rhetorical strategy. Two thousand and five hundred years ago, Confucius famously admonished his disciples not to probe the other world where devils, or spirits of the deceased, dwelled. Demonizing Westerners as *yangguizi* (foreign devils), the Chinese not only mystified the "barbarians" coming from outside the Middle Kingdom but also warned their countrymen, in their increased interaction with the West, to guard against foreign products and influences that would endanger their Chinese essence.

A distinct history of English inevitably carries forth a distinct set of values and practices associated with English teaching. When I first arrived in the United States to work toward my doctoral degree, I was surprised that writing was studied in a discipline called composition studies. I had to take courses such as "classical [Western] rhetoric," "modern [Anglo-American] rhetoric," "postmodern [Western] rhetoric," "cultural studies," and "post critical qualitative methods." In China, I studied writing in literacy classes before and during college and in applied linguistics in graduate school. Shuttling between English-teaching communities in both countries, I further found that they shared so much, but at the same time so little, in teaching writing. For example, teachers in both countries emphasize topic sentences, logical arrangement and paragraph development, and correct grammar in student writing. But they differ about what English writing can do in students' lives, what good writing is, how to teach and assess writing, how to train writing teachers, and many other matters. How can American composition scholars make claims about saving the world or globalizing the discipline while other English-teaching communities do not share with them many fundamental values and practices in teaching writing?

This book intends to draw both American and Chinese communities' attention to values and practices that they share but also those that they do not share. By understanding our common and our different grounds, we may not be able to save the world, but we may achieve goals that matter to individual English-teaching communities instead of goals that only matter to American composition studies. I contend that this aim should be the global vision of composition studies, a discipline that, while residing in the United States, also has played (and continues to play) a crucial role in the world of English teaching and learning. The book has been written for both composition teachers in the United States and English teachers in the rest of the world. The purpose is to bring the parties together to generate productive conversations. I am privileged to have the opportunity of building such a transnational bridge.

Such a bridge, which is long overdue, could not have been built without help. The project was first conceived in the spring of 2001: I took a graduate seminar on second language writing with Tony Silva at Purdue University and under his guidance became discontented with its exclusive focus on the post–World War II U.S. context. Ensuing conversations with Braj Kachru, Margie Berns, and Yichun Liu convinced me that it was my responsibility to rewrite the modern history of second language writing. In particular, I wanted to tell a Chinese story about how the Chinese encountered and transformed English composition. Once the project took off, I benefited from Margie Berns, April Ginther, Paul Kei Matsuda, Thomas Rickert, Tony Silva, and Patricia Sullivan, all of whom offered constructive criticisms of my dissertation writing.

Since coming to Penn State, I have received additional generous collegial support, which enabled me to bring the project to fruition. I am grateful to Dean Susan Welch, to my former English Department head, Robert Caserio, and to my Penn State colleagues Keith Gilyard and Richard Doyle for early encouragement and for believing in the significance of my project. Many others, most notably Suresh Canagarajah, Arabella Lyon, LuMing Mao, Carolyn Matalene, Stephen Schneider, Jack Selzer, Jan Swearingen, and Hui Wu, offered extremely helpful criticisms on the book manuscript. A number of colleagues also read parts of the manuscript with care: Jonathan Benda, Kevin Eric Depew, Jenny Edbauer, Lin Gui, Julia Kasdorf, Xing (Lucy) Lu, Gretchen Nauman, and Stuart Selber. Students in my graduate seminar on the "Theory and the Teaching of Writing" in fall 2007 also commented on the manuscript: Kim Andrews, Gabriel Ford, David Green, Tyler Hollett, Paul Johnston, William Lee, Rebecca Wilson Lundin, Ersula Ore, and Mark Sturges. My dear colleagues Cheryl Glenn, Nicholas Joukovsky, Mark Morrison, and Robin Schulze provided me invaluable guidance in various aspects of manuscript preparation.

Finally, I thank archivists Seth Kasten of Columbia University's Burke Library, Martha Smalley and Joan Duffy of Yale Divinity School Library, and Nanci Young of Smith College Library: their expertise made my archival research both efficient and fruitful. Archivists at Beijing University, Fudan University, Nankai University, Qinghua University, Tianjin University, Wuhan University, and Zhongshan University also provided me assistance of various sorts. I thank all of these people for joining my effort to understand the intricacies of "the devil's tongue." Unless otherwise noted, all translations into English are my own.

I am also thankful to the Southern Illinois University Press staff. Editor-in-chief Karl Kageff offered me encouragement and guidance when I prepared the manuscript. Copy editor John Wilson was patient with me.

I also want to express my gratitude to family and friends. Bart and Kelly Alexander embraced me into their family as soon as I arrived at Purdue. Charles and Barbara Walters invited me to stay with them every time I visited Yale. Liu Ping and Liu Huiying showed me hospitality in Guangzhou. My family also extended material and spiritual support. My parents, Mingkeng and Meixiang, and my sister, Xiaoqiong, helped me collect source materials in China. I thank Scott Baxter, Huiling Ding, Christine Tardy, Gigi Taylor, and Hsiao-Hui Yang for their comradeship in my scholarly pursuit. My research interns Ali Ferguson and Candace Shultz edited the manuscript for me.

Finally, I want to dedicate the book to my former teacher Lynn Walters, a graduate of Smith College. Like numerous Anglo-American teachers who taught in China over the last two centuries, she devoted her young life to this foreign land. She always hoped to do research on Ginling College, a sister school of Smith College in China. She was never able to do so. I am pleased that I have done that for her.

Early versions of portions of this book were previously published in *Rhetoric Review* ("Conflation of Rhetorical Traditions: The Formation of Modern Chinese Writing Instruction," copyright 2005 by Xiaoye You, reproduced by permission of Taylor & Francis Group, LLC, http://www.taylorandfrancis. com/) and *The Politics of Second Language Writing: In Search of the Promised Land*, edited by Paul Kei Matsuda, Christina Ortmeier-Hooper, and Xiaoye You ("Globalization and the Politics of Teaching EFL Writing," copyright 2006 by Parlor Press, adapted with permission). Archival materials appear courtesy the Lindquist Papers, Yale Divinity School Library (by permission of Rhio Harper and Thomas Imboden). Professor Michael G. Yetman generously allowed me to use an excerpt from his unpublished manuscript "China Days." Part of my archival research was supported by the Penn State College of the Liberal Arts research fund startup for tenure-track faculty and the Smith College travel to archive grant. The book project was also sponsored by the MOE Project of the Research Center for Linguistics and Applied Linguistics, Guangdong University of Foreign Studies.

Writing in the Devil's Tongue

INTRODUCTION

Writing is always contested for residents of what Mary Louise Pratt has called "contact zones," or "social spaces where cultures meet, clash, and grapple with each other" (34). There has been no exception to this rule for Chinese students who write in English, as my early encounters with English writing reveal. In the late spring of 1989, China Central Television (CCTV) devoted its primetime news coverage entirely to students' political demonstrations in major Chinese cities. I was in my first year of high school and, as a country boy, hardly understood why college students were refusing to eat while demanding Western democracy in front of the Gate of Heavenly Peace in Beijing. Against this backdrop, our English teacher asked us to write a passage reporting a recent event in our lives. Living in a small town in the south, my family almost every evening watched CCTV Channel One, the only channel that our black-and-white TV received, so I wrote about the demonstrations following the government-censored news. The writing did not seem daunting to me. I simply drafted a Chinese passage in my mind, or *da fugao* 打腹稿, as our Chinese teachers always instructed us, and then translated it into English. When the teacher returned the paper, I was disappointed by the many red-inked corrections. However, I was thrilled that I could compose, however imperfectly, in the language of the "foreign devils," as Westerners were popularly nicknamed in Chinese colonial history. In retrospect, my first English piece encapsulated a high-school student's situated cultural experience: using an international medium, namely English, I tried to make sense of a political struggle resulting from China's reengagement with global political and economic orders after the Cultural Revolution (1967–76).[1]

Two years later, I entered a local teachers' college and took my first and only college writing course. Gary, a teacher from Canada, often copied sentences and short passages on the blackboard to illustrate rhetorical strategies, ones that I can hardly recall now. What I do remember is the prevailing anxiety that my fellow classmates suffered when they ran out of ideas for their journal entries. Some students later boasted in the dormitory about their coping strategy. They simply translated Chinese folktales into English, such as "The Legend of Miss White Snake" and "Lady Mulan Joins the Army." Stories that we grew up reading in picture books or hearing from our parents turned out to be a treasure trove for our English compositions. Gary seemed to be enchanted by these Oriental myths, so he gladly passed my fellow classmates. In retrospect, I would argue, translating Chinese folktales for English journals was more than a student gimmick; it was, rather, an unconscious cultural strategy designed to assert these students' Chinese heritage when it was being besieged by the influx of transnational ideas and products.

A postcolonial perspective continues to lead me into global contact zones. Reflecting on these personal anecdotes, I have come to realize that my experience in learning English writing in fact reflected an important slice of the history of English composition in China. As these anecdotes show, English composition was always deeply rooted in local and global politics, Chinese literary tradition, and the everyday lives of students. Resembling the "underlife" that operates in the American composition class (Brooke), Chinese students negotiate the requirements with their teachers when they appropriate local folklore to demonstrate unexpected agency in the English classroom. Considering that English was first taught in government schools in the 1860s, when China was being encroached on by Western powers, the history of English composition in China has definitely been a complicated one. How has English writing been taught over the last one and a half centuries? Did students fifty or one hundred years ago write in English the same way my generation did in high school and college? How did English writing affect the lives of Chinese students and, more broadly, the lives of their compatriots in the process of Chinese modernization? Because English was widely taught in many former colonial countries, similar questions can be raised about these nations in their struggle for national independence and modernization. A postcolonial perspective allows us to reconsider issues of ethnicity, modernization, and English composition in a global context.

Indeed, in the history of colonialism, indigenous people were often forced to learn the language of the colonial power—the "foreign devil's tongue"— to inscribe their lived experiences. In their encounters with Westerners, the indigenous often invented names to signify those that were "not one of us," names such as "foreign devils" (*yangguizi* 洋鬼子) in China,[2] "red-haired people" (*komojin* 紅毛人) in Japan, "white people" (*barang, falang,* or *far-angi*) in South Asia, and "outsiders" (*gringos*) in Central and South America. Among the indigenous, these "terministic screens" (Burke) immediately conjured up exotic images of the "other," including their physical appearances, clothing, language, mannerisms, and customs. Besides inventing local nomenclature to describe imagined "devilish" cultures, the indigenous often had to learn Westerners' languages to limn their own feelings, experiences, and dreams. English was one of the devil's tongues historically forced upon indigenous people. When British, and later Anglo-American, colonial powers stretched to different parts of the world, the English language accompanied the colonizers and became a tool of cultural dominance. Either for its pragmatic function in trade or as a symbol of prestige, English was widely taught in regions with British and American colonial interests. Students who had to learn English in those regions invariably bore the burden of trying to reason, speak, and write from the foreigner's mind-set while entangled in local political and cultural dynamics. They had to juggle multiple languages, multiple identities, multiple cultures, and multiple worldviews. Learning English was thus a struggle for those students as well as for their teachers. Even in an age of global economy, as my own experience shows, learning to speak and write in the devil's tongue remains highly contested in many regions.

Over the years, I have been troubled by the indifference in American composition studies shown toward worldwide teaching of English writing. There has been little awareness among composition scholars and teachers of the transnational nature of their undertaking. Bruce Horner and John Trimbur attribute this deep-seated parochialism to a tacit policy of English monolingualism underlying first-year composition. Due to the monolingual policy, they observe, "U.S. college composition, from its formation to the present day, operates for the most part within national borders, at worst justifying writing instruction for reasons of economic productivity, cultural integration, and now perhaps homeland security, while at best imagining a more inclusive, pluricultural, and participatory civil life in the U.S." (623). Thus, it is not surprising that historical narratives of English composition have largely focused on the United States, reinforcing an egocentric national imagery. When composition historians do venture outside the United States, they are predominantly interested in transatlantic intellectual exchanges, ignoring those that have happened or are happening across the Pacific Rim.

Despite the fact that cross-national information and human flows have made composition classrooms virtually global, composition studies have not yet broadened their scope to an international level. Although the number of international and generation 1.5 students significantly increased in American universities over the last several decades, composition studies have, until recent years, paid little attention to them, treating them as no different from U.S.-born students or as needing to be assimilated into the mainstream. Due to the isolationist mentality and an assimilationist stand, a majority of teachers are little informed of the diverse cultural, literary, and rhetorical traditions that their students have to wrestle with when writing in English.[3] Composition scholars keep going back to Western rhetorical canons for theoretical and pedagogical inspirations. Influenced by a colonialist mentality, they assume that English is *the* language of the WASP (white, Anglo-Saxon, Protestant) and thus the national language of the United States; therefore, English writing must be and only can be taught in light of Western tradition.[4] The interpellative force of monolingualism "hails" both composition teachers and scholars, making them susceptible to colonialist and nationalist assumptions and practices.

Only in recent years have scholars critically examined American composition practices against the backdrop of worldwide teaching of English writing. In 1995, Mary Muchiri, Nshindi Mulamba, Greg Myers, and Deoscorous Ndoloi raised complex issues related to the exportation of American composition practices into several African countries. A series of studies by Suresh Canagarajah revealed the discriminating and marginalizing tendencies of Anglo-American writing conventions that have exacerbated writing practices in postcolonial countries ("'Nondiscursive' Requirements"; *Geopolitics*). He argued that rhetorical assumptions and pedagogical practices need to accommodate writers who are shuttling between linguistic communities in an age of globalization ("Toward"; "Place"). Min-Zhan Lu suggested that composition studies develop more responsible and responsive approaches to the relation between English and its various users in the world. LuMing Mao underscored the possibility of a creative understanding of cultural and rhetorical traditions when people live and work in "rhetorical borderlands," a term that succinctly describes contemporary composition classrooms ("Rhetorical Borderlands"). These scholars not only have critiqued the parochial, monolingual mentality in composition studies but, more important, also have suggested ways American composition can both benefit from and contribute to the worldwide teaching of English writing. Their egalitarian and inclusionary political stances have opened up a space for new rhetorical assumptions, pedagogical approaches, and writing practices in composition instruction.

In second language (L2) writing studies, a field that traditionally has focused on ESL (English as a second language) writing in North America, scholars have also articulated their international visions and responsibilities.[5] At a colloquium addressing the future of L2 writing in 1999, Terry Santos argued that as ESL students tend to be mainstreamed at American universities, the increasing number of students with English as a foreign language (EFL) in the United States promises an optimistic future for L2 writing studies. Furthermore, she said, "Perhaps we should look beyond the United States when considering the future of the field, and appreciate the opportunities the larger world offers our profession" (10). Ilona Leki further alerted the field of L2 writing that as English writing is taught in many non-English-dominant countries for various reasons, EFL writing teachers, particularly expatriate teachers of North American background, will be looking toward North America for innovation. And when an L2 specialist researches or teaches in an EFL context, Leki suggested, at minimum he or she should conduct "a careful analysis of the local needs, goals and possibilities" (205). Although remaining U.S.-centric, Santos and Leki have advocated a transnational response to the worldwide expansion of English composition. Their proposals to learn from and work with composition specialists in other parts of the world break new ground in L2 writing and American composition studies.

What should be the future role of composition studies in worldwide English writing, research, and teaching? What kind of knowledge in composition studies might cross geopolitical boundaries and become more universally useful in teaching English writing? When considering the values of American composition theorists and theories, what kind of relationships do composition studies hope to foster with English teaching professionals in other parts of the world? As American composition has, like it or not, funneled many theories to other parts of the world, can it continue to stand as a purely American enterprise? Current practices can easily evoke fears of cultural imperialism among English teachers in other countries if compositionists do not develop an international perspective "capable of understanding the study and teaching of written English in relation to other languages and to the dynamics of globalization" (Horner and Trimbur 624). Historically, English composition in many other countries has sprung from the colonial influences of Britain and the United States and their academic institutions. However, Muchiri et al. argue, "What we need is not a colonial metaphor, as conventionally applied, but some way to go from the global circulation of writing research to the local contexts of writing" (194). The "global circulation of writing research" has only perpetuated more of the same monolingual, monocultural assumptions developed in North America. If we agree with

Muchiri et al.'s postcolonial stand, what strategies will allow us to enter into "the local contexts of writing" and to make our work more ethically global? One way to start engaging these questions may be by taking a close look at the history of composition in other countries. Through examining alternative composition histories, we may move beyond anachronistic assumptions and practices.

This book investigates English writing instruction in China since the Second Opium War (1856–60) as a Chinese response to the realization that traditional native literacy education was inadequate in the pursuit of national modernization. A key theme is the Chinese pursuit of versions of modernity since the Opium Wars through their relentless fight against feudalism, colonialism, imperialism, bureaucratic capitalism, and, nowadays, transnational capitalism. Embedded in the Chinese endeavor for modernization, English composition has always been a contested educational practice ridden with conflicts of multiple dimensions—rhetorical, pedagogical, and professional. In their rhetorical practices, some scholars sought to develop new rhetorical assumptions responsive to the new societal demands, such as scientific rhetoric, current-traditional rhetoric, and proletarian rhetoric, while others clung to old assumptions, such as Confucian rhetoric, in both Chinese and English writing practices. In the pedagogical arena, writing teachers struggled to balance between indoctrinating students into Chinese mainstream ideology and providing them with a practical tool for making a living. They wanted to adopt innovative writing pedagogies or simply to spend more time on teaching writing, but sometimes their material conditions did not allow them to do so. In their writings, students strove to inscribe their lived experiences, feelings, and desires by meshing traditional Chinese and Anglo-American rhetorical strategies; they also wrestled with their relatively low English proficiency, political turmoil, and fierce competition in the job market. In the professional arena, Chinese scholars actively sought new pedagogical theories from overseas and tried to tailor them to local pedagogical traditions and material conditions. Continuous conflicts created tensions as well as propelling forces. The interweaving of these conflicts, tensions, and forces shaped English composition instruction in China.

The Chinese pursuit of modernity, an overarching theme of this history, ideologically sustained and shaped writing instruction. Louis Althusser defines ideology as "the expression of the relation between men and their 'world,' that is, the (overdetermined) unity of the real relation and the imaginary relation between them and their real conditions of existence" (89). The school system helps the state exercise its ideological control in a silent way.[6] Through an apprenticeship in various kinds of knowledge coated by the ruling class's ideology, students reproduce and perpetuate the relations of production in a class society. As a required part of schooling, English composition in China reproduced the mainstream discourse of modernization and, hence, the relations of production and subjectivity. For example, at the beginning of the People's Republic, English teaching was motivated primarily by political needs, such as training military interpreters and producing candidates for the field of diplomacy. Not only the fear of war but also the hope for world peace among the Chinese prompted English teaching at that time. In their English writing, students were excited by, and thus identified with, the fantastic idea of building a "new China," and they pledged to study hard to become competent socialist workers. Nowadays, English is hailed in Chinese mainstream discourse as an indispensable tool for participating in the global economy. Students conscientiously study the language to enter fields of industry, business, trade, education, and culture. Historically, English writing practices engaged Chinese students first in the nationalist imagination of modernity and later in the discourse of globalization.

Mainstream Chinese ideology seeped into composition partly through pedagogical discourse. Examining the relationship between ideology and pedagogical discourse, Basil Bernstein suggests that every discourse in the educational field is "ideologically repositioned" (200) in relation to its original field of production.

> [P]edagogical discourse is a principle for appropriating other discourses and bringing them into a special relation with each other for the purposes of their selective transmission and acquisition. Pedagogic discourse, then, is a principle which removes (delocates) a discourse from its substantive practice and context, and relocates that discourse according to its own principle of selective reordering and focusing. In this process of the delocation and the relocation of the original discourse the social basis of its practices, including its power relations, is removed. (183)

In the present study, I explore how the discourses of mainstream Chinese society were ideologically repositioned in the schools through the rhetorical traditions represented, the pedagogical approaches chosen, and the essays written by students. Thus, the architecture of the study consists of two key trajectories with students' writing cutting across them. First, underneath the overarching trajectory of the Chinese pursuit of national modernization, Chinese society moved from feudalism to bourgeois capitalism (1911–49) to Communism (1950–89) and to transnational capitalism (1990–). Second, every social formation and its ideology produced a dominant pedagogy, such as Confucian pedagogy in feudal society, current-traditional models under bourgeois capitalism, and social realist pedagogy under Communism. Students' writing cut across both trajectories and produced various discourses.

Despite the imposition of cultural ideologies and pedagogical models, students managed to negotiate composition in ways that allowed them to address their concerns in historical contact zones. Writing opened up a space for them to work out alternative or counter discourses against both Chinese and foreign establishments. Students in early English-language schools, for example, not only translated Western texts in science and technology but also wrote about their understanding of Christianity. Their religious essays, as I show in chapter 1, challenged both authoritative biblical interpretations and Chinese emperors' self-proclaimed heavenly power. After China gradually shifted from Communism toward transnational capitalism at the end of last century, students described their material desires, often rendering critical reflections on China's intercultural changes. Thus, Chinese mainstream ideology not only shaped students' writing practices but also carved out a textual space for students to engage, to subvert, and to modify the mainstream discourses and cultures.

Any historical narrative comprises multivalent voices: the voices of institutions, teachers, students, and composition scholars. Embracing fragmentation and ephemerality in an affirmative fashion, postmodernists such as Foucault and Lyotard refute the notion that there exists any metanarrative or metatheory through which all things can be connected or represented (Harvey). For them, one of the desirable methods for historical representation is allowing different voices the legitimacy and authenticity to speak for themselves and to explore and to build up the transparent qualities of human discourse. Following this line of thinking, the present study, while not totally forsaking a metanarrative centering on Chinese modernization, tries to treat all parties involved in the history as members of an equal "interpretive community" (Fish) and explores ways of ensuring that all voices are heard. Due to unequal material conditions, historical figures are, of course, not always given an equal chance to be heard. In the Chinese history of English composition, some have spoken louder than others, and some have occasionally even silenced others because of their discursive power, resources, and traditions of record keeping.[7]

This study pays particular attention to students' voices. Previous composition histories have tended to focus on institutional, disciplinary, and pedagogical issues, marginalizing student actors in the social drama of composition instruction. I try to bring students back to center stage by featuring several passages written by them in each chapter. These passages not only showcase rhetorical and linguistic features of their writings but also serve as representative anecdotes that reveal the complex ways in which students, responding to their situations, performed multivalent, intercultural discourses. As Kenneth Burke explains: "Critical and imaginative works are answers to questions posed by the situation in which they arose. They are not merely answers, they are *strategic* answers, *stylized* answers" (77). These passages are students' strategic and stylized answers to their historical contact-zone situation and acts of forming and re-forming their experiences through language. They are students' unique voices, vocalized in a devil's tongue, mediated by the evolving dialogue of modernity, inside a Chinese Burkean parlor.

By retrieving the Chinese history of English composition, I argue that English is no longer a language owned by any particular people or nation. It is not only the language of the Americans or the British, the WASP or the scientific community, but also the language of all its monolingual and multilingual users in the world. The historical narrative reveals that over the last one and a half centuries educated Chinese strove to acquire an additional language to inscribe their experiences, feelings, and dreams and to resist feudalism, imperialism, and bureaucratic and transnational capitalism in their pursuit of national modernization. Mediating in local cultural politics, English shared important duties with Chinese. Chinese writers used English alongside Chinese in political, pedagogical, rhetorical, and linguistic terms. Analogous composition histories are found in many other Asian nations, such as India, Japan, Malaysia, Sri Lanka, and the Philippines. With an altered assumption of English language ownership, composition scholars and teachers will have to modify their rhetorical assumptions, pedagogical approaches, and writing practices in the age of globalization.

In this transnational investigation, representation of rhetorical traditions has become a particularly thorny issue. Yameng Liu has identified a dominant paradigm in comparative rhetoric that works under the assumption that "there exists an easily abstractable and consistently definable set of 'essential' characteristics in Chinese or any other rhetorical tradition" (322). In a postmodern era marked by fragmentation, multiplicity, and fluidity, how can one represent a non-Western tradition of rhetoric and composition without committing reductionist, deterministic, and essentialist missteps? Comparative rhetoricians have generally agreed that a non-Western tradition needs to be studied and represented on its own terms. LuMing Mao explains: "If our larger goal is to study these [non-Western] traditions on their own terms, . . . attention can be directed toward materials and conditions that are native to these traditions and so that appropriate frames and language can be developed to deal with differences as well as similarities between different traditions" ("Reflective Encounters" 417–18). However, Mao suggests that non-Western traditions will not stand on their own terms forever because comparative rhetoricians always bring in Western frames and concepts to arrive at a creative, reflective understanding, or "a fresher perspective on the internal dynamics of their object of study" (418). In other words, representation of a non-Western tradition will always be a dialectical process in which the rhetorician mobilizes available frames and concepts of all traditions.

In my discussion of the Chinese tradition of rhetoric and composition, I rely on Chinese terms and use Western concepts reflectively. I try to introduce Chinese concepts and traditions succinctly while allowing some degree of breadth and depth. Three key terms in the Chinese discourse of communication and composition run through the entire book. The first is *dao* 道, or the Way. In metaphysical speculations of ancient China, the universe did not start from a clear distinction of different worlds but rather from a chaotic mess. What most attracted the ancient Chinese was not something that would transcend this chaotic state, but the innermost essence of the chaos that remained hidden and mysterious. The answer to everything about this world that lay at the heart of the chaos is called *dao*. The Confucian school, which was endorsed as state orthodoxy in the Western Han Dynasty (260 B.C.E.–24 C.E.), was particularly interested in seeking out the Way. For them, the Way offers not only the answer to how the natural world operates but also the key to the moral-spiritual order and the prosperity of human society. Therefore, Confucius once said, "In the morning, hear the Way; in the evening, die content" (*Analects* 103). The Way, as all one needs to know, marks the realm of Confucian ontology and epistemology.

The second term is *wen* 文, or writing. *Wen* originally referred to patterned marks on natural objects like the striped and spotted variegation of tigers or the sculptured colors of clouds. In ancient times, Chinese forebears invented writing by recording natural objects and events in imitation of their natural patterns. Through a particular stroke order, a Chinese character captures the essence of a natural object graphically. As Confucian rhetorician Liu Hsieh (ca. 462–520) explains, "When birds' markings replaced knotted cords, writing first emerged" (10). Once pictographic writing was created, Chinese sages used it to explore and transmit the Way of the universe. Liu further explains that the sages "observed heavenly patterns in order to comprehend their changes exhaustively, and . . . studied human patterns of behavior in order to transform them" (12). Therefore, writing is a rhetorical means to understand the Way and to transform the people in light of the Way.[8] The Confucian school always stressed a dialectical balance between substance (the Way) and form in writing. The Chinese literati traditionally preferred writing to speaking because writing captures and promotes the Way, in contrast to ancient Western civilizations, such as the Greeks, who tended to value orality over writing because, allegedly, the former directly comes from the soul and conveys truth better (Plato).

The third term is *li* 禮, meaning rites. While writing signifies the Way of both the natural world and human society, for the Confucian school, ritual helps humans restore, maintain, and communicate about the Way. *Li* originally referred to a code of rites and ceremonies governing specific religious observances, and later it was extended to embody the total spectrum of social norms, customs, and mores, covering increasingly complicated relationships and institutions. Through ritual performance, a human community comes together and takes on order. Appropriate ritual brings the Way—peace, harmony, and structure—to human society. Therefore Confucius once admonished his disciples, "To look at nothing in defiance of ritual, to listen to nothing in defiance of ritual, to speak of nothing in defiance of ritual, never to stir hand or foot in defiance of ritual" (*Analects* 162). In other words, to observe the ritual codes, one needs to mind his or her acts of looking, listening, speaking, and gesturing because these multimodal acts generate profound symbolic meanings in society. The ultimate goal of human communication is to maintain the established ritual codes, thus sustaining the right path, the Way, of human society and the natural world. Speaking is an integral part of the ritual. Confucius, however, was suspicious of speaking because in reality it is often performed without a balanced or coordinated use of other ritual acts. Getting ritualized for the Way thus constitutes the full course of one's education. While classical Western education emphasized grammar, logic, and rhetoric for reaching truth, ancient Chinese education centered on ritual for seeking the Way. Together, the three concepts—the Way (*dao*), writing (*wen*), and ritual (*li*)—constituted the essence of rhetorical education in ancient China.[9]

To sum up, this book brings a transnational perspective to composition studies by retrieving the Chinese history of English composition. When the Chinese sought to build a modern nation one and a half centuries ago, they realized the inadequacy of native language education and adopted English as an additional language. They negotiated with rhetorical, linguistic, pedagogical, and professional issues when teaching English writing. As English has served the Chinese for more than a century, it has virtually become a Chinese indigenous language rather than a devil's tongue. The goal of examining the history of bilingual writing instruction in an East Asian country is to challenge American composition teachers' and scholars' English monolingual mentality and to alert them to other rhetorical assumptions, pedagogical approaches, and writing practices. Further, this history also challenges us to more thoroughly attend to what Robert Connors calls "composition-rhetoric" in our scholarship and teaching, that is, to the specific rhetorical form that composition takes in response to social context and social demands (*Composition-Rhetoric*).

My study is presented in six chapters. In chapter 1, I examine the emergence of English composition in Chinese colleges at the conjuncture of nationalist and colonial discourses in the late nineteenth century. I first introduce the Confucian rhetorical tradition as embodied by the civil service exam essays that were required of students in imperial China and abandoned in the early 1900s. The English writing that was systematically taught in Chinese colleges by the end of the nineteenth century exhibited significant American influences. I explore the possible reasons for and the main characteristics of these influences. I also assess how Chinese students participated in nationalist discourse through English writing in the late Qing dynasty.

Chapter 2 deals with college English composition in republican China after 1919. This period featured a conscientious national struggle for cultural reformation and decolonization. I focus on the broad conflation of Confucian and Anglo-American rhetorical traditions in pedagogical theory, public speaking, translation, and student writing. I also explore how English writing affected both teachers' and students' everyday lives amid battles against feudalism and imperialism for national independence. During this period, scholars started to consider theoretical and pedagogical issues unique to English composition in the Chinese context.

Chapter 3 focuses on English writing instruction from the establishment of the People's Republic in 1949 to the end of the Cultural Revolution in 1976. This period marked a drastic decline in the societal demand for English as well as in politicized themes in composition. I trace the formation of Chinese proletarian rhetoric and the ways that it shaped both Chinese and English composition.

Chapter 4 examines the redefinition of English composition from the late 1970s to 1989. Economic reform and the opening up of China to the outside world stimulated the teaching of English writing. Once again, Anglo-American influences entered the country, coming mainly from the fields of composition studies and applied linguistics. English writing instruction proliferated in colleges, and composition research revived. I suggest that English composition explicitly supported a political agenda, namely to advance the Four Modernizations project orchestrated by Communist Party reformers.

In chapter 5, I assess the development of English composition after 1990. As China moved into a new phase called "socialism with Chinese characteristics," a series of reforms took place in higher education to enhance its flexibility and accountability in a market economy. Chinese composition, while retaining the Marxist style of writing, emphasized creativity and individuality. In contrast, English composition was portrayed as a neutral technology governed by static rules in both pedagogy and assessment. Research on English composition became more systematic and vigorous in the 1990s, and Chinese scholars actively negotiated with imported theories and pedagogies in light of the local context.

Chapter 6 focuses on issues of English composition in the age of globalization. I first introduce the recent redefinition of English literacy in the Chinese discourse of globalization and indicate that English is no longer conceived of in explicitly ideological terms in Chinese society. As English composition historically mediated in Chinese modernization on political, pedagogical, rhetorical, linguistic, and discursive terms, I argue that, rather than a foreign devil's tongue, English has always/already been "our" tongue for the Chinese users of the language. I conclude the book with some deliberations on how composition studies may respond to the worldwide teaching of English composition.

1

ENCOUNTERING THE
DEVIL'S WRITING

1862–1918

When English was first taught in Chinese schools in the nineteenth century, the majority of literati despised it. They firmly believed that only Confucian classics embodied the worthy knowledge of the human realm and that Western learning mainly dealt with practical matters, which Confucians looked down upon. After repeatedly losing wars to Western powers, the Chinese were compelled to learn their enemies' craft in order to defend themselves. English as well as other foreign languages served the purpose of appropriating Western science and technology; thus, they were regarded as crucial for political functions but inferior on cultural terms. The Chinese clearly demarcated native and foreign tongues, conceiving the former as a mainstay of Chinese cultural essence and the latter simply as a transient tool for solving an imminent crisis.

Despite its low cultural status, English opened up an array of new possibilities for the Chinese users. First, English, along with other foreign languages, was a gateway to Western scientific developments. Chinese students translated many English books on science and technology before 1900.[1] Second, recognizing the inadequacy of native language education in fashioning a modern nation, the Chinese picked English as the most important foreign language in their new school system in 1901, a move that spurred other ways of viewing the world. Third, Chinese students were exposed to Anglo-American rhetoric through translating English books and composing in English.

They used a mixture of Anglo-American and Chinese rhetorical strategies to express their feelings and desires and to join the national discourse of "self-strengthening," a movement arising amid Western intrusion and terrorization. Despite its status as a "devil's tongue," thus, English gained a foothold in Chinese cultural reformation, which ironically defied the "tool" metaphor that Chinese educators had assigned to it.

Tong Wen Guan

English first entered government schools when China was faced with an unprecedented national crisis. Before its encounter with Western imperialism, China was a self-contained, multiethnic empire in East Asia, proud of its political, economic, and cultural superiority. Although held in contempt by the Chinese, who considered them "barbarians" from the outside, Westerners had been conducting business and evangelistic work in China for centuries, but their activities were strictly controlled by the Chinese government. The East India Company began trading with China in southern coastal areas in the mid-eighteenth century, with Indian opium being one of the major commodities. Unhappy with the proliferation of opium use in the south and the massive outflow of silver into foreigners' pockets, the Manchu Qing government sanctioned a campaign in 1839 to confiscate and burn opium in south China. The opium-banning campaign triggered the First Opium War in 1840 between the militarily ill-prepared Qing government and Great Britain. In the end, China lost the war, after which treaties were signed and monetary compensations made, Hong Kong was snatched away, and some port cities were forced to open or lease to Britain, France, and the United States. After losing the Second Opium War to Britain and France in 1856, the Qing government bitterly realized that China had lagged far behind the West.

In treaty-signing moments, some Qing officials felt the urgency of foreign language education. All treaties related to war were written in English after 1862, creating a large demand within the imperial government for translators who could make sense of the documents. Therefore, in 1862, the Qing government decided to establish an institution called Tong Wen Guan 同文館 (Academy of Interpreters) in Beijing and later in other port cities to train agents for international communication. The academy opened an English class first and then French, Russian, and German classes in subsequent years. Students were recruited through the imperial civil service exam and were taught mostly by Western evangelists. Thus, the acceptance of English as a school subject was a reluctant choice made by the Chinese, a choice that was emblematic of a feudal society struggling to respond to the worldwide expansion of colonialism and capitalism. The reluctant choice also signaled the beginning of a concerted educational undertaking to enhance transnational understanding and world peace in modern Chinese history.

Originally designed to provide training in foreign languages, the academy quickly found it of little use for the students to master a Western tongue without any Western learning. Therefore, Western subjects such as astronomy, chemistry, geometry, physics, economics, and international law were incorporated into both the five-year and eight-year language curricula. In the department of English, students focused on English reading, speaking, and writing in the first year and moved on to practice translating dispatches and books on various subjects in later years (*Tong Wen Guan* 19). The pedagogical emphasis on Western subjects and translation reflected the government's nationalistic intent. That is, foreign language education should furnish professionals versed in Western affairs who could defend Chinese interests in international conflicts and introduce Western learning to their compatriots.

Whereas Tong Wen Guan was founded on a nationalistic agenda, its daily operation was largely colonialist in nature. From the day the academy opened, it was under the gaze of Sir Robert Hart, the inspector-general of the Imperial Maritime Customs Service, who earmarked funding and appointed teachers for the school for over three decades.[2] The Customs Service was established in 1854 jointly by the Qing government and Western consuls in China to enforce control over the existing Chinese customs system. In fact, Western personnel controlled the service until the 1920s because the Western powers wanted to regulate the taxes and duties imposed upon them.[3] Hart well understood that the expansion of Western interests in China depended on a growing cadre of natives who could communicate with Westerners.

In the classroom, English mediated a colonial discourse, enabling students to critically examine and reconcile cultural values East and West. Western teachers secretly taught religion, a subject forbidden by the Chinese government. In fact, William A. P. Martin (1827–1916), a graduate of Indiana State University and president of the academy in 1869–94, requested professors "not to allow their classes to skip the religious lessons in the reading-books" (*Cycle of Cathay* 325). Students practiced writing in English on religious topics, often tacitly challenging and resisting established authorities. One of Martin's students, for example, deliberated on the Christian God as follows:

All the human beings of the various nations throughout the world should respect the God; because he is the source from which the wealth, happiness, blessing, etc., are derived, and it is he who gives fortune or misfortune to the people. Although people cannot see his appearance, yet they should respect him as though he is in the presence before their eyes;

because he can secretly give rewards to those who have done good deeds, and punishment to those who are bad. (qtd. in *Cycle of Cathay* 298)

On one hand, like Homi Bhabha's depiction of Indians' encounter with the Bible (146–48), the Chinese student displaced and disturbed the authoritative Christian teaching in the text. He rearticulated biblical teachings through culturally mediated terms. For example, "the God" has never been standard usage among Anglo-American Christians. The Bible says relatively little about receiving wealth because of faith, and the connection of "wealth," "happiness," and "blessing" is unusual from an Anglo-American Christian point of view. Similarly, "respect" God is an unusual Christian expression; usually "worship" or "fear" would be used. The use of "respect" may come from the Chinese expressions *bai* 拜 or *jingbai* 敬拜. Through mimicry, the student undermined the narcissistic authority of his evangelical professors who were obsessed with proselytizing and converting their Chinese students and subverted the authorization of their biblical representations. On the other hand, the student mocked the arrogance of the Chinese monarchy. Portraying an omnipresent and omnipotent God transcending all nations, he challenged the emperor's self-proclaimed heavenly power, which explains why the government opposed religious matters in the academy. The Qing government desired only that Western language and science subjects be taught; however, because they were taught by evangelists, who wanted to convert their students, these subjects were naturally tinted with Christianity. In the selective adoption of Western learning, as the student essay shows, English played a catalytic role, enabling students to ruminate and respond to Western subjects in a linguistic code more resistant to government censorship.

Despite the political pragmatism, the establishment of Tong Wen Guan stirred a heated debate in Chinese educational circles. Conservatives in the government vigorously opposed Western learning. Woren, the Mongol neo-Confucian moralist and head of the Imperial Academy, argued that Western barbarian subjects were unfit for teaching in state institutions, where attention should focus on the sagely learning of ritual sanctity to rectify the mind and pacify the realm. Western learning in astronomy and mathematics was of very little use in efforts to establish a nation; rather, according to Woren, establishing a nation required, above all, "propriety and righteousness . . . in the minds of the people" (qtd. in Yeh 9). The "sagely learning" refers to the Confucian canon, works such as the Four Books and the Five Classics that deal with Confucian teachings and Chinese antiquity. Thus, the opposition of the conservatives is revealing. Also concerned about the nation's future, the conservatives upheld the centrality of traditional humanistic education in constructing a harmonious and prosperous nation-state. They were nervous and distrustful of Western learning not simply because it was "barbarous" but because it departed drastically from Confucian epistemology. In this debate, English was linked to Western learning, hence to the issue of nation building, which concerned both the liberal and conservative officials. Such vociferous opposition was gradually silenced after Woren's death in 1871.

Although Western languages and sciences were the prominent subjects at Tong Wen Guan, students also studied Chinese classics conscientiously in the academy. Besides reading the Confucian canon, all students were urged to practice so-called eight-legged, policy, and discourse essays, which I shall discuss shortly. To secure government positions, like students in traditional schools, they needed to score high on the civil service exam, which only assessed these three genres for literary degrees.[4] Although Western subjects were studied in the academy, they were not tested in the provincial exam until 1887,[5] testifying to the resilient status of Confucianism-centered classical learning in the country. Like U.S. education before the Civil War, traditional Chinese education was elitist and centered on classical learning. However, while U.S. education prepared students for professions in ministry, medicine, and law, Chinese education prepared students for government service. The Chinese educational system at that time was virtually monolithic, embodying a rich Confucian tradition of rhetoric and writing, as we shall now see.

Writing in Traditional Chinese Education

Traditional Chinese education was deeply shaped by neo-Confucian views of individual responsibility and agency. For thousands of years, the family offered the individual a conceptual framework to define the relationship between the self, the state, and the universe. In *The Great Learning*, one of the Four Books, Confucius teaches that an individual's education matters greatly to the peace and order of both the family and the state: "Things being investigated, knowledge became complete. . . . Their persons being cultivated, their families were regulated. Their families being regulated, their states were rightly governed. Their states being rightly governed, the whole kingdom was made tranquil and happy" (358–59). To regulate the family and to govern the state properly, the self ultimately must be cultivated. As part of personal cultivation, learning to write bore heavy ethical burdens.

Self-cultivation, according to Confucianism, develops largely through ritualization (*li*). Confucius was extremely concerned about various means for ritualizing individuals in order to align them with symbolic acts that reflect the true spirit of the Way (*dao*), the natural harmony of the universe. In the *Analects*, Confucius laments the deterioration of complex ritual systems established in previous dynasties. He attributes the deterioration of both family and state rites to the lack of true spirit that bolsters them in contemporary society. Being good or virtuous is what Confucius advocates as the true Way, or the true spirit, of a human community, which will sustain a tranquil and happy kingdom. Only through restoring the Way will the social rites prosper; only after the rites prevail will the disintegrated society come together again. This Confucian logic establishes ritualization as an overarching frame of philosophy and rhetoric.

As family regulator and state governor, the individual naturally lies at the heart of Confucian ritualization as both the agent and the subject of transformation through symbolic meanings. Confucius places tremendous faith in the agency of the individual for achieving what is good. Individuals ritualize themselves through probing and identifying the good character (*yi* 義) within. To comply with ritual codes, they must monitor closely their acts of looking, listening, speaking, writing, and gesturing because human acts carry profound and powerful symbolic meanings in society. Ritualization takes place when the individual negotiates symbolic meanings by actually performing multimodal ritual acts within both the family and the state. Confucius's emphasis on ritualizing the self parallels Pierre Bourdieu's depiction of the consecration of the ritual performer, which must come after the severity and painfulness of rites of initiation.

Confucius also considers it a gentleman's responsibility to affect others with his goodness—to influence them, to persuade them, to transform them, and ultimately to lead them toward goodness. Success in ritualizing others depends, for the most part, on the consecration of the ritual performers, or the rise of true gentlemen. Once instituted by the community, a gentleman's goodness can be compared to the wind. As Confucius says, "The essence of the gentleman is that of wind; the essence of small people is that of grass. And when a wind passes over the grass, it cannot choose but bend" (*Analects* 168). Therefore, the Confucian gentleman is entrusted with the responsibility of overseeing the well-being of Chinese society.

Ritualization is a lifelong process of learning and investigation for the gentleman. Confucius emphasizes learning from antiquity. He says, "Let a man be first incited by the *Songs*, then given a firm footing by the study of ritual, and finally perfected by music" (*Analects* 134). The *Book of Songs* is the first anthology of Chinese folk songs. The songs describe the simple, everyday lives of the multitude, lives of the rich and powerful, and ritual performances in the court. Through studying the songs, Confucius suggests, individuals will sharpen their skills in handling situations rhetorically both at home and in public—the skills to express their own feelings, to incite others' emotions, to observe their feelings, and to influence them. Music conducted on the occasion of ritual performance is another subject for learning from antiquity. Music is a subset of ritual, but it is different from rites, which separate individuals according to their different social roles. As Haun Saussy explains the Confucian view, "[music] in its distinguishing and arranging operates not directly on human beings but on sensory givens whose relationships create an auditory simulacrum of the social world, to which every hearer has, in principle, the same degree of access" (13). Furthermore, Confucius celebrates great masters of rites in previous dynasties for their moral sublimity. He encourages his students to study them and to follow their paths as recorded in the Book of History. Therefore, since ancient times, the study of antiquity as encapsulated in the Book of Songs, Book of Rites, Book of Music, and Book of History becomes the exclusive means for drawing the self close to the ideal gentleman.

Confucian canons also ritualize individuals by instilling in them the preferred means of persuasion. The canons generally include the Four Books (Analects, Great Learning, Mencius, and Doctrine of the Mean) and the Five Classics (Book of Changes, Book of History, Book of Songs, Book of Rites, and Spring and Autumn Annals). These books codify Confucian thinkers' rhetorical preferences, including a predominant use of dialectic argument through chain reasoning,[6] reasoning by analogy, and historical examples (Garrett, "Classical Chinese"; Jensen; Kirkpatrick, "Chinese Rhetoric"). These rhetorical strategies reflect the traditional Chinese perception of the evolving world, which consists of intertwined particulars in constant motion and conflict. In their continuous, intimate interaction with the natural world, the Chinese cultivated a preference for dialectic and holistic reasoning. Through chain reasoning, analogy, and historical precedents, Confucian rhetoricians confirmed and perpetuated this particular ontology. Connecting the past with the present, dialecticism was opportune in ritualizing, or building, the Confucian gentleman.

After the Tang dynasty (618–907), ritualization of the Confucian gentleman was institutionalized through the civil service exam system. As candidates who successfully passed the exam were given esteemed official titles, the exam system served as the rite of passage for the Confucian gentleman. In both the Ming (1368–1644) and the Qing (1644–1910) dynasties, the high-stakes civil service exam played a doorkeeping function mainly through essay tests, including the eight-legged, policy, and discourse essays. Through these genres, the candidates' task was to convince the examiners that they were capable of regulating the family and governing the state in the Confucian spirit. Because the exam selected officials based on scholastic merits rather than patronage, it appealed to the West and eventually influenced civil service reforms in England, France, Germany, Prussia, and the United States during the eighteenth and nineteenth centuries. For example, Tong Wen Guan president Martin and Thomas A. Jenckes of Rhode Island introduced the exam to the American public in 1868, and it influenced the U.S. civil service reform in the 1880s (Teng).

The exam essays instilled in students unique rhetorical sensibilities with a Confucian conscience. Students became particularly familiar with expository (*yi* 議, *lun* 論, *shuo* 說) and persuasive (*shui* 說) styles through deliberating on questions concerning moral philosophy, classical studies, history, and government. However, in most cases they were not expected to express their critical views when answering these questions, though they constantly did. The exam essays fully served the function of ritualization that Confucius himself had so enthusiastically performed through his teaching. Essay writing engaged the students in examining themselves against the moral codes prescribed in the classics, as well as in reflecting upon how they could enlighten rulers to nurture a morally sound society. In short, writing was to promote the Way of Chinese feudalism.

The most important type of writing required in the provincial and metropolitan exams was the renowned eight-legged (*bagu* 八股) essay. A sentence or a short passage would be quoted from each of the Four Books. The examinees would write an essay to elucidate each quote, maneuvering through six to eight rhetorical moves in several hundred Chinese characters. The logical structure of the eight-legged essays, as R. Kent Guy observes, resembles the deductive reasoning style in the American collegiate debate format, but it values a quite different kind of proof when someone is making an argument: "As the burden of proof in an essay in the [modern] Western tradition would be borne by evidence, in Chinese examination essays it was borne by elegantly stated perception" (170). Exemplifying what Guy means by "perception" are the annotations of the Four Books by Zhu Xi (1130–1200), a neo-Confucian exegete. Students were instructed to explicate the quotes by strictly following Zhu's interpretations. In a sense, writing the eight-legged essay was a kind of translation in which students appropriated Confucian and neo-Confucian thoughts creatively within certain organizational constraints. Through an archaic, "foreign" language, students brought home to the reader the haunting voices of the Confucian masters who lived two thousand years ago.

To fathom the philosophical and rhetorical depths of the eight-legged essay, it is beneficial to closely analyze such an essay, an ingenious "translation" of Confucian words. "I Have Never Yet Seen One Who Really Cared for Goodness" was an essay widely read by students in the Qing dynasty.[7]

Written by Tang Xianzu (1550–1616), who later became a famous essayist and playwright, this exemplar was praised by Fang Bao (1668–1749), another neo-Confucian scholar, for two stellar merits. First, Tang used simple, familiar language and refrained from making elusive quotes from different sources. Second, he spoke in an unambiguous Confucian voice, thus establishing a neo-Confucian *ethos* successfully (Wang Kaifu 205).

Tang's essay conforms to the standard structure of the eight-legged genre. The essay usually opens with four introductory sections. First, two sentences are required to introduce the topic (*poti* 破題, "opening the topic"). Second, the essay topic is explained in several more sentences (*chengti* 承題, "carrying the topic forward"). Third, a more profound discussion about the subject matter is provided (*qijiang* 起講, "elaborating"). Here the writer is expected to shift to a neo-Confucian moralist's voice. Fourth, a few sentences are used to further clarify the essay topic (*ruti* 入題, "revealing the topic"). To connect the introductory sections and the full explication of the essay topic in the forthcoming "legs," the fourth section is optional. Tang followed the four standard sections to introduce the topic. He opens the essay by directly revealing the source of the essay title (*poti*): "The Master regretted the difficulty in becoming a virtuous person; thus he said that so many people had forsaken their pursuit of virtue" (202). Unequivocally identifying the source of the essay title demonstrates Tang's adequate knowledge of Confucian classics, a first step in establishing his *ethos* to the reader. Then he alludes to Confucius's remarks in the *Analects* and explains the Master's thoughts from a third-person perspective in the *chengti* and *qijiang* sections. He performs the role of a cultural exegete like the renowned neo-Confucian scholar Zhu Xi. We need to note that Tang starts to shift to Confucius's voice in the last sentence of the *qijiang* section:

> One who cared for Goodness and abhorred wickedness did not decline virtue. Those who gave up their pursuit of virtue simply had not used their whole might. That is what the Master had regretted again and again.

> Consider what the Master meant: a gentleman learns in order to do Good; he realizes Goodness because he can exert his strength. That one cares for Goodness, but does not have strength to realize it, how can *I* not regret that today? (202)

Then Tang naturally enters the topic in a first-person voice, pretending to be the master conversing with his disciples (the whole rhetorical move is *ruti*). He adopts parallelism, one of Confucius's favorite rhetorical strategies, for exposition:

Today, Goodness is worth being cared for, but I have not yet seen one who cared for Goodness. Wickedness should be abhorred, but I have not yet seen one who abhorred wickedness. (202)

The opening four sections are followed by the parallel legs, the basis of the eight-legged essay's name. Unlike the four introductory sections, each of these "leg" sections requires at least two sentences, and they have to provide stylistic balance. It should be noted, however, that the essay form varies in some ways. The *ruti* section is optional. Among the four sections of parallel legs, the final parallel leg is also optional. An essay that omits the final two legs will have only six legs. Each parallel leg may have more than two legs. Some eight-legged essays have as many as twenty legs. Tang starts the first parallel structure (*qigu* 起股, "opening legs") by providing an overview of his thesis that most people crave a good reputation rather than goodness itself:

The reputation as one who cares for Goodness is what most people crave. However, the one whom I consider as not yet having appeared does not crave such satisfaction but prefers not letting any other consideration (than Goodness) come first.

The reputation as one who abhors wickedness is what most people crave. However the one whom I consider as not yet having appeared does not abhor what excites his anger but wickedness that (through his constantly doing Good) will not have a chance to get at him. (202)

Tang does not move on to the next parallel structure (*zhonggu* 中股, "middle legs") immediately, but rather uses an optional section (*guojie* 過接, "transition") to connect the opening legs and the middle legs. Here, he mounts a rebuttal against those hypocrites who excuse themselves for lacking sufficient strength to do good:

Because everyone only seeks reputation, it is difficult to do Good. However, Goodness may not be truly that difficult to realize. When one acts, he sees the difference between Goodness and wickedness; later considering carefully what he has done, he has actually used strength that favors wickedness. (202)

Following the textual norms, Tang next presents the middle legs in which he explains why he (the master) had not seen one who really cared for goodness:

I know there are people who care not for Goodness. When one cares about Goodness, it will follow him. One's preference for letting no other consideration (than Goodness) come first starts from a momentary desire for Goodness. As I have not yet seen one who cares for Goodness, how can I expect to meet one who cares for Goodness but who is without sufficient strength?

There are people who abhor not wickedness. When one abhors wickedness, it will disappear. One's abhorrence of wickedness getting at him starts from a momentary dislike for wickedness. As I have not yet seen one who abhors wickedness, how can I expect to meet one who abhors wickedness but who is without sufficient strength? (202–3)

As expected, Tang further explicates the rarity of people who truly cared for goodness in the third parallel structure (*hougu* 後股, "latter legs"):

People are not born the same, and they bear varying qualities. Therefore some people may not possess sufficient strength.

However, there have been too few people who aspire to pursue Goodness and too many who do not. I have not yet seen even one of the former. (203)

In the fourth parallel structure (*shugu* 束股, "closing legs"), again Tang refutes those who had excused their failure to achieve goodness because of their insufficient might:

One may or may not have sufficient strength; it will manifest when it is in use. If one never uses it, how can he blame his strength (as being insufficient)?

Whether one realizes Goodness or not depends on the might he uses. If one never uses his might, how can he lose hope on Goodness? (203)

In the eight-legged essay, the fourth parallel structure is optional. However, by asking the two rhetorical questions, Tang's exposition reaches its emotional climax in the last parallel leg. Finally, Tang concludes the essay by restating Confucius's exclamation that he had not met one who really cared for goodness (*dajie* 大結, "conclusion"):

Thus, for those people that I have seen, they are not constrained by Heaven but rather by themselves. It is not because Goodness stays away from them, but they choose to stay away from Goodness. Where can I find such a person who truly exerts his strength and rises as the type of Good person that I have expected? (203)

The eight-legged essay's emphasis on rigid rhetorical moves instead of free exposition is in keeping with Confucian ritualization. Confucius lays more stress on the individual's disciplined internal examination than on self-expression. According to the *Analects*, ideal communicators are virtuous individuals who have cultivated a good understanding of the universe and their place within it. They establish good character through daily self-examination and public behaviors in agreement with the morally appropriate rituals of the time. The exam essays were part of the social ritual for the consecration of the individual, encouraging self-examination in light of the Way. In the essay, the students were not expected to articulate unique thoughts about the universe that differed from neo-Confucian philosophy. Instead, they should exemplify their *ethos*, or "correct" voices, through skillful manipulation of Confucian concepts, commentators' interpretations, and historical events within an expected structure—like skilled ballet dancers who express their feelings and emotions through performing formal steps gracefully. The multiple rhetorical moves constituted a set of rites through which students could examine and cultivate themselves.

The second type of exam essay, which was undervalued in the grading process, was a group of five policy (*ce* 策) essays. Given concrete problems of national significance, such as famine relief, frontier security, military provision, local order, economic development, and public education, the examinees would elaborate on the problems and discuss how to handle them properly. While their own voices were suppressed in the eight-legged essay, the examinees' opinions on state matters were sought in the policy essays. As one of the oldest Chinese essay genres, the policy essay entertained the Confucian notion of a gentleman's political responsibility; that is, he needed to advise the ruler in state governance. However, in the late Qing dynasty, because many of the issues raised in the writing tasks were politically sensitive, the examiners would often write politically correct answers into the questions. Therefore, the question "often was so lengthy and comprehensive that little was left for a student to do except to paraphrase, converting the question into his answer" (Wejen Chang, "Legal Education" 295).[8] Thus, as often happened in the eight-legged essay, the examinees' opinions were often trampled in the policy essay. Further, as the examiners were trained in moral philosophy and philology, they tended to read policy essays narrowly through moral and philological lenses (Elman, *Cultural History of Civil Examinations*).

The third type of writing task was an essay called *lun* 論 (discourse) in which the examinees would be asked to comment on a certain historical figure or event. The question dealt with early dynastic histories, such as *Hanshi* 漢史 (History of the Han Dynasty) and *Shiji* 史記 (Records of the Grant Historian) as well as Confucius's *Chunqiu* 春秋 (Spring and Autumn Annals), one of the Five Classics but essentially a historical chronicle (Elman, "Changes"). This type of essay normally started with a statement followed by an elaboration of the topic; next, the historical significance of the person or event in question would be thoroughly discussed; finally, the essay would be wrapped up by the writer in a manner suggesting the topic's relevance in the present, which might carry subtle mockeries of the government and criticisms of society.[9] The rationale apparently goes along with the Confucian emphasis on the study of antiquity for self-cultivation and state governance.

Under the influence of the exam, Ming and Qing schools emphasized a full-time devotion to reading the Confucian canon and to writing essays in classical Chinese. In private schools at the county and township levels, students started with some primers and then moved on to study the Four Books and the Five Classics. They practiced yoking together double characters, constructing parallels, and writing species of composition.[10] In the academies at the provincial level, besides reading the canon, students studied a few other classics selected by each academy and practiced exam essays. We should note that this curriculum excluded a majority of the writing produced in Chinese history, including such genres as non-Confucian philosophical prose during the Spring and Autumn period (770–476 B.C.E.) and the Warring States period (475–221 B.C.E.), rhymed essays in the Han dynasty (206 B.C.E.–220 C.E.), dramas in the Yuan dynasty (1271–1368), and novels in the Ming and Qing dynasties (1368–1911). Daily recitation was the pedagogical norm in private schools and academies. Much like American schools before the mid-nineteenth century, recitation was valued for mental discipline (Berlin, *Writing*). It was also considered indispensable to the mastery of the classical writing style, which differed markedly from vernacular Chinese of the Ming and the Qing dynasties.

Therefore, with a fairly restricted reading list and intense preparation for the imperial exams, students of the late Qing (except students of foreign affairs schools such as Tong Wen Guan) were exposed only to Confucian classics and exam essays, even though these only constituted part of the Chinese rhetorical tradition.[11] The *bagu-ce-lun* pedagogical system was in full dominance when students studied Western subjects at Tong Wen Guan. When Western learning made its presence increasingly tangible in the 1870s, Chinese students encountered a rhetorical system markedly divergent from that represented by the Confucian classics and the exam essays.

The Infiltration of Western Rhetoric

Western learning spread when reformist officials in the Qing court entrusted national defense and economic development to Western technology. After China had lost the two Opium Wars (1840–43; 1856–60), some Qing officials clearly saw the inadequacy of the traditional humanities education. In contrast to conservatives like Woren, the reformists felt the pressing need to learn Western technology to save the nation from further foreign exploitation. To navigate between the two epistemological systems, they embraced a *ti-yong* 體、用 dualism, which regarded Chinese learning as essential versus Western learning as useful for practical purposes. The dualism later became the archetypical frame for Chinese educators to conceptualize the relationship between Chinese and foreign languages. The reformists founded foreign affairs schools (*yangwu xuetang* 洋務學堂) in several port cities, such as Guangzhou, Fuzhou, Shanghai, and Tianjin. In those schools, students studied not only Chinese classics but also a variety of Western subjects, including foreign languages, physics, chemistry, engineering, communication technology, and ship building—thus extending the Tong Wen Guan curriculum to a larger student body. In the *ti-yong* epistemology, these Western subjects were supposed to promote the Confucian vision of cosmological order and social advancement rather than to trample on it. It was for this ideal that the reformists held Western learning dear.

In the foreign affairs schools, students made their initial contact with Western scientific rhetoric. Like students at Tong Wen Guan, they focused on studying Western subjects and translating foreign science books into Chinese. Students of both Tong Wen Guan and Shanghai Polytechnic also published their homework or exam papers in scientific journals edited by their teachers (Elman, *Cultural History of Modern Science*). In the process of studying Western sciences and translating science books for their compatriots, students had an intimate encounter with Western scientific rhetoric.

Science lessons at Tong Wen Guan epitomized the character of this particular rhetoric. Students used *Gewu rumen* 格物入門 (Elements of Natural Philosophy and Chemistry, 1868), a seven-volume science primer written in Chinese by William A. P. Martin. The course moves from the study of water and fire to the study of electricity, mechanics, chemistry, and mathematics. The text adopts a dialogic scheme that mimics the question- (*chuti* 出題) and-answer (*poti* 破題) routines traditionally performed in Chinese academies (ii). The first volume deals with hydraulics. The first lesson opens as follows:

Q: What is the study of water (*shui xue* 水學)?

A: It investigates the nature of water to facilitate ordinary people in using it (*yi li minyong* 以利民用).

Q: What are the branches in the study of water?

A: There are two branches in the study of water: first, water statics (*jing shui* 靜水); second, water dynamics (*liu shui* 流水).

Q: Do water drops have attracting force (*xiangxi zhi li* 相吸之力)?

A: Although water flows and it is easy to both disperse and gather, its thin drops have attracting force. There are two pieces of evidence.

Q: What is the first piece of evidence?

A: For example, dews on grass are as round as pearls. Or, when water is spread on a dry ground, thin drops will temporarily congregate and form round shapes. The round shapes are all caused by the attracting power. (1)

Despite the traditional dialogic form, the passage departs from Confucian classics and the exam essays in several salient ways. First, the subject matter deals with natural objects rather than metaphysical, historical, or political matters. Second, the style is rather colloquial—familiar, plain, vivid, and straightforward. Third, the study of water (hydraulics) claims to benefit ordinary people like peasants and craftsmen, not just literati.

Western scientific rhetoric clearly introduces a whole new set of beliefs—ontological, methodological, and ideological—into human communication. Its fundamental belief system is rooted in a realist ontology, that is, the belief that there exists a knowable reality, driven by immutable natural laws. Scientific rhetoric is a continuation of classical Western rhetoric in terms of its modes of inquiry and its political and ethical concerns (Zappen, "Scientific Rhetoric"). Scientific rhetoric, as manifested in science books, is marked by the wide use of syllogistic and inductive logic and a plain style with the Aristotelian ideals of clarity, brevity, and appropriateness, and the rhetoric is applied to report objective observations and experiments. Zappen argues that this style, advocated by Francis Bacon, was extremely "suitable for the general participation in a particular kind of democratic science" in which average people are invited to learn about and respect nature and to make use of nature for the benefit of human life ("Francis" 75).

The *ti-yong* epistemology thus opened a Pandora's box, incrementally challenging Confucian rhetorical practices. Confucian rhetoric, as exercised by a small number of social elites, was concerned with philosophical, political, ethical, and emotional topics, but much less with natural phenomena or technology. Confucians embraced the notion of looking inward rather than outward for true knowledge; they had disdained the native Mohist tradition[12] in scientific investigation and formal logic ever since Confucianism was enshrined as the intellectual orthodoxy (Jensen). For the majority of Chinese who received little education, the philosophical, political, and ethical topics, which were addressed in an archaic code unintelligible to them, were far beyond their daily concerns. By contrast with the Chinese classics, Western subjects, through imported or translated books, introduced natural science and technology to a sizeable body of Chinese students in a plain, objective, and descriptive style.

The percolation of Western learning into Chinese society gradually shook loose classical humanities education. In 1898, after repeated petitions from government officials and enlightened intellectuals, the Qing government started to add more practical subjects to the civil service exam, including domestic politics, foreign affairs, business management, military science, natural sciences, and engineering. In 1901, the government elevated discourse and policy essays to primary importance in the exams by requiring four more discourse essays and downplayed the eight-legged essays by reducing them from eight to three (Elman, "Changes"). Although these changes did not immediately eliminate Confucianism-centered education, they oriented Chinese students to alternative, practical means of rightly governing the state.

The introduction of Western learning also challenged the male-centered elitism in the Chinese educational tradition. Under the influence of Confucianism, formal education for women was neither approved nor systematically provided for in Chinese society before the twentieth century. Evelyn Sakakida Rawski observes that "basic literacy was unevenly distributed between males and females, with perhaps 30 to 45 percent of males and only 2 to 10 percent of females possessing some ability to read and write" (23). In 1901, the emperor ordered a new grade school system to be established nationwide that was modeled after those in the West and Japan. The new system consisted of primary schools, middle schools, technical schools, normal schools, and universities.[13] For the first time, women were officially allowed to enroll in school, a development that raised the level of literacy and altered the pattern of male-dominated cultural politics. In 1905, the civil service exam system was completely abandoned. However, the humanistic spirit of reading Confucian classics and writing civil exam-styled essays lingered on in the new school system.

The establishment of the new school system led to a widespread familiarity with scientific rhetoric and reshaped rhetorical education in China. The new system confined reading and writing to a narrower curricular space. Required courses in lower primary schools included self-cultivation, classics, Chinese, mathematics, and physical education. In both higher primary and middle schools, more courses were added, such as foreign languages, physics, chemistry, and biology. Studying English and other Western subjects exposed a larger number of students to Western rhetoric for the first time. They had to move beyond the Four Books and Five Classics to ponder a wider variety of subject matter in their schoolwork. Consciously or unconsciously, they had to swing between two different epistemological and rhetorical systems. Western courses reconstructed the whole "noetic" field, that is, the specific relationship assumed to exist between language and reality (Berlin, *Rhetoric*), and thus altered how rhetorical education was understood in China.

Western rhetoric was explicitly taught in English composition classes. Systematic teaching of English writing can be traced to the first group of modern colleges established after Western models. These colleges fell into three subgroups: those established by the central government, by the provincial government, and by private organizations. At the Capital Teachers Learning Institute (later Beijing University), the first Western-style university established by the imperial government in 1898, five foreign-language courses were offered: English, German, French, Russian, and Japanese. Students were taught grammar, translation, and composition in their English class.[14] At Tianjin University, an institution established by a provincial official in 1895 and allegedly modeled after Harvard and Yale, English was a mandatory course. Students practiced both English exposition and English-to-Chinese translation (Li , Zhang, and Liu). In private institutions, many of which were American mission colleges, English composition was emphasized even more. These mission colleges were run independently or jointly by Baptist, Baptist Episcopal, and Presbyterian denominations. Before their final integration into the national university system in the early 1950s, foreign mission colleges enrolled 15 to 20 percent of the total number of college students in most years.[15] Although educating a relatively small proportion of students, those colleges were the national leaders in teaching English, ushering in Western learning, and internationalizing Chinese education. They introduced Anglo-American language pedagogies and produced a large cadre of Chinese teachers of English. Now we, therefore, turn to these colleges, which heavily influenced the teaching of college English writing for more than half a century.

American Influences in English Composition

Prior to government-initiated educational reforms, foreign forces had already infiltrated Chinese educational territory. After the Second Opium War, the government officially allowed foreign missionaries to conduct evangelical work in the country. When port cities along the coasts and major rivers were forced open by war treaties, mission schools mushroomed and gradually penetrated the hinterland. The primary goals of these schools were to train Christian leaders, provide religious training for Christian children, and convert non-Christians (Sinclair). In the beginning, these schools were small, teaching only Christian subjects and only in Chinese. Soon they included Chinese classics in their curricula because teaching Christianity exclusively did not attract Chinese families who valued traditional classical education for procuring social prestige. The civil service exam system dictated what education meant to the Chinese, namely joining the esteemed officialdom, something of which the missionaries were keenly aware.[16]

There was hardly a place for English in mission schools until the late nineteenth century. English was not taught in the early years because missionary educators believed that only a mastery of Chinese could help future Chinese clergy reach their parishioners (Brockman; Silsby). St. John's College in Shanghai (est. 1879) was one of the first schools to teach English. In 1881, it started to offer English courses in one of its departments, mainly at the request of some business patrons (Lamberton), reflecting a rising demand for English in business and trade. When mission schools began integrating Western science courses into their curricula in the 1890s, English started to be widely taught. Because translated works on science subjects were scarce at that time, students had to learn English first in order to understand their English-language textbooks. Thus, economic and scholastic factors prompted English teaching in mission schools.

By the turn of the twentieth century, English writing had become a prominent part of English education in mission schools. One of these early schools was Christian College in China (est. 1898), located in Macao. In 1900, freshmen and sophomores studied both English grammar and literary works in their English classes, and the school offered "independence and facility in the use of English cultivated by a carefully selected and graded series of exercises in original composition" (Christian College in China 20). Hangchow Presbyterian College (est. 1845) also taught English composition at that time. In 1904, English was one of four major subjects in both its preparatory school and college, along with Christianity, mathematics, and science. In the first two years of college, students studied English grammar and selected readings in English literature and wrote English compositions. They studied the art of letter writing in their freshman year and composed expositions on current affairs in their sophomore year. In the next three years, they practiced translating English into Chinese and vice versa, studied rhetoric and debate, and continued reading selected English literature (Hangchow Presbyterian College, *Hangzhou*).

Though English teaching in mission colleges was still relatively obscure in China at the turn of the twentieth century, by the 1910s it began to resemble its practice in American colleges in several remarkable ways. Most strikingly, like their American counterparts, almost all mission colleges consistently emphasized composition training for freshmen and sophomores and literature study throughout English majors' entire college education. Also significant was the fact that most of these schools listed English grammar as part of their freshman English curriculum. Emphasis on grammar makes sense because Chinese students might not have developed proficiency in English before they entered college.[17] But why did almost all mission colleges require students to study English composition just like American college students at that time?

Wen-Hsin Yeh highlights the utilitarian value of English in major port cities as the chief reason for teaching writing: "English in these private colleges of Shanghai and Tianjin, taught by native English speakers and studied with an emphasis on speech and composition, was the language that prepared students to take advantage of the opportunities presented by trade, finance, manufacturing, and the rise of new professions in the urban centers" (17). She also points out that English was a service course designed to facilitate the teaching and learning of other content courses, which were taught in English at those schools.

English composition was also routinely required as part of an administrative policy choice aimed at internationalizing Chinese higher education. All of the mission schools were funded by foreign missions and controlled by foreign boards and trustees from overseas. Managing a college in China, a foreign administrative staff made up primarily of Americans naturally would have to choose an administrative system that was familiar to them. A. W. March, a missionary educator, spelled out the administrators' sentiment at that time in terms of transplanting the entire Anglo-American higher education system to mission colleges in China:

> It is far easier for Americans and Englishmen to use their own mother tongue as the medium for their work. We can follow the curricula worked out by Western educators. We can pattern our schools much after those in which we received our degrees. We can follow their systems of classification, recording, discipline, and even the methods for teaching by which we were taught. We can easily compare the standards of our schools with those and estimate the comparative values of our degrees. . . . We are simply conducting in China the same kind of a school that we have been accustomed to all our lives. (110)

Despite March's ethnocentrism, his remarks unveil the challenges to Westerners who were running a college in China. To teach all subjects in Chinese would mean securing a sufficient number of books written in Chinese and managing a large number of Chinese-speaking teaching staff, which would be daunting for foreign administrators. March also suggested that a standardized international system of education would facilitate both degree comparison and knowledge transfer. Modeling themselves after American colleges, mission colleges, established mostly by American missions in China, were thus consistent in their English courses. Influenced by the new discipline of English studies in the United States—"a discipline based on English as the language of learning and literature as the specialized province of study" (Berlin, *Rhetoric* 22)—the missionary educators deemed composition part and parcel of the relocated English education in Chinese colleges.

Following their American counterparts, all mission colleges required that students demonstrate satisfactory English ability before entering college. The catalog for Fukien Union College (est. 1916), for example, stipulated that "the standard of admission to the University should correspond to that of London and Yale University" (5). English composition, grammar, conversation, reading, dictation, and English literary works were tested in the school's entrance exam in 1916. The composition section involved "analysis and synthesis of sentences; paraphrasing; direct and indirect narration, punctuation, correction of errors, and letter and essay writing" (10). At Ginling College (est. 1913), the first women's college in China, students needed to demonstrate in the entrance exam their competence in oral and written English and their knowledge of English literature. Requirements for oral and written English were spelled out as "accuracy in spelling, [in] grammatical construction, and in pronunciation; ability to converse on ordinary subjects, to write from dictation, to translate from Chinese, and to compose simple paragraphs" (Ginling College, *Bulletin* [1915] 11–12). Stringent requirements for English grammar, speaking, and writing ensured that entering freshmen were prepared for the challenging course work conducted mostly in English.

Once students entered college, they were taught English composition in as diverse ways as American students were taught. However, an examination of school catalogs, course schedules, and textbooks reveals some of the conceptual resemblances in the composition teaching in the two locales, resemblances deriving largely from the use of similar texts in Chinese colleges (both mission and state) and in the United States.[18] For example, *The Mother Tongue*, volume 1 (Sarah L. Arnold and George L. Kittredge, 1908) and volume 2 (Kittredge and Arnold, 1908) were commonly used in Chinese middle schools. *New Composition and Rhetoric for Schools* (Robert Herrick and Lindsay T. Damon, 1911), *Outlines of Composition and Rhetoric* (John F. Genung and Charles L. Hanson, 1915), and *Written and Spoken English* (Erle E. Clippinger, 1917) were widely used in Chinese junior and senior colleges. All written by American scholars, these texts systematically introduced Anglo-American rhetoric and composition into China. To see those conceptual resemblances in English composition teaching between the two countries, a scrutiny of these textbooks is thus warranted.

Originally writing for American children, the authors of *The Mother Tongue* (volumes 1 and 2) conceive of composition in close connection with speaking, grammar, and literary taste. As the authors state, the book was designed "to guide children to an intelligent appreciation and enjoyment of good English, to help them to speak and write correctly, and to introduce them to the study of grammar" (Arnold and Kittredge iii). The first volume furnishes numerous interesting short narratives and poems for the children to read and then imitate in speaking and writing exercises. The authors hoped that children would cultivate their taste and develop a love for literature in their mother tongue. In volume 2, the authors offer a systematic treatment of English grammar. They emphasize that grammar is a science of language and that "the rules of grammar agree with laws of thought" (xvi). Therefore, following American children's natural, cognitive sequence of acquiring English, they introduce elements of grammar. As they explain, "[some difficult elements or constructions] are inserted in their natural and logical places, in accordance with the expressed wish of many teachers to have the treatment continuous" (iv). Thus, as illustrated by *The Mother Tongue*, writing at the elementary level was taught in conjunction with speaking, leading American children to the study of Anglo-American literature. The study of grammar directed the children to methodically analyze their thoughts and words employed in speaking and writing.

Immersing Chinese students in American school texts, and hence in the U.S. national culture, created both obstacles and opportunities for learning. Used in the Chinese context, *The Mother Tongue* oriented Chinese students with reading, writing, and reasoning the way American children did. However, since English was a "devil's tongue," students' imaginations had to be permitted to run wild sometimes. For example, students were asked to study the verbs in the following narrative adapted from Charles Dickens's "A Christmas Carol":

> Mrs. Cratchit made the gravy hissing hot. Master Peter mashed the potatoes with incredible vigor. Miss Belinda sweetened up the applesauce. Martha dusted the plates. Bob took Tiny Tim beside him in a tiny

corner at the table. The two young Cratchits set chairs for everybody, and, while they mounted guard at their own posts, crammed spoons into the mouths lest they should shriek for goose before their turn came to be helped. (Arnold and Kittredge 190)

Filled with rich cultural references, the lighthearted narrative would quickly bring the cozy aura of Christmas dinner to American or British children. However, the same references—gravy, mashed potatoes, apple-sauce, and plates—threw Chinese students into bewilderment. They would have to work hard to imagine a group of "foreign devils" meeting to conduct a fiendish family ritual, and doing so would make it nearly impossible to appreciate Dickens's light humor. However, such colloquial narratives could be liberating for the students. Departing from the morally and politically charged classics that continued to dominate the required reading in Chinese schools, these narratives freed students from such confines, allowing them to imagine other peoples, other cultures, and other worlds.[19]

The other three widely circulated texts, originally written for American high school pupils, conceive of composition as a realm independent from literary studies. Their authors concur on what systematic training in rhetoric and English writing mean for high school students. All three texts offer detailed treatment of elements of English grammar, rhetorical effectiveness of words, sentences, and paragraphs, and modes of written composition. Unlike *The Mother Tongue*, volume 1, which employs numerous literary texts to foster children's love for literature, these texts mainly use student writings and real-life practical writings as examples. Their treatment of these three major areas without the use of literature suggests that rhetoric and composition at the more advanced levels was conceptualized as a realm independent from literature courses.

Although all three texts focus on writing, like *The Mother Tongue*, they reinforce the connection between speaking and writing. For example, Genung and Hanson explain the preparatory function of speaking for writing in *Outlines of Composition and Rhetoric*. They hold that "small talks, particularly on subjects about which the pupil knows a good deal, are always valuable in themselves and useful as a step in the preparation of written compositions. . . . Some of the energy expended by teachers in correcting written work might be used more profitably in a discussion of oral compositions" (iv). To that end, all three texts present speaking exercises alongside writing exercises.

Furthermore, the three texts maintain the lineage of classical Western oratory and are meant to prepare students for a liberal democracy. When introducing argumentation, all three texts illustrate this discursive mode with examples of public debates. Genung and Hanson focus on the procedure of parliamentary debates in the chapter "Argumentation." Clippinger devotes an entire chapter to reasoning, parliamentary law, and debate in *Written and Spoken English*. Herrick and Damon simply define argumentation in relation to public debates: "We may attempt to convince others of truth or falsity of a given statement. Compositions of this kind are called arguments; oral arguments in which two speakers or groups of speakers support opposite sides of a question are called debates" (38). Both connecting writing with speaking and locating argumentation in public debate clearly indicate the lineage of classical Western oratory tradition in English composition instruction. Furthermore, behind argumentation and public debate resides the notion of liberal democracy commonly celebrated in the West. Although China had its own oratorical tradition (Garrett, "Classical Chinese," "Chinese Buddhist"), there was little if any pedagogical connection between public debates and writing. Confucian educators valued writing rather than speaking as the means of ritualizing an individual in Chinese feudalism. Even in imperial court debates, writing was much preferred. The connection between speaking and writing would enhance college students' deliberative engagement with the politics of republican China (see chapter 2).

Another striking feature of the textbooks is the predominance of the modes of discourse. All three texts devote a large section to description, narration, exposition, and argumentation, the hallmark of what was later called current-traditional rhetoric in the United States. As described by Berlin, current-traditional rhetoric originated in the faculty psychology of eighteenth-century rhetoric and kept its most mechanical features. Vastly different from the Confucian emphasis on seeking truth through internal examination, faculty psychology located reality in the external world and attempted to account for all features of human behavior—the sensory, the rational, the ethical, and the aesthetic—characterizing each of them as a different mental faculty that functions independently of the others. Current-traditional rhetoric retained the mechanistic part of faculty psychology and the most elementary emotional considerations in its concerns. Rhetoric's sole appeal is "to the understanding and reason, with its highest manifestation to be found in exposition and argumentation" (Berlin, *Writing* 63). In an atmosphere of relentless academic pursuit and scientific investigation for building a strong nation, current-traditional rhetoric found a home in Chinese colleges. Starting in the 1910s, English writing curricula in almost all mission and state colleges featured a sequenced instruction of description, narration, exposition, and argumentation in the freshman and sophomore years.[20] For the first time in Chinese history, writing was taught in the four modes of discourse, a development that in turn influenced the teaching and practice of Chinese writing (see chapter 2).

Current-traditional rhetoric reduced style to correctness in the writing class. For example, the three American texts stressed the importance of correct forms in speech and writing. Herrick and Damon instructed the student: "Carefulness in pronunciation, in the use of words, in grammar, and in spelling will bring its own reward in the form of a justifiable self-respect. Failure to talk and write correctly brings much the same penalty as bad manners" (16). By comparing correct forms to good, ritualistic manners, the authors tried to humanize style for students. However, against the backdrop of U.S. nation-building, the emphasis on correct form and the ensuing penalty for its violation was in fact disciplinary, taming American citizens' tongues to Standard English, the de facto national language. While stressing correctness, Genung and Hanson also elaborate on how to enhance the rhetorical effectiveness of every word, sentence, and paragraph.

In Chinese colleges, emphasis on correct form was already the prevailing composition pedagogy. Graded written work tended to precede any sort of free writing. When students had the chance to write freely, their papers were often returned dotted with red symbols marking only language errors rather than anything related to the content.[21] It is not surprising that a student at Ginling College ended one of her compositions quite wittily, pitying her teacher's grueling work in grading student papers: "I thought Miss Stendel will be very tired to correct this poor writing. I want to save her spirit and her red pencil so I dare not write any more" (Tsai). As also revealed in the quote, the American emphasis on correct forms discouraged the student from expressing herself further in writing. While style did not exclusively mean correct forms in composition textbooks, pedagogically such a focus was certainly rampant in Chinese colleges. The analogy comparing poor writing to bad manners made by Herrick and Damon implied that striving for correct forms was simply part of the English composition ritual that Chinese students had to perform.

With current-traditional rhetoric dominant, other rhetorical forms were marginalized in composition classes, such as expressionistic rhetoric. According to Berlin (*Rhetoric*), expressionistic rhetoric was derived from the liberal culture of higher education in the United States. For liberal educators, literature courses would put students in touch with the civilizing influences of Western culture, thus providing a basis for ethical behavior. Writing, if it were to be taught in the university, should be taught through cultivating the individual in literary study and through the individual's seeking the truth of his or her unconscious world in sensory experiences. This rhetorical form was apparent in *The Mother Tongue* used in some Chinese middle schools. Reading and writing were developed together to cultivate students' love for Anglo-American literature.

In mission colleges, expressionistic rhetoric was reflected in the combination of literature and composition. Students were asked to write literary analyses, short stories, and personal diaries. For example, Ginling College offered a short story course in 1913 in which students read published short stories, wrote their own short stories, and presented them to the class. Starting in 1931, literature and composition were completely merged into one course among those required for both freshmen and sophomores. A similar trend also occurred at other schools. At Shanghai College (est. 1918), students studied both literature and composition in freshman and sophomore English. The University of Nanking (est. 1889) required sophomores to take "Readings in English Prose" beginning in 1914. Besides reading English prose, students studied the principles of rhetoric and composition, emphasizing the development of literary appreciation. Both Peking University (est. 1870) and Shanghai College also offered creative writing courses to their English-major juniors and seniors during the 1920s.[22] Despite these instances in which literature and composition were integrated, most freshman composition courses in both mission and state colleges followed the four modes closely and required little literature reading. In contrast, expressionistic rhetoric prevailed in Anglo-American literature courses, which, however, were only required of English majors.

Another commonality shared by American and mission colleges was the service function of English composition for other content courses: composition classes prepared students to study other subjects and to communicate in their own disciplines.[23] At some mission colleges, attention was paid to studying the nature and principles of writing in the student's discipline. Canton Christian College, for example, stressed the close relationship between English study and other courses in its 1909 curriculum: "There can be no fast and hard lines drawn between the work in many classes and the English course. . . . Thus is given part of the general cultural and elementary scientific course within the time allotted to English" (*Catalogue, 1909–1910* 27). In 1923, the college offered an English composition course exclusively for freshmen in the College of Agriculture. Students practiced themes on subjects taken from both their practical work and agriculture textbooks. The emphasis on writing for the benefit of subjects across the curriculum was also highlighted in Shanghai College's 1922 catalog: "All classes are required to hand in written work on a theme each week. . . . An attempt is made to correlate this theme-work with the work in other departments, so that the themes may be prepared on subjects furnished by other courses as well as English" (57). All freshmen in Shanghai College took a course called "Rhetoric," which required a detailed study of the rhetorical principles illustrated in texts used in other departments. Students also took three other rhetoric and composition courses in their freshman and sophomore years—"Composition," "English Essay," and "Public Speaking"—which all correlated the students' theme work with their work in other departments. Since science and engineering courses were taught with texts imported from the United States and Britain, English composition prepared the students to function effectively in English.

Compared to Americans, the British had limited influence in college English composition. Primarily interested in elementary and secondary education, they never established any colleges in China except the University of Hong Kong (Davin). However, in secondary schools, the British played a role no less important than that of the Americans. Students in those schools sometimes studied for the Oxford and the Cambridge local exams or the London University matriculation.[24] A series of grammar and composition textbooks written by John C. Nesfield achieved the widest circulation in Chinese secondary schools. They included *English Grammar, Past and Present* (1889), *Oral Exercises in English Composition* (1905), *Junior Course of English Composition* (1901), and *Senior Course of English Composition* (1903). These texts formed a systematic way of teaching composition, but with no significant departure from American methods. Students started with oral composition of sentences and paragraphs and learning grammar rules. Then they moved on to study rhetorical effectiveness in composition and practiced writing descriptive, narrative, reflective, expository, and argumentative essays. The British texts displayed two unique features though. First, they were written to be accessible to students who did not speak English as their mother tongue, particularly those in British colonies. Second, they were extremely exam-oriented. In the *Senior Course*, for example, the author listed numerous essay topics from previous civil and scholastic exams held in Britain and India. These aspects contributed to the appeal of the texts in Chinese schools, thus subjugating Chinese students to British cultural and literary taste. By structuring composition instruction in ways compatible with American mission schools, British-controlled secondary schools adequately prepared their students for state and mission colleges.

The conceptual and pedagogical commonalities between Chinese and American colleges in teaching composition occurred for several reasons. First, most mission colleges were controlled by American church denominations and staffed largely by North American teachers, with the result that academic departments and course offerings were structured following the Anglo-American model. Second, college courses in science and engineering were commonly taught with texts written in English, which made English composition an indispensable service course. Third, and most important, English composition at both mission and state colleges was supported by the wide use of texts published in the United States. These books, written within the framework of current-traditional rhetoric, fortified the dominance of this rhetorical paradigm in Chinese colleges. The British influence was tangible but limited to middle school composition. Underneath these pedagogical commonalities lay the most salient political reason—the inability of the Chinese government to defend its educational territory against the colonialists and to furnish its people with the kind of education they most needed. It also should be noted that the Anglo-American influences not only gave rise to these conceptual and pedagogical commonalities but also found nuanced expression in students' English writing.

New Sensibilities in the Devil's Tongue

While English composition served its institutional purposes, at the individual and more personal level, it mediated between the student's inner self and the outside world. Students of Tong Wen Guan, as the earlier student essay shows, tried to make sense of Christianity in relation to the traditional Chinese ontology through writing. English lent them a sense of distance so that they could examine themselves and relativize Chinese society, and it allowed them to imagine and describe the world in the foreign devil's terms. English writing opened up a network of novel references, which forced students to compare and contrast different aspects of human experience. The past and the future, the East and the West, the personal and the universal all converged underneath the students' pens. Through the newly acquired symbol system, they vocalized their new sensibility and in the process made the devil's tongue less devilish. To delve into this new sensibility for a vantage point, we might examine a student magazine of St. John's College.

Publishing in the English magazine meant learning to negotiate with cultural, linguistic, and rhetorical challenges in contact-zone discourses. Founded as a bimonthly publication in 1890, the *St. John's Echo* claimed to be "the first paper published in the Orient by Chinese youths in a tongue foreign to them and only acquired after hard years of study" ("Greeting" 1). Most articles published in the early years were originally written in English classes. Some students were fully engaged in the editorship and gained much experience in English writing. Writing and reasoning in English, however, was extremely challenging. One of the student editors recalled the amusing difficulty of having to explore an idea in Chinese and express it in English:

> To those who desired to make contributions to *The Echo* and aspired to become editors, they made resort to the Library a great deal in order to read current news from the English papers and also to read a large number of standard novels, especially those by Scott, Lytton, Washington Irving and the like. Once a young editor was assigned the political subject of the "Open Door Policy and the Spheres of Influence." He worried for days and mumbled to himself their Chinese translation as "the way of opening a door and balls of powers." He thought to himself the best [way] was to turn the knob in order to open the door and that to develop balls of power, all that was necessary was to learn to pitch hard. (St. John's University, *St. John's University* 49)

The essay topic dealt with the fact that after the Second Opium War the Chinese market was forced open by foreign powers who claimed exclusive trading rights to certain parts of the country ("spheres of influence"). The quite comical acts of turning the knob and pitching the ball ironically capture the complexity of transculturation, the process whereby the subordinated or the marginalized select and invent from materials transmitted by a metropolitan culture. Both "open door policy" and "spheres of influence" were political terms too foreign and complex for the student to decode. For students who struggled with the basics of English, writing was a recursive process of translating between multiple cultural and linguistic codes. They tried to understand an English topic by translating it into their mother tongue; and they formulated ideas in Chinese and translated them into English. Empirical studies have revealed the recursive processes of first language composition (Emig; Flower and Hayes; Perl). When one composes in a second or a third language, the processes are further complicated by the additional mental translation between multiple languages (Yichun Liu; Wang and Wen; Zhang Zuocheng). To express their new sensibility in English, Chinese students had to struggle on multiple levels with cultural, linguistic, and rhetorical terms.

The *St. John's Echo* encouraged expression of students' personal feelings, desires, and experiences, which were undervalued if not forbidden in their Chinese school essays. In the 1890s, some St. John's students seeking government positions continued to take the civil service exam. Thus, they practiced the exam essays in their Chinese classes. However, in their English essays, they were freed from any formal constraints. The following passage is quoted from the essay "The Great Chinese Garden in Shanghai" in the opening issue of the magazine. In several remarkable ways, the passage differs from every essay genre that the students had ever practiced in their Chinese class:

> It is the greatest and the most famous garden which has ever been known in our country. It is situated on the banks of the river Haw-ha-poo, near the city of Shanghai. It is about two hundred Chinese miles in circumference. It is full of beautiful houses, pleasant walks and many interesting things. When the climate is very mild flowers grow there abundantly. If you look deeper, you will find different kinds of animals, such as the lion, tiger, elephant, monkey, &c.; different sorts of birds, such as the peacock, ostrich and canary; and also different kinds of fish swimming in the fresh water. Besides these, there are green lawns, tea-houses, lotus-ponds and small bridges, which have nine curves. This is a public garden, whose keeper allows every person to enter, if he will pay him twenty cents. If you are a boy, the keeper only receives from you ten cents. The garden keeper will tell his servants to receive you either on a steamer or a carriage, if it is too far for you to walk, and you shall give him ten cents again. (Wong 3)

Reading through this piece, one is easily attracted to the author's delightful description of "the most beautiful garden" in China. Such a topic, showing a "trivial" personal interest, would never make its way into the Chinese exam essays. Through this seemingly insignificant topic, the student shared his pride, enchantment, and humor with the reader and used both expository and descriptive strategies, the latter of which were rarely seen in the Chinese exam essays. His remarkable choice of topic and rhetorical strategies might be influenced by his awareness of a particular audience, namely the Western audience. As the magazine indicated in the same issue, "The West is still ignorant of many things concerning the Chinese nation, its literature and customs, and we will strive to tell you something about them in a simple and unpretentious way" ("Greeting" 1). To enlighten the ignorant West about the Chinese nation, the student chose a topic and rhetorical strategies that he deemed appropriate for his audience. Despite being considered a devil's tongue, English enabled the student to share his personal world with a larger world; in doing so, he also extended the English codes by adding new cultural nuances.

The *Echo* was pervaded by an air of national crisis at the turn of the twentieth century. Students lamented the weakness of the Qing government and the great inertia among the Chinese facing foreign aggression. Their essays revealed Chinese literati's traditional aspiration for the state as demonstrated in the civil service exam essays. In an essay entitled "The First Step of China's Independence" published in 1904, the author exclaimed:

Look at the present condition of China—inside, the government extremely corrupt; outside, the ever increasing foreign encroachments[;] above, the governing class selfish and unjust[;] and below[,] the governed, ignorant and disunited—who but the cold-blooded or indifferent will not shed his tears?

Any mines she possesses, are opened by demand; any railroad she constructs is claimed by treaty; any ambassador she sends, is accepted at will; nay any province she has is limited by the sphere of influence. Who but the foolish and shameless will not say that China is independent in name but dependent in reality?

Alas! The majority of the nation are blind. The enlightened who understand China's position are but few. The majority care nothing more than for drinking and eating. Allowing national affairs to be managed entirely by the government, they have no political thoughts. Whether China is dependent or independent makes no difference to them. A minority are ambitious, energetic, eager to wash away the national shame and zealous to regain their country's historical glory. To gain national independence, reformation has been considered by them as a necessary step. Were there no Chinese of such type, China would be dependent for ever. (Dzung 19)

Permeating the text is the student's critical voice—a mixture of his disappointment, anger, and frustration with both the government and the people. Compared to the Chinese exam essays, however, this piece marks a sharp departure in the student's reasoning. Instead of evoking antiquity as evidence for his argument or as precedent for the solution, the student carefully examines the present to argue that, without reformation, China would be dependent on the West forever. Further, the author challenges the Confucian depiction of ordinary Chinese as "grass" to be bent by the "wind," or the ruling class, by trying to arouse the political consciousness of the former. Although the student reasons differently from Confucian teachings, he employs figures of speech highly favored by Confucius, such as parallelism, rhetorical question, and metaphor. The parallel structure in the first paragraph even rhymes with the repeated final *ts*, reminiscent of classical Chinese four-line poetry (*jueju* 絕句): "inside, the government extremely corrupt; outside, the ever increasing foreign encroachments; above, the governing class selfish and unjust; and below, the governed, ignorant and disunited." The juxtaposition of both traditional and nontraditional rhetorical strategies offers a fresh breeze to the student's argument.

China's hope was not diminished though. In the same issue, another student described changes in "the Chinese mind" in the wake of new Chinese literature, saying, "it was inactive and blind, narrow and bigoted, but is now alive with new ideas, new energy, new spirit, new sentiments, new motives, far nobler and freer than those of the past" (Y. Y. Tsu 13). The opening of the Chinese mind was attributed to the rise of new literature published in hundreds of emerging newspapers and magazines in the late Qing dynasty. The new literature introduced Western thoughts, employed written Chinese to unite the reading class, and revolutionized the political conception of the people. Thanks to the new literature, the author observes, "They, the reading class—the most influential people in China—begin to understand the relation they bear to each other. Instead of being proud of their literary aristocracy, they now extend their pity to the ignorance of even the common people" (14). These united and mentally liberated people, the author suggests, would bring about a new nation.

These two excerpts demonstrate the students' solid English; more important, they exemplify the transforming power of the devil's tongue in modern Chinese culture. English afforded the students a broader vision, or the ability to view objects from the vantage point of multiple cultures, inspiring them to critically examine their own world. A foreign language hypothetically implied an outside, detached audience for the students, one that encouraged them to speak their minds without fearing criticism or punishment. English writing engaged them to closely observe the happenings in their country and to make sense of them. It allowed them to depart from traditional Confucian thinking and to respond to new contingencies with open minds. Students also "played" with English, mixing in preferred Chinese rhetorical strategies to vocalize their experiences and perspectives; thus, they enriched the English language by adding new rhetorical and cultural nuances to it. Their use of and experimentation with English prose style contributed to the rise of a new Chinese literature and culture.

Apparently, English transcended the "tool" metaphor that the Chinese had assigned it earlier. When English was introduced into Chinese schools, Chinese educators wished to contain the devil's tongue by articulating the *ti-yong* dualistic frame. Conceiving national cultures as discrete, static entities, they naively hoped to use their own culture as points of anchorage from which to put Western learning to practical use. However, my historical narrative has revealed a dialectic rather than a dualistic relation between Chinese and Western cultures. The introduction of Western learning helped to reform Chinese schools and their curricular systems, hence the traditional Chinese epistemological framework. Through English, students assimilated, reworked, and reaccentuated Western cultural values in the formation of modern Chinese culture. At the same time, students added Chinese expressions and values to the English language, making it incrementally less Anglo-American. This dialecticism would continue to play out through the teaching of English and other Western subjects, despite the periodic evocation of the *ti-yong* dualism in Chinese mainstream discourse in later years.

To conclude, the introduction of English composition into Chinese schools can be attributed to both Chinese impulses and colonialist forces. The dominant Chinese school curriculum until the turn of the twentieth century consisted of Confucian classics and the exam essays. They embodied the full course of literary, moral, and rhetorical education in Chinese tradition, dating back two thousand years. This tradition valued writing as one of the rhetorical means to ritualize individuals and to engage them in state governance. However, writing-centered humanistic education proved to be ineffective in building a strong, modern nation. Thus, at Tong Wen Guan and other foreign affairs schools, the curriculum shifted to studying Western subjects and to translating dispatches and foreign books. As the Chinese government was unable to defend its educational territory and to furnish the kind of education that its citizens most needed, foreign mission schools flourished. Both state and mission colleges imported English composition texts from the United States, and thus arose the unanimous teaching of Anglo-American rhetoric and composition. While the first half-century of English teaching was marked by the importation of American composition pedagogies, the following years shifted towards conscientious negotiation with and domestication of the imports amid the Chinese struggle for political and cultural independence.

2

WRITING AND DECOLONIZATION

1919–49

By the time the First World War ended and a half-century of English teaching had passed, Chinese literati no longer despised the devil's tongue quite so much. They keenly understood that, rather than a makeshift strategy, mastering foreign languages was indispensable in pursuing their modern dreams. The country was partitioned and controlled by local warlords with the complicity of foreign powers. Western missionaries continued to proselytize as freely as before. A Japanese militarist regime coveted China as well as other Asian countries as it set about building its Greater East Asian Empire. The national crisis that emerged in 1840 deepened in the beginning of the twentieth century. In the continual "self-strengthening" movement, the literati came to realize that not only political and educational structures but, more fundamentally, Chinese culture would also need a revolution. In a new cultural overhaul starting in the late 1910s, again, English played a pivotal role.

After many years of wholesale adoption of Anglo-American composition pedagogy and textbooks, the 1920s saw conscious efforts to absorb and reform them according to local traditions. In the early years, the Chinese had to depend on native speakers to teach them English. With a sense of cultural superiority, Anglo-American teachers brought their pedagogy, texts, and values into the classroom as if they were teaching at home. More and more Chinese entered the field of English teaching in the 1920s. Trained in both classical Chinese and Western learning, they well understood what the former could not offer for a modern nation. They critically adopted Western language theory and pedagogy to reform Chinese language and its pedagogical practices. They taught English with an acute sensitivity to students' strengths and weaknesses. As English teaching increasingly came to the service of Chinese, it was brought to the heart of Chinese cultural reformation.

The New Culture Movement

As more Chinese were exposed to Western political and intellectual traditions, they came to embrace liberal democracy as a political ideal for the nation. No longer wanting to preserve the Qing regime, some bourgeoisie argued that hereditary feudalism was a major obstacle to the rise of a modern China. Led by Sun Yat-Sen (1866–1925), the bourgeoisie battled with the regime for two decades and finally established a republic in 1912. The republic was founded on Sun's "Three People's Principles" (*sanmin zhuyi* 三民主義), which is a compromise between Western political philosophy and Chinese tradition. The first principle is nationalism, the movement to unite all ethnicities of China and to free them from imperialist domination. The second principle is democracy, under which people have rights to express their political wishes and exercise their political power through the National Assembly. The government operates through the checks and balances among five branches—legislative, executive, judicial, control, and examination. The third principle is social welfare, or cultivating an industrial economy and ensuring equality of landholdings for peasant farmers. The rise of a republic kindled a hope among the Chinese for ending foreign exploitation.

However, the republican government was too weak to defend the national interests. At the end of World War I in 1918, the terms of the Treaty of Versailles once again permitted foreign powers to encroach on Chinese sovereignty. Despite being a member of the victorious Allied Powers, China's request to reclaim control of Qindao in Shangdong Province from the defeated Germans was rejected by the Allies. Instead, they ordered the port city to be handed over to Japan, an action that provided a steppingstone for a full-scale Japanese invasion of China in the 1930s. The republican government's impotence enraged the masses and led to nationwide student and worker protests in the spring of 1919. Inside China, with the help of local warlords, Western powers exercised their influence by directly or indirectly controlling parts of the country. China fell deeper and deeper into the hands of foreign imperialists.

In educational affairs, the government continued to relinquish its central control. Its weakness was repeatedly ridiculed by foreign missions and cited as one of the reasons that they should play a commanding role in the educational sector. For example, Peking University (later Yenching University), controlled by American church denominations, made this point clear in a statement in 1920: "The government of China is hopelessly weak and corrupt, the people of China are pitifully poor and ignorant. . . . The only hope for China lies in the training of a new type of young manhood and womanhood who have the education and the character to bring about a better political and social order" (*Announcement of the College* 15). The statement evoked a notion, popular in the West after the Opium Wars, that Chinese civilization had declined and its ignorant people were unable to envision and build a modern nation (following the Western model); therefore, Westerners saw themselves as the Messiahs for the wretched Chinese. This idea echoed the criticism made by the St. John's student we encountered in chapter 1, who also censured the frailty of the government and the inertia of the people. Both the university statement and the student essay corroborated the imposing presence of Western imperialism. They also revealed that colonialist discourse had deeply saturated Chinese minds, making them adopt colonialists' worldviews.

In such a disappointing sociopolitical climate, some intellectuals advocated democracy and science as ways to replace the *ti-yong* dualism in nation-building. Instead of safeguarding traditional Chinese culture, they wanted to crash it. In the New Culture movement (1915–23), they promoted democracy to counter China's feudal social structure and ethics; they promoted science to counter Confucianism, idol worship, and superstition that were deeply seated in traditional Chinese mentality; and they called for the birth of a new culture to replace old Chinese literature and language. Under the leadership of Hu Shi (1891–1962) and Chen Duxiu (1879–1942), two returnees from overseas studies, writers began to use the modern vernacular to produce literary works. They imitated Western language styles to innovate the Chinese language. They introduced Marxism as well as other Western political philosophies to their compatriots. The movement was a cultural battle against the feudalism and imperialism that had shackled the Chinese minds.

In their efforts to engender a new culture, the intellectuals advocated a transactional view of language and reality. They saw truth as arising out of the interaction of elements of the rhetorical situation rather than as residing in either the objective or the subjective worlds. Appealing to the positions of American philosophers C. S. Peirce, William James, and John Dewey, Hu Shi expressed this epistemological position most ardently: "Truth is simply a tool used [by humans] to adapt to the environment. As the environment changes, so will truth. . . . Knowledge that humans need is not the absolute '*dao*' 道 or '*li*' 理 but truth here and now that is particular to myself" (Hu, "Shiyan zhuyi" 295). Denying absolute truth, Hu emphasized truth as historical, contingent, socially constructed, and instrumental. Language, such as the terms *dao* (the Way) and *li* (reason), mediated the traditional Chinese discourse of truth. As truth was contingent and particular to a writer, Hu argued, the writer's thoughts and feelings, rather than Confucian ethics, became the most valued substance of his or her writing. To produce modern writing, Hu suggested, one needs to observe life closely and to delve into various social issues. Furthermore, one should make good use of detailed description when writing about people, the environment, social matters, and personal feelings ("Wenxue"; "Jianshe"). The transactional view of language encouraged Chinese writers to strategically battle against the old culture.

The "struggling to survive" sentiment also infused composition instruction, positioning composition as a cultural battlefield for both teachers and students. The continual, critical contact with Western culture gradually gave rise to a new cultural development in Chinese schools, manifesting in the intersection of Chinese and Anglo-American rhetorical traditions in composition, translation, public speaking, student writing, and pedagogy. Born out of the New Culture movement, the new culture of rhetoric and composition, with English playing a strategic role in it, contributed to the Chinese struggle for decolonization and modernization.

Conflation of Rhetorical Traditions

As Chinese intellectuals became increasingly open to Western learning, they ushered Western rhetoric into Chinese writing practices. English and Chinese composition in republican China went through two parallel paths in adopting and transforming Western rhetorical and composition theories. Anglo-American teachers introduced Western rhetoric via imported textbooks; Chinese scholars and teachers studied it conscientiously and brought it into Chinese school writing. Although Chinese writing was emphasized in secondary schools and English writing in colleges, the historical trajectories of their teaching showed both parallels and intersections.

Western rhetoric was formally introduced into Chinese writing practices through the mediation of Japanese rhetorical works.[1] Several Chinese rhetorics, such as Chen Jiebai's *Xin zhu xiucixue* 新著修辭學 (New Rhetoric), Wang Yi's *Xiucixue* 修辭學 (Rhetoric), and Long Baichun's *Wenzi fafan* 文字發凡 (An Introduction to Language), appeared in the first three decades of the twentieth century. In one way or another, they were indebted to at least two Japanese works—*Shin bijigaku* 新美辭學 (New Rhetoric, 1902) and *Shujigaku* 修辭學 (Rhetoric, 1908) (Yuan and Zong). Both were heavily influenced by Western rhetorical theories. In *Shin bijigaku*, Shimamura Hogetsu claims that he studied Western rhetoric (particularly Adams S. Hill's work), grammar, aesthetics, ethics, and psychology when writing the book. He defines rhetoric as "the study of the principles for achieving aesthetic effects, that is, a type of study on written composition" (1) and then discusses four sub-definitions of rhetoric; the evolution of both Western and Chinese rhetoric; elements of rhetoric; diction; figures of speech; style; and psychological, ethical, and scientific aspects of aesthetics. In *Shujigaku*, Takeshima Hogoromo lists four books that he had referenced: John F. Genung's *Practical Rhetoric*, Adam S. Hill's *Foundation of Rhetoric* and *Principles of Rhetoric*, and Barrett Wendell's *English Composition*. Hogoromo's book first defines rhetoric as "a field of study aiming at teaching people how to express their thoughts and feelings most effectively through language" (1). Also focusing on the rhetoric of written texts, the book is divided into two parts: style (rhetorical styles, elements of a text, and figures of speech) and organization (description, narration, exposition, and argumentation).

Apparently, the two Japanese rhetorical works represented Anglo-American rhetoric at that time in quite a comprehensive fashion. Western rhetoric since Hugh Blair and George Campbell had been increasingly influenced by new developments in psychology, logic, and aesthetics. In addition, scientific approaches to rhetoric gave rise to so-called current-traditional rhetoric in American composition instruction in which writing was taught for the purpose of learning new information and engaging in free inquiry, with special attention to style and arrangement (Berlin, *Rhetoric*; *Writing*; Brereton; Crowley, *Methodical Memory*). Modeling their Japanese counterparts, most Chinese rhetorics in the early twentieth century framed their discussions of the definition of rhetoric, figures of speech, and modes of discourse from the perspective of psychology and aesthetics. They were early attempts to study the Chinese language using Western frames.

In Chinese composition instruction, the greatest impact of Anglo-American rhetoric was on the modes of written discourse. Traditionally, Chinese literati followed a discursive typology that associated a piece of writing with a particular sociopolitical occasion or purpose. For example, Liu Hsieh (ca. 465–520) offered an elaborate discussion of more than thirty genres in the Chinese literary tradition, such as *ce* 策 (policy essay), *fu* 賦 (narrative poetry), *lei* 誄 (elegy), *lun* 論 (discourse), *meng* 盟 (oath of agreement), *xi* 檄 (war proclamation), *yuefu* 樂府 (musical poetry), and *zhen* 箴 (exhortation). A somewhat similar way of labeling written discourses was also found in rhetorics published in the pre–Civil War United States. The five most common belletristic forms, according to Robert Connors, were letters, treaties, essays, biographies, and fiction ("Rise and Fall"). The modes of discourse that started to dominate U.S. composition instruction in the second half of the nineteenth century had never been among the most prominent ones in traditional Chinese rhetoric (Yuan and Zong; Zhu Binjie).

These new modes become conspicuous in Chinese composition instruction in the early twentieth century. Their earliest pedagogical use probably took place at the Capital Teachers Learning Institute (later Peking University) in 1903. In the four-year program of its teachers' college, students composed with *jishi* 記事 (narrative and descriptive styles) in their first year and *lunli* 論理 (argumentative and persuasive styles) in their second year (Beijing daxue).[2] In his 1915 treatise, "Xiaoxue zuowen jiaoshou fa" 小學作文教授法 (Composition Pedagogy for Primary School Students), Yao Enming divided composition into two general categories: general composition and practical writing. The former includes *xushi* 敘事 (narration), *jishi* 記事 (description), *shuoming* 說明 (exposition), and *yilun* 議論 (expository argumentation). The latter consists of letters, telegrams, invitations, government documents, contracts, advertisements, and so on. As the new modes began to dominate Chinese writing instruction, the *bagu-ce-lun* pedagogical system soon came to a dead end.

When the modes were incorporated into Chinese composition pedagogy, as their English translations show, they were strategically modified to reflect the Chinese literary tradition. For example, there was hardly a counterpart to the clear-cut argumentative essay in traditional Chinese writing. Instead, an argument was often supported by a full-fledged exposition on related matters, as in the three civil service exam essay genres. Therefore, Yao used a Chinese term, *yi-lun* (expository argumentation essay or opinion essay), as a compromise between Western modes and traditional Chinese essay genres. As essay genres, *yi* focuses on deliberating or debating issues in order to make a decision, and *lun* deals with logical reasoning and judgment. In the contact zone of transnational composition, translating Anglo-American concepts using terms familiar to Chinese scholars and teachers would help to fend off any conservative reaction toward foreign ideas and practices.

Pedagogically, the civil service exam essay genres were no longer the structuring elements in the writing class, but their influence persisted. By the 1920s, although the modes dominated Chinese composition, not every mode was treated equally. In middle schools, the most emphasized mode, as can be expected, was the one that came closest to the old exam essays, the expository argumentation (*yilun*) type. Liang Qichao (1873–1929), a renowned scholar who avidly called for reforming Chinese composition instruction, thus lamented, "How many people have suffered from the civil service exam-oriented teaching! Unfortunately now the schools are practicing the same thing. Although the form has been slightly altered, the spirit remains unchanged. They only tailor some Four Books topics into those of fashionable, modern subjects" ("Weishenme" 81). Liang believed that the exclusive focus on expository argumentation essays in middle schools created serious problems for students' intellectual and moral growth. In his view, as the students were still cognitively and intellectually immature, most of those essay topics encouraged them to parrot what their textbooks or teachers said. Without doing extensive research on those topics, the students could only contrive unrealistic ideas in their writing to please the teacher. Therefore, they developed the bad habit of playing with words without developing argumentative substance.

Thus, echoing Hu Shi's suggestions for vernacular writing, Liang strongly proposed that narrative and descriptive writings be emphasized to counterbalance the expository argumentation type ("Weishenme"). Writing narrative and descriptive essays, students would focus on concrete, objective matters and develop skills in observing life, collecting data, and organizing information. Through the process of data-gathering, they would learn to seek scientific truth and to develop their abilities in analyzing and synthesizing information. Liang's emphasis on narration and description coincided with the prevalence of scientific rhetoric in many school subjects, which featured an empirical rather than metaphysical pursuit of truth. His low regard for expository argumentation underscored the inadequacy of Confucian tradition for developing students' intellectual and moral well-being in modern times.

Soon new composition theories appeared, which completely altered traditional rhetorical assumptions. The most influential works were published in the early 1920s, including Chen Wangdao's *Zuowen fa jiangyi* 作文法講義 (Lectures on Written Composition, 1922), Liang Qichao's "Zuowen jiaoxue fa" 作文教學法 (Composition Pedagogy, 1923), and Ye Shaojun's *Zuowen lun* 作文論 (On Written Composition, 1924). These authors were all advocates of Chinese-language reform and influential educators. All three works were structured according to the new modes. Chen followed the Anglo-American typology most closely— *jizai* 記載 (description), *jixu* 記敍 (narration), *jieshi* 解釋 (exposition), *lunbian* 論辯 (argumentation), and *youdao* 誘導 (persuasion). Liang used three modes, namely *jizai* 記載 (description and narration), *lunbian* 論辯 (exposition and argumentation), and *qinggan* 情感 (expression of feelings). Ye followed Liang but categorized description and narration as two different modes. All three authors selected examples from both classical and modern Chinese works to illustrate their discussions of the modes. In doing so, rather than conceiving of writing as a means to the Way, these authors emphasized writing as a means of creating psychological effects on the audience, or the Ciceronian triad as elaborated by the Scottish rhetorician George Campbell, "to enlighten the understanding, to please the imagination, to move the passions, or to influence the will" (145). The theoretical reframing of Chinese composition, on the one hand, corresponded with the prevalence of scientific rhetoric in school subjects; on the other hand, it reoriented writing from its traditional metaphysical and political intents to its technical, psychological effects.

The use of these modes unleashed personal experiences and individualistic voices in Chinese composition. The mode of *qinggan* (expression of feelings) that both Liang and Ye adopted resulted from the influence of traditional Chinese writing. Besides politically charged essays, such as the exam essays, there were some ancient essay genres broadly called *sanwen* 散文 (scattered writings) that focused on personal feelings. In creating this particular mode, the authors revolutionized Chinese composition by incorporating a personal dimension, which had been marginalized in previous dynastic academies. The attention to personal feelings and voices was in tune with the cultural shift from a feudal authoritarianism to a liberal democracy.

Compared with the exam essays, argumentative writing took on some scientific dimensions. For this mode, all three authors included similar suggestions, with Chen's being the most encompassing. Chen emphasized that the thesis of an argumentative essay should be formulated in concrete and assertive terms. He instructed that such an essay should consist of three parts—thesis statement, proof, and conclusion. For the thesis statement, the writer might discuss the origin of the topic, define the issue, draw upon the common ground of both sides of the debate to expose their disagreements, and then state the main argument of the essay. Next, for the sections involving proof, the writer needs to collect both direct and indirect evidence of various kinds and to follow inductive, deductive, or analogical reasoning to present the evidence and make the argument. To conclude the essay, the writer should restate the main argument and round up this part to make the whole essay unified. Although Chen's prescriptions for the argument structure do not deviate markedly from the logical structures of exam essays or of other classical essay genres, the emphasis on the writer's seeking proof by collecting empirical evidence was uncommon in the Confucian tradition, particularly in the *bagu-ce-lun* pedagogical system.

The conflation of rhetorical traditions was accelerated by the success of the vernacular writing movement. Seeking new forms of expression, some Chinese writers, looking to the West, wrote essays, novels, short stories, poems, and news reports. They imitated Western language styles as a way to disrupt the archaic lexical-syntactic patterns of classical Chinese.[3] By 1920, the movement was so successful that many works were produced in the vernacular, and the government had to order vernacular reading and writing instruction in primary and middle schools. In the new Chinese language curriculum, students were exposed to both classical and vernacular works, with the latter manifesting clear Western stylistic features. The movement not only exposed the Chinese to Western styles but also made modern Chinese writing more accessible to the general public and expanded the popular basis of literacy. Clearly, the vernacular movement shared the democratic underpinnings of Western scientific rhetoric, which emphasizes a plain, clear style as well.

Amid the enthusiasm for Western modes, scholars also raised criticisms about mechanical imitation. Some writers blindly followed the rules of expository argumentation without quality or substance. This style of writing was ridiculed as a foreign eight-legged style (*yang bagu* 洋八股), reminiscent of the old-fashioned eight-legged essay. For instance, Chinese teacher Pan Chen criticized the clumsy use of formal logic in one of Hu Shi's essays. Following new school curriculum standards in the 1920s,[4] one of Hu's essays was selected in a middle school textbook to serve as an example of expository argumentation. Hu begins his essay, "New Life," as follows: "What kind of life can be called new life? I thought much about it and came up with a sentence, i.e., new life is meaningful life. Once you hear this statement, you will surely ask me again, what does meaningful life look like? Let me tell you one or two real-life incidents as examples, and then you will understand what I mean" (qtd. in Pan 487). Next, Hu offers an example of meaningless life. A Chinese man gets drunk and starts a physical fight with another person. After the man comes out of his drunkenness, he apologizes to the person whom he has fought with. Then he is invited to stay and play cards with some people. He gambles with them and loses a lot of money. For Hu, this type of life is meaningless because the man cannot clearly explain why he has done those things later. A meaningful life is one that can be explained and defended. Therefore, he concludes, "We hope that the Chinese could all live this kind of meaningful life. In fact this kind of life is not difficult to lead. One only needs to keep asking why he or she does things this way instead of that way. This is what I have called new life" (489).

Although it was an instructive piece for average Chinese, Pan criticized Hu's essay for strictly following formal logic in the Western philosophical tradition. Pan contended that Hu's superficial employment of formal logic could not reach the essence of the issue and that mechanical imitations like Hu's essay were pedagogically harmful:

> Hu asked the question, "What does meaningful life look like?" to lead the reader to his own thesis. It is the old trick of W-ism [asking What? Why? and How? about everything] and the common approach taken by

experimentalist philosophers. What comes next is exemplification and then judgment, which again is an outdated pattern. Once the student has mastered this formula, at best, they can expose an issue cursorily. They will never be able to take a new standpoint, collect sophisticated materials, look through profound phenomena, or express insightful opinions. (490)

Pan was concerned that students might be led to formulaic rules of expository argumentation instead of seeking worthy substance for their writing. If a renowned writer like Hu faulted on the mechanical use of formal logic, a student would be even more vulnerable to the formulaic rules of argumentation.

Pan shared a deep concern with Liang Qichao. Both worried that students would be engrossed by rigid textual rules in both the eight-legged essay and the Anglo-style argument. Instead, they believed students should observe life closely, identify critical issues, collect and examine rich materials, and come up with insightful opinions, which, ironically, were also advocated by Hu Shi during the vernacular movement. Students should learn how to solve problems in life creatively through writing. Overemphasis of the structural elements of expository argumentation would divert their attention from more crucial matters in their lives. A similar concern was later raised by Sharon Crowley, who condemned current-traditional rhetoric as not being rhetorical in American composition classrooms. She argued that rhetoric needs to engage critical issues arising from contingent, shifting relations between rhetor, the composing process, rhetorical context, and audience. However, current-traditional rhetoric tends to treat these rhetorical factors as being static and free from sociopolitical influences (*Methodical Memory* 167). Pan's criticism underscored the peril of blind, mechanical adoption of the Western modes, which, like the Chinese exam essays, might suffocate rather than liberate students' sensibility, creativity, and their love of life.

Not only in secondary schools but also in college composition courses, Anglo-American and Chinese traditions of writing intersected, turning academic writing into another contact-zone space. I will trace writing instruction in two mission colleges as case studies. Tengchow College (est. 1864) was renowned among the mission colleges for its strong emphasis on Chinese classical education during the late Qing dynasty; English was not taught there. Shanghai College (est. 1918) represents the norm of mission colleges in the 1920s in that it provided both classical Chinese and English education. A comparison of writing instruction in these two colleges can provide a starting point for investigating how rhetorical traditions clashed and grappled with each other in colleges.

Tengchow College in the late Qing implemented a typical archaic form of Chinese education. First, students studied the Four Books and the Five Classics through recitation and teachers' lectures. Second, students wrote essays on themes chosen from those classics that they had studied. According to the 1891 college catalog, students spent six years in college practicing eight-legged essays, parallel prose, and rhymed poems while studying Chinese classics, the sciences, and Christianity. The college justified this tedious composition training by pointing to the value of traditional education: "Emphasis is laid upon writing these [exam] essays because they are required in the government examinations for degrees and because public opinion demands proficiency in them as essential to respectable scholarship" (Tengchow College 4). Because of social expectations, even a mission college could not afford to deviate from the classical Chinese curriculum.

However, the growing presence of Western scientific rhetoric encouraged the reform of the archaic Chinese curriculum, gearing it towards current, practical matters. Although mission colleges emphasized Chinese composition at the turn of the twentieth century, eight-legged essays were often supplemented by writing on current affairs. John Ferguson, a missionary educator, pronounced this curricular shift at the first triennial meeting of the Educational Association of China in 1893[5]: "Would it not be better to teach them to compose '*yu*' 諭[superior's instructions], which will fit them for the practical duties of a writer on current subjects? . . . The freedom of thought developed by the study of mathematics, science, or foreign languages prepares the student for the ready and vigorous expression of thought" (20). The call for writing about current topics, rather than posing quotations from Confucian classics, anticipated the coming change in the civil service exams; that is, the importance of eight-legged essays would be surpassed by policy and discourse essays in 1901. The teaching of Western subjects created mounting pressure on Chinese college composition in the late nineteenth century, moving it from the metaphysical rendering of antiquity to dealing with current, practical matters.

Gradually, the Chinese composition curriculum came to resemble that of English composition. Students were no longer asked only to write expository arguments on themes from the classics; they also practiced description and narration by modeling both classical and modern Chinese writings. The curricular expansion can be noted by comparing the 1921 and 1924 course descriptions at Shanghai College. In 1921, "Rhetoric and Composition" was offered to freshmen, sophomores, and juniors in the Department of Chinese Language and Literature. In this curriculum, there was a strong emphasis on studying model writings from different dynasties, moving far beyond the

Confucian classics. The ordering of the models was grounded in Chinese dynastic history.

Nevertheless, the linkage to classical writings was weakened in the 1924 curriculum with the addition of current-traditional rhetoric. Freshmen and sophomores were required to take "Chinese Prose." The model writings that the students read in the class were changed little from those of the 1921 curriculum, but the models were conceived of and organized from a more rhetorical perspective. The chronological method of selecting models was replaced by the Western modes, which were also treated in Erle Clippinger's *Written and Spoken English* and Charles Ward's *Theme-Building*, two English texts used at Shanghai College at that time. Similar curricular shifts in Chinese composition were also noticeable in course descriptions of other universities in the 1920s and 1930s, such as National Peking University, National Wuhan University, the University of Nanking, and Yenching University. Framing Chinese classical works in the modes indicated an increasing openness among Chinese intellectuals toward Western values in the scholarly contact zone.

The modes-guided curricular shift was also supported by college entrance exams. For example, the writing topics for students hoping to enter National Peking University before 1921 were all of the expository argumentation type, such as "On common sense as the foundation of academic research" (1918), "Knowledge ought to be derived from empirical studies" (1919), and "On the benefits and drawbacks of civil service exams" (1920). Into the late 1920s and the 1930s, writing tasks for students applying to this university expanded to include narrative and descriptive types, valuing the individual's unique life experience and voice: "Describe a most memorable event in your life (it must be a true experience, whether it is the happiest, the saddest, or the most interesting event)" (1935) and "Describe an unforgettable moment in your childhood" (1942) (Guoli Beijing daxue, *Guoli Beijing daxue yuke ruxue*; "Guoli xinan"). Therefore, through another institutional means, Chinese composition revitalized both narrative and descriptive styles, which had been devaluated by the *bagu-ce-lun* pedagogical system.

Another point of contact between Chinese and English composition was the somewhat different traditions of documentation. Documentation was always a concern in traditional Chinese writing. In the late twelfth century, for instance, rhetorician Chen Kui (1128–1203) addressed the function and methods of citations in his book *Wen ze* 文則 (The Rules of Writing). Rather than focusing on the ownership of a text or of the knowledge within it, Chen explored the circumstances and purposes for using citations. He noted two general citation methods being used in classical Chinese texts: "The first was to use citation as evidence about an event that had taken place; the second was to use citation to verify or confirm what had been said" (qtd. in Kirkpatrick, "China's First" 124). However, Chen suggested that copying another person's work without acknowledgement could not be condemned.

Western notions of plagiarism and copyright were not emphasized because the Chinese entertained a different epistemological perspective in their literary practice. Sharon Crowley suggests that modern Western discourse theory privileges a single authorial mind and conceives of texts as "reflections of the workings of this sovereign authorial mind" (*Methodical Memory* 12). The framers of the U.S. Constitution also believed that "nothing is more properly a man's own than the fruit of his study, and protection and security of literary property would greatly tend to encourage genius" (qtd. in Patry 911); therefore, they wrote the Patent and Copyright Clause into the Constitution. In contrast, Chinese literati emphasized transmission of the Way, which resides deep in the Confucian classics, as the only worthy knowledge to the public. A Chinese writer might extensively quote renowned writers without indicating the sources. Such a practice was permissible also because high literacy was only available to a relatively small number of literati, who had all studied the classics painstakingly for the civil exam. Being so familiar with the classics, they would know where the quotes came from. Writing always offered the author a chance to demonstrate his wide range of reading and to share his thoughts with persons of a similar educational background.

Such a literary tradition inevitably collided with the "no plagiarism" etiquette of English writing in colleges. In mission colleges, it was not uncommon to find statements like the following "college standards of honesty":

> For class work the following requirements are made in all departments:
> (a) The writing of papers, exercises, and note-books must be done individually and expressed in the student's own words.
> (b) All borrowing of ideas must be indicated by references or foot-notes.
> (c) All borrowed phrases must be indicated by quotation marks. "Use without quotation is theft." (Ginling College, *Handbook 1918* 4)

These moralized rules prescribed a ritual of honesty that disciplined all students.[6] Besides reinforcing the conscientious practice of citation in English composition as it was practiced in scholarly Chinese writing, these standards established a particular epistemology ingrained in modern Western traditions. On one hand, they perpetuated the capitalist notion of ownership of one's work or one's knowledge, a notion that was alien to Chinese students. On the other hand, they encouraged the students to seek their own words and, hence, their own voices in their English writing. Thus, the rules promoted the betrayal of the Confucian notion of the self, a notion that encourages self-examination through conversing with his or her inner self rather than on pompous, individualistic expression for an external audience. Thus, to be an "honest" writer in English composition meant transforming oneself into an immoral maverick in the Confucian culture, something that was a challenge for Chinese students.

Translation and English Writing

By the end of the First World War, translation had become a time-honored link between Chinese and English writing. Translation, from a rhetorical perspective, shares a common ground with writing in that both deal with textual mediation. For a body of themes, forms, or ideas, the translator or writer tries "to find a new form which can do justice to the material, transporting (translating) it so as to bring it home to a more or less clearly defined public, deploying what [Roland] Barthes would have called the 'codes' that govern discourse in a given society" (P. France 255). Translation, like English writing, was also a type of language appropriation for Chinese students. Students gained control over English or Chinese texts in a previously inaccessible linguistic form. After the Second Opium War, a large number of Western texts were translated and, thus, appropriated for a Chinese audience. For instance, Thomas Huxley's *Evolution and Ethics* was translated into Chinese as *Heavenly Evolution* (a familiar term for the Chinese) by Yan Fu in 1894. In his paraphrastic translation, Yan used Chinese traditional categories such as *dao* 道 (Way), *sheng* 生 (production), *ren* 仁 (benevolence), and *tian* 天 (Heaven) to help readers understand the Darwinian idea concerning the struggle for existence; he recast Huxley's cosmos/ethics dichotomy by evoking Chinese concepts of *xing* 性 (nature) and *qun* 群 (group); and he introduced a moral universe into Huxley's amoral vision (Xiao Xiaosui, "China Encounters"). Introducing a Chinese audience to foreign texts, the translator had to deploy traditional Chinese concepts and rhetorical strategies to engage the Chinese minds.

When discussing college English teaching before 1937, Yeh Wen-Hsin claims that it had different emphases in mission and state schools. State colleges prioritized translation instruction, while mission colleges paid greater attention to written and oral expression. The difference, according to Yeh, could first be observed in the college entrance exams during the 1930s. State colleges often tested students' translation abilities, but mission colleges did not. She further argues that translation requires an understanding of both Chinese and Western cultures and languages. Mission colleges placed much more emphasis on Western education; state colleges, remaining the center of traditional classical research, were better prepared to teach translation. Her argument is partly correct because ever since the opening of Tong Wen Guan, translation has always been the primary focus in state schools. However, the clear line Yeh draws between state and mission colleges in terms of teaching translation is, in fact, inaccurate.

While mission colleges set high standards for oral and written English, many of them were also committed to the nationalist agenda of teaching translation. Some mission colleges, such as Hangchow Presbyterian College and West China Union University in the 1910s and 1920s and the University of Nanking in the 1940s, offered translation courses for juniors and seniors in their English departments. Some offered translation training under the course title "Composition" or "Advanced Composition," as was the case at the University of Nanking in the 1910s and Yenching University in the 1920s. Sometimes translation was offered in Chinese departments. The earnest desire to produce students versed in both Chinese and English even made the Chinese department of Canton Christian College fully devote itself to teaching the art of translation in the 1910s (*Catalogue, 1909–1910*). In 1915, students were required to take courses in composition in Chinese for two years, which, in fact, were all about the art of translation in their disciplines. The following passage is quoted from the course description for Chinese composition at the college:

> The aim of the course is to guide and encourage the student to make use of the knowledge which he has acquired through the medium of the English language by expressing it in Chinese. This is so essential in the preparation of the increasing number of men who are looking forward to teaching in primary and middle schools that its importance must be emphasized. Students are classified according to the general lines of study which they pursue and are required to reproduce English works in substance in modern and idiomatic Chinese. Opportunity is afforded for collateral reading of books already translated by acknowledged authorities and for informal class discussions. (*Catalogue of the College Department* 72)

The course description, on one hand, underscores the school's expectation that students will take responsibility for transmitting Western learning to their compatriots. On the other hand, it indicates a significant venue through which Western rhetorical styles learned in college could be incorporated into both Chinese and English teaching in middle schools. Therefore, like the state schools, some mission colleges also recognized the value of translation in their curricula and committed themselves to the Chinese nationalist endeavor of acquiring Western science and technology through training competent translators.

Both state and mission colleges taught translation partly because postcollege exams invariably stressed transnational exchange capacities. Students who wanted to enter the civil service after graduation were tested in English writing and English-to-Chinese translation (Kaoshiyuan). In the 1930s and 1940s, students who aspired to study abroad with government sponsorship were tested in English writing and in their ability to translate both English and Chinese. In the English-to-Chinese translation, the passages dealt with general Western civilization, democracy, sciences, and technology. In the Chinese-to-English translation, the passages dwelled on the current national crises and social issues and occasionally included fictional excerpts (see Lin Qingfen). These topics, reflecting the international communication concerns of a nation struggling for survival, effectively turned mainstream discourse into pedagogical discourses. To prepare for the exams, students would have to practice these topics and thus become absorbed in the Chinese discourse of modernization.

Transposition between Chinese and English required students to develop great linguistic and rhetorical dexterity and acute intercultural knowledge. The translation procedures moved far beyond mere faculty psychology and a technical emphasis on moving an audience and into significant cultural and cognitive accomplishments and depths. For example, since the passage chosen for Chinese-to-English translation often embodied many Chinese syntactic and stylistic preferences, literal translation might sound strange to the intended English-speaking audience. To illustrate the point, I have taken one such Chinese passage from an exam for government-funded overseas studies (Lin Qingfen 53) and given it both literal and paraphrastic translations:

In the reform of Chinese society, we can see the social classes and changes in both their social status and nature. The traditional four social classes of intellectuals, peasants, workers, and businessmen have been completely turned upside down. In contrast, new social classes are increasing day by day, being discovered day by day, and enhancing their importance day by day.

In the reform of Chinese society, we observe changes in the social classes in both their social status and nature. The traditional social hierarchy consisting of intellectuals, peasants, workers, and businessmen has been completely turned upside down. New social classes are increasing, emerging, and enhancing their importance day by day.

The literal translation, although loyal to the Chinese discursive and syntactic structures, might seem a little fragmentary and repetitive to an English-speaking audience. It captures a parallelism favored in Chinese writing—"In contrast new social classes are increasing day by day, being discovered day by day, and enhancing their importance day by day." However, having the same subject ("new social classes") perform the three actions ("increasing," "being discovered," and "enhancing") might seem less stylistically polished to English-speaking writers. In contrast, the paraphrastic translation, abiding by Anglo-American rhetorical and stylistic preferences, might read more coherently and cogently to the intended audience. Working with such a Chinese text, students thus had to position their translations along a spectrum—either foreignizing the text by taking the audience to the Chinese author or domesticating the text by taking the Chinese author to the audience. Either way, the translation would keep and simultaneously lose something original from the Chinese text. How a student appropriated the text would depend on his or her understanding of the audience, the Chinese author, and the Anglo-American and Chinese rhetorical preferences. In these ways, translation offered students a field test for their knowledge of both Chinese and English writing.

Public Speaking and Extracurricular Writing

English writing in Chinese colleges was taught not only through lectures, weekly themes, and conferences but also through public speaking. China has its own oratorical tradition. Public speaking was studied during both the Spring and Autumn and the Warring States periods (770–221 B.C.E.), approximately the same period during which classical Greek rhetoric emerged. Warfare frequently broke out between small kingdoms in northern China. Some eloquent individuals traveled between these kingdoms to advise the kings, sharing their philosophical wisdom and promoting their political visions. Their oratorical activities gave rise to the beginning of Chinese civic rhetoric (Xing Lu, *Rhetoric in Ancient China*).

Rhetoric never became a disciplined study in ancient Chinese academies, even though it was constantly studied informally.[7] The study of rhetoric, as conceived in the West as the search for the available means of verbal persuasion (Aristotle), was suppressed by Confucianism, which emphasized reconciliation of conflicts through internal deliberations and appropriate interpersonal behaviors rather than through adversarial argumentation. Public speeches, as revealed by the dynastic histories, were often delivered from the ruler to his ministers or his political advisers, and vice versa, but seldom to the masses. Discussions among scholars about delivering public speeches often focused on addressing the ruler or their fellow scholars. For thousands of years, students studied famous speeches and theories about delivering speeches in light of the Confucian inspiration. Once they joined officialdom, those speeches served as models when they addressed the ruler or their colleagues.

The formal art of public speaking came into China along with Western learning or, to be more specific, Western political philosophy. After the mid-nineteenth century, Chinese scholars became increasingly interested in Western sociopolitical thinking and institutions. The works of Adam Smith, Lord Russell, Charles Darwin, Thomas Huxley, and Herbert Spencer were avidly studied. Western superiority in various social dimensions was oftentimes attributed to its tradition of public debates taking place in the parliament, the court, and the academy. For example, in *Zuixin xiongbian fa* 最新雄辯法 (The Principles of Argumentation, 1910), an early translation on Western argumentation, the Chinese translator Lu Ce expressed his indignation at the perennial influence of Confucian moral philosophy on Chinese minds, and he aspired to encourage the masses to discuss matters of national importance. He declared: "China is a sleeping lion, a sick thing. We need to beat drums to wake it up, prescribe bitter medicine to cure it, and confront it with questions. For the fields of politics, academia, military, diplomacy, and industry, if they want to make any changes, how could they do so without engaging any debates?" (5). Lu's determination to alter the traditional attitudes toward public debates was one of the growing efforts to engage the masses in discussing the country's future. At the turn of the twentieth century, the concept of democracy had already been introduced and advocated by the Chinese bourgeoisie. Through nationwide public speaking activities, they shared their visions of the country with the masses and suggested strategies to solve ongoing national crises. Public speaking planted seeds of democracy among the people and allowed them to dream of a modern China together with the bourgeoisie.

On college campuses, public speaking therefore provided students a training site for exercising the imported notion of freedom of speech. Colleges began offering public speaking, debate, and/or parliamentary law in their English departments in the 1900s. In public speaking classes, students studied Western rhetoric and famous English speeches, wrote their own speeches, and delivered them in class. In their composition classes, they also studied parliamentary law and argumentative writing, as featured by the imported composition texts at that time. Thus, a close connection was forged between public speaking and English composition. If the modes that students practiced in their composition classes were too "rudimental and mechanical"

(Crowley, *Methodical Memory* 95) to allow real rhetorical practice, students would move beyond the restrictive rules to truly practice (Western) rhetoric in public speaking.

Public speaking created transnational epideictic moments in which both domestic and foreign audiences were invited to examine current issues, to compare China with the West, and to envision a strong, modern Chinese nation. In the 1920s and 1930s, intercollegiate English debates were regularly held in the Greater Shanghai area. Like in the late Qing dynasty, the destiny of the nation remained a central concern for the students. The following is the beginning of a winning debate speech given by a student of Shanghai College in 1922. The speaker managed to set the stage for the other three speakers in his team:

> The question for debate tonight is, "Resolved, That the coming of western industrialism is likely to do more harm than good to China." We recognize the vast extent of this proposition, reaching as it does into the fields of geography, history, politics, engineering, economics and sociology, and we solicit your sympathetic consideration. We shall try to make our statements comprehensive enough to embrace all the essential phases of the subject; and at the same time specific enough to base our arguments on concrete facts. The essential characteristics of western industrialism may be stated as follows:
>
> *First*, large scale production by power driven machinery. *Second*, this machinery is owned and controlled by a relatively small number of persons, who may be designated as employers, proprietors, or capitalists. *Third*, the machinery is operated by employees, or laborers, who receive wages for their labor, and in return for their wages surrender all control over the organization of production, and over the products of their labor. *Fourth*, the entire system of production and distribution is conducted by the owners on a basis of competition, and for the primary motive of pecuniary profits.
>
> If time permitted, we could quote many authorities in support of this definition but believe it is not necessary. We assume that these are universally recognized as the distinguishing marks of that system which is commonly referred to as *modern* or *western industrialism*. It is this system, with these characteristics which we of the affirmative maintain will, if it comes to this country do more harm than good to China. (Tung 1)

Then the speaker moved on to critique Western industrialization for establishing itself on "wrong principles": profit making, competition, and autocratic ownership and control of industry. The student successfully adopted the formality of Anglo-American parliamentary law in his speech pattern. He stated his team's adversary position both firmly and courteously. In his speech, the student quoted American scholarly works extensively to support his assessment of Western industrialization, revealing his solid footing in Western learning. He no longer resorted to Confucian masters or Chinese historical precedents to bolster his argument, as older generations of intellectuals would have done. Exemplifying a contact zone between Western learning and twentieth-century Chinese culture, the student chose modern experts' knowledge rather than common Chinese knowledge to appeal to the domestic and foreign audiences.

More important, speeches like this one planted seeds for social change. Adopting a perfect Anglo-American debate form, the student boldly castigated capitalist values, which some of his international audiences represented. By calling attention to the imperfections of Western industrialization, the speaker invited the audience to consider alternative forms of modernity. As he later stated, "I ask you tonight, ladies and gentlemen, which appeals to you as more reasonable, and more attractive: a system of industry based on competition, which degrades and brutalizes and disgraces our civilization; or [one based] on cooperation, which is productive of life and progress" (2). This statement suggests the urgency of choosing an appropriate mode of social development amid foreign aggression. Through English speeches, students connected their intellectual training with urgent social issues, artistically turning public forums into international sites of an anti-imperialism campaign.

English speeches were also practiced in literary societies in both mission and state colleges.[8] English teachers often required their students to participate in literary activities. Students at St. John's College, for example, founded a literary and debate society in 1898. The society's activities were of great value in that they trained students to speak and write the English language: "Often days and weeks were spent to compose and learn by heart orations or debates and such efforts repeated gave the novices a very thorough drilling, far more than would the corrections made by the teachers in class-room" (St. John's University, *St. John's University* 49). This description illustrates how the literary society functioned as another site of rhetorical education in which students composed English speeches, memorized them, and practiced delivery—the full circle of classical Western rhetoric. Through extracurricular opportunities such as English publications and literary societies, classroom writing became more meaningful and stimulating for students.

The intersections of Chinese and Anglo-American rhetorical traditions occurred not only in the teaching of Chinese composition, translation, and public speaking but also in the students' writing, particularly in the writing of Chinese women. Next, we turn to a particular women's college to assess the role that English writing played in college women's search for and assertion of their new selves.

Writing in a Gendered Voice

Although their numbers were small in republican China, college women infused new meanings into education and writing instruction. They were "pioneers" of their times, as the first group of Ginling students called themselves (Ginling College, Class of 1919). They changed the educational landscape and shaped the rites of college for women. The first rite they performed in college was the entrance exam. The subjects drastically departed from those tested in the old civil service exams. Students applying to Ginling College in 1915, for instance, were tested in Chinese, English, history, mathematics, religion, and science (*Bulletin*). Religion dealt with the narrative sections of the Old and New Testaments. History extended beyond domestic history to include the histories of East Asia, the United States, Britain, and Europe. As Christianity replaced Confucianism (which was minimally assessed in the Chinese test) and as world history sidelined classical Chinese history, Ginling students were no longer confined to the Confucian sense of the self. Alternatively, they could refigure their obligations to both their families and the state as serving a divine being, God. They had to reevaluate the purpose of Confucian ritualization against a widened knowledge of human existence. They had to juggle competing frames of reference while trying to make sense of them.

Indeed, the Confucian self metamorphosed into something hardly recognizable in Confucian terms. It experienced not simply gender change but also novel obstacles in self-cultivation that came with such a change. In their compositions, students often voiced their determination to receive a higher education that was unimaginable to women before. The struggle to make these decisions and to face the consequent challenges was daunting. Some Ginling students' English essays can offer us a glimpse into the minds of liberated women in the early 1920s. One such student confessed her struggle in pursuing her ideal self as follows:

> My father's letter came to me at breakfast time. My tears fell in my bowl when I read it. I went upstairs to read it over and over. He said that it was very difficult to jump the stairs of study. He always knew I would have a very hard time in Ginling. He did not agree with me when I came to Ginling for this sake. He did not forbid me for he wanted me

to get the experience of [being] a poor student. He hoped that I would change my pride which I possessed a long time during the first year in Ginling. He promised [to allow] me to stay at Ginling [for] five or six years and hoped [for] my success some day. . . . I put down the letter and sat as a statue [for] about one hour. (Tsai)

Educational pursuit defined the Confucian self. Women were long denied formal schooling in the old social structure. Once the school door opened, this talented woman did not hesitate to "jump the stairs of study" (skip grades) and entered college successfully. However, her aspirations for modern education did not fare well with her well-educated father, who doubted his daughter's academic competence and warned her against her overbearing pride. English writing opened an outlet for the student to reflect upon her dreams and the realistic challenges with which most girls of her time would have to reconcile—fulfilling their traditional roles in the family, securing financial support, and meeting stringent academic requirements. This student confided her struggle to her American teacher, a sympathetic reader who probably shared a limited understanding of the Confucian self, which had long excluded women.

Studying in a mission college, most Ginling girls clearly sided with Christianity and nearly forsook their Confucian heritage. They reconsidered their social commitment as a result of the Christian rituals in which they participated at the college. Many related their conceptual changes in their English compositions. Student Chen Guh-Hsiang reflected on her freshman year at Ginling as follows:

Now my freshman year will nearly pass away; and my mind is full of a grave and wide question. What is the question? The question is my duty to my beloved nation, China. What makes me think about that question? Well there are many places. But the most striking place or source is at the chapel of my college. Every time, every guest said, "You are the one out of the thousands, who has such opportunity to receive the blessing." At first I did not understand what the word "blessing" means. I thought I paid the college, and I had the right to get anything from the college. It was foolish to say that we were blessed. But now on the contrary, I really know it is my great blessing for entering college. The reason is because I know there are thousands and thousands of men, women, and children in China who have no chance to enter any school. They are shut out from the world, know nothing about their own nation and humanity.

Chen's account underscored the new ritualization that took place at the college. Students were encouraged to attend chapel service on a daily basis. There, they not only listened to religious sermons but often speeches given by renowned thinkers, such as Liang Qichao, Hu Shi, and Jane Addams. Like other girls, Chen learned at the chapel services that being able to attend college was a blessing from God. Bewildered at first, she accepted the new meaning of her education later. This marked a phenomenal departure from the Confucian self in at least two aspects. First, when Confucianism had served as the inspiration for Chinese schools two decades before, women had not been allowed to attend schools. Getting a higher education was a man's privilege, unimaginable for a woman. Second, the Ginling girls were led to perceive higher education as a duty commissioned by a divine being rather than as the ritualization of the self for the Way. The student's reorientation to Christian ontology and epistemology, derived from a particular education in colonial China, starkly contrasted with traditional Chinese philosophy.

The only part of the self imposed upon by Christian teaching that resonated with Confucian epistemology and ideology was the students' enthusiasm expressed for human enlightenment and world peace. Chen's essay goes on to spell out her social obligation, seemingly echoing the whispers of the Confucian self:

> My recent decision is how I can do with those people. I say to myself, "I must go forth to face the world, give and share with them what I have, to raise the standard of the rotten society." Within these few days, I always hear a voice calling "You are the person whom China needs and is waiting for; and do not say 'I am not the person, because I feel I can not do it, and I am not qualified.'" . . . If I cast away my duty, then how about those children? Who is going to lead and teach them? Those children are the great men of China later. China is depending on them. From this point of view those children's careers depend upon me. Though I am weak, I ask God to give me the strength and ability to perform my grave work.

At first, Chen articulated a mission seemingly in agreement with the social responsibility of the Confucian self. That is, Chinese society is in crisis, or is "rotten"; there is a need for righteous individuals to stand up, to lead, and to "ritualize" others. However, she heard a voice from God, quoting Old Testament writers who were chided by God for regarding themselves as unqualified to serve Him. She first painted herself as someone underqualified, but then, in light of the nation's needs, she decided to take part in meeting the needs, which expressed the humility Christians think appropriate. Rather than matching up to the ideal Confucian self, she looked to Old Testament prophets as her role model in conceptualizing her social responsibility. Despite the heavy influence of Christian ontology, one does not fail to sense in Chen's words the communal bond between the self and the nation. Her patriotic Christian self is congenial with the Confucian ideal of a virtuous person who regulates his family, governs the state, and finally achieves a tranquil and happy kingdom (Confucius, "Great Learning" 357).

Also remarkable about this essay are the places of cultural mediation and mixing. The student sought her ideal self by negotiating with various cultural frames, including Christianity, Confucianism, nationalism, and commercialism. Most noticeably, she was still in the process of acquiring Christian concepts and worldviews. She managed to make sense of the term "blessing" as used in biblical discourse and engaged in deferential conversations with God. At the same time, she was entangled by both Confucian political ideals and the ongoing nationalist discourse. She pondered her duties at school chapel meetings and thought about her obligation to the nation in terms of her obligation to God. She was also influenced by ideas of commercialism, once believing that education could be bought and sold. The juxtaposition of and reconciliation with multiple "terministic screens" were inevitable rites of passage for college women like Chen.

As pioneers in Chinese higher education, female students enjoyed an unprecedented liberty in celebrating their unique life experiences and voices. Besides offering serious reflections on the relationship between the individual and the state, young women's compositions were permeated with innocence and joy. Writing to an imagined American friend, for example, a Ginling student recounted the following memorable story in her "Autobiography":

When I was eleven years old I went to Zau-Shun with my second brother. My home is situated beside a small brook. Not very far from our home there are several high mountains. Every day we could see the beautiful scenes of sun-rise and sun-set. When I stayed there I liked to catch the frogs and the grasshoppers. One day I went out with my second brother. When we walked a little while, my brother wanted to fish, so he sat on a big rock beside the brook and fished. When he was fishing, I went to the farm to catch the grasshoppers. At that time the farms were very wet. Suddenly I saw a very big green grasshopper hopping among the wheat. I loved it very much, so I bent my body forward in order to catch it. Unfortunately, I slipped and fell in the farm. I was very much frightened and called my brother loudly to help me. When he heard it, he quickly came to me and found me in the mud. He pulled me out and led me home. (Tien)

Despite appearing "trivial," personal accounts like this were widespread and meaningful to the students writing them. Such narratives were rare in Chinese school writing two decades before this time. In the *bagu-ce-lun* paradigm, little space existed for personal narratives, let alone a personal voice and individual experience for women. Instead, writing focused on ruminating over Confucian precepts and government policies. Personal narratives enabled women to explore themselves in a gendered voice and to confirm their new agency. The narratives also liberated them from the bondage of male-gendered Confucian epistemology. Women students described not only their personal experiences but also their dreams and desires, which were vital to collectively design a new nation.

Writing as Anti-Imperialist Warfare

Through English, students struggled not only with rhetorical traditions and gender inequality but also with foreign imperialists. Republican China was marked by constant political and military turmoil, agitated by both foreign and domestic political forces. Immediately after the establishment of the republic in 1912, battles sprang up among local warlords who represented the competing interests of Western colonial powers. Starting in 1927, military confrontations between the Nationalist troops backed by Western powers and the Communist troops dominated the domestic scene until the Japanese invaded the country in 1931, triggering the Anti-Japanese War. After the war with Japan ended in 1945, a civil war between the Nationalist and the Communist troops broke out again in 1946. The war lasted until the Communists led by Mao Zedong took over the mainland and the Nationalists retreated to Taiwan in 1949. Not spared from the turmoil, students wrote English essays amid various kinds of warfare, protesting against foreign imperialist exploitation and intervention.

The most devastating impact on China came from the war with Japan, which sought to build a Greater East Asian empire. When Japanese invaders attacked cities on the eastern seaboard in 1937, colleges in those cities had to either downsize their classes, evacuate entire schools to the western part of the country, or completely close. In the notorious Nanjing Massacre in December of 1937, Japanese troops slaughtered over a quarter-million Chinese civilians (I. Chang). Despite numerous atrocities like this one, many schools continued to operate, with extremely limited resources, fewer books, scarce teaching facilities, and poor student accommodations. Frequently, English classes were taught in between Japanese air raids. Esther Tappert, for example, while teaching at the National Chungking University in Sichuan Province during the war, found that her English classes were diminished in number and spirit by the nerve-racking war. However, she extended spiritual support to her students on 8 May 1939 after a night of nonstop Japanese bombardments. She told her students that the little amount of English they were learning in class was not of much importance, but "faithfulness to little duties helps keep up moral courage, and each time we refuse to let ourselves be demoralized by emergencies, we have gained a victory, however small, over those whose chief purpose is to terrorize and make normal life impossible." Constrained by such a severe condition, English writing instruction was reduced to the minimum during the Anti-Japanese War.[9] However, language can be viewed as both a ritualistic act as well as a symbolic action. As Tappert said, any English reading and writing performed in the classroom signified students' unyielding dignity. By engaging students in those small duties, Anglo-American teachers like Tappert acted as Chinese people's allies rather than as colonialist agents.

In their English compositions, students struggled to describe their experiences and feelings. At St. John's University, for example, the war with Japan was a popular topic in writing classes despite the life-threatening risks such a topic could bring to the students. Mary Lamberton, an English teacher at St. John's during the war, recalls those dangerous scenarios:

> In the fall of 1940 the College was closed for two days because all streets leading to Jessfield were barricaded by Japanese gendarmes. The faculty and staff had to be continually on the watch to keep the students from doing provocative things. Boats commandeered and officered by the enemy were continuously passing on the creek flowing around the campus and these were loaded with property taken from the Chinese who lived in Soochow and were on their way to Japanese homes in Shanghai or Japan. This sight the students did not find easy to bear quietly. Often they expressed their hatred of the Japanese in their English compositions, so that the instructors in English often tore up the essays rather than risk their being found on the persons of students who might be searched on their way home. If they had been discovered and read by someone who understood English, punishment would have been swift and severe. (184)

Thus, unlike in the comparatively peaceful United States at that time, English writing instruction in China was severely taxed by the war. Nevertheless, English writing provided the students who lived in those dreadful circumstances with an underground venue to express their sadness, indignation, and hatred. Student writing subverted the disorder and terror imposed by the Japanese imperialists. Through English writing, students and their foreign teachers co-constructed a transnational anti-Fascist discourse—a discourse that sustained the Confucian tradition of seeking peace and harmony in a turbulent human society. This time, the Chinese and the foreign devils all spoke the same language in their fight against imperialist encroachment in China and other East Asian countries.

Clearly, English in republican China again transcended the *ti-yong* dualism that resided in most Chinese's minds. Instead of being used on the anchorage of a static, monolithic Chinese culture, English continued to participate in the reformation of local literary and political culture as the Chinese fought against imperialism and colonialism. Contact with English and the rhetorical tradition that followed enabled Chinese scholars to reform modern Chinese language, its literary production, and its teaching. As revealed in their writing and public speaking activities, students acquired Anglo-American rhetorical forms to engender public and private discussions on political issues, which infused ideals of liberal democracy into modern Chinese culture. The widespread use of English in the country changed the nature of the language, making it less a foreign devil's tongue and more an international language for decolonization and national independence.

Localizing English Composition Pedagogy

English composition pedagogies, however, continued to perpetuate monolithic assumptions about English and Anglo-American people and thus clashed with Chinese students' writing practices. Composition, together with other English courses, stressed the basics of the English language. Skimming over college catalogs published during the first half of the twentieth century, one can easily notice an unequivocal emphasis, for freshman and sophomore English, on grammar and oral practice alongside literary readings and weekly themes. Students often failed writing tasks because they composed with a strong Chinese accent. An American teacher, for example, complained about Chinese logic in students' English essays: "Students rarely place the subject of the sentence first. I have checked composition after composition where every sentence began with a prepositional phrase or clause. The key to clear, simple, and direct writing is the location of the subject in the sentence. It usually goes first" (W. Brown 77). In the eyes of native speakers, beginning a sentence with a prepositional phrase to denote the time or the place of an action or a state of being appeared to be disturbingly confusing, complicated, and indirect. The monolithic notion of English and its native speakers thus deeply troubled and inconvenienced both students and teachers.

Like Western rhetoric, American composition pedagogy was critically adapted to the Chinese context. After the 1920s, a growing number of Chinese teachers joined the English teaching staff, including those who had recently graduated from college and those who had returned from overseas studies. Western scholars with graduate training in language and education also increased their presence in China. Chinese and Western scholars conversed on how to teach English composition effectively in a non-English dominant country. Some of them published textbooks with Chinese students' particular challenges in mind. Their pedagogical practices and scholarly work sustained the development of context-sensitive pedagogical theories, often challenging the monolithic, static notion of English and its legitimate users.

The most influential composition theory that grew out of the Anglo-American encounter with the Chinese context was developed by Lawrence W. Faucett (1892–1978), who was an English professor at St. John's University (1922–25) and Yenching University (1927–30). He laid out some "scientific" principles for teaching composition in *The Teaching of English in the Far East* (1927), a book widely used in English pedagogical courses in Chinese colleges in the 1930s and 1940s.[10] These scientific principles were later applied in a textbook series, *Oxford English Course* (1933), which he compiled for Oxford University Press. As the series was quickly adopted by African, Middle Eastern, and Asian countries, his English teaching theory that grew out of East Asia was popularized in a wider non-English dominant context.[11]

Appealing to the most recent theories in educational psychology and linguistics, Faucett emphasized the importance of oral work. Influenced by linguists' interest in modern spoken language, he asserted that teaching English as a foreign language (EFL) needed to start with daily conversations instead of the archaic language of literature. He suggested that grammar and translation be replaced by a direct method, involving object lessons, picture lessons, and oral explanations in English. In the later stage of one's English learning, written work would be introduced. However, EFL ought to be taught differently from English as a native tongue because the language was used for restricted functions and domains in East Asia. As he explained, "Many students have been taught literary English in the Far East when their own aim was to secure English for business or professional purposes" (*Teaching of English* 34).

Devoting an entire chapter to composition instruction, Faucett emphasized the importance of controlled writing exercises in helping students form good habits. He said, "Original composition attempted too soon leads to the formation of bad habits because the students will naturally construct English sentences by vernacular models" (*Teaching of English* 147). Therefore, he proposed a syllabus of written work that would lead to free composition. The syllabus consisted of seven kinds of controlled writing: copying, dictation, grammatical transformation and conversation exercises, sentence work (question-and-answer exercises), paraphrase work, short themes, and finally composing original paragraphs.

While the graded writing pedagogy clearly mimicked the fairly traditional pedagogy in American schools, it also took EFL students' particular difficulties and needs into consideration. According to nineteenth-century compositionists John Walker and William Russell, American pupils were urged to first master grammatical and rhetorical rules through rote learning; they were judged incapable of inventing their own subject matter. Theme writing on general, abstract, and impersonal subjects came later in one's composition training (cited in Schultz). Besides evincing a similar distrust of students' invention ability, Faucett's emphasis on a balance between and integration of different skills was derived from an awareness of EFL students' relatively lower English proficiency. Therefore when students learned how to write in English, they practiced composite skills—copying, spelling, speaking, listening, using correct grammar, and writing.

Controlled composition was equally emphasized at an advanced level. Faucett suggested reproducing texts or portions of texts that have been read; recasting poems, especially ballads, into prose; retranslation; and free letter-writing both for social and business correspondence. He encouraged teachers to correct errors because "it is often more profitable to correct and recorrect one short assignment than to receive a great deal of written work without giving the student a chance to benefit by his discovered mistakes" (*Teaching of English* 152). Apparently, current-traditional rhetoric undergirded Faucett's conceptualization of advanced composition. For him, written products were valued over topical exploration. He conceived of writing as a technical tool for accuracy and precision and regarded error correction as a vital part of a student's apprenticeship for mastering such a tool.

Chinese scholars also criticized the lack of EFL awareness in teaching English writing. In view of the heavy reliance on American pedagogy, Ge Chuangui (1906–92) published *Yingwen zuowen jiaoben* 英文作文教本 (A Textbook of English Composition) in 1941 to stage his arguments for teaching composition in light of local characteristics. Ge pointed out that college English composition at that time had neglected the special needs of Chinese students. For example, he contended that authorship was not an appropriate goal for average Chinese students. Rather, students needed to learn how to express themselves effectively for "practical purposes." He also criticized school composition for its underlying intention of producing professional writers. "While most students may never wish to write professionally, it does not follow that all that they will ever have to do in the way of English composition is to write short essays on given subjects, or what are called in

American schools 'themes'" (i). Ge suggested that students needed to acquire skill in other practical genres that they would encounter in their respective disciplines and future professions. He underscored the traditional demarcation between Chinese as representing the Chinese cultural essence (*ti*) versus English as the devil's tongue, only worthy of use for practical purposes (*yong*). Therefore, when English composition was taught in Chinese schools, as both Ge and Faucett argued, its pedagogical goals should be adjusted to reflect the situated needs of the students.

To develop a composition pedagogy suitable for the local context, Ge then delineated students' strengths and their challenges with English writing. Their greatest strength came from the fact that English was not their mother tongue. They did not need to unlearn many erroneous or colloquial expressions that native speakers often use that are unsuitable for written English. As Ge claimed wittily, "Much of the material that is usually found in books of composition written for English-speaking students is therefore quite useless to you—perhaps as useless as any method of getting rid of the cigarette habit would be to non-smokers." While celebrating students' strengths as nonnative speakers, Ge pointed out the special difficulties that they would have to confront: "But you find it much more difficult to express many common ideas and thoughts than he [an Anglo-American student] does; you are far less good at the use of many common words than he is; you may even make such ridiculous mistakes as he never dreams of" (2). While Ge's assessment of Chinese students' strengths and weaknesses would help writing teachers make informed pedagogical decisions, it also would reinforce the monolithic notion of English and its native-speaking peoples.

Thus, Ge's book was not immune to the influence of current-traditional rhetoric. He discussed over two hundred topics of English composition in light of Chinese students' difficulties. These topics were grouped into eight chapters: "Introduction," "Mechanics of Composition," "Learning to Write," "Writing Correctly," "Write Correctly (Continued)," "Writing Well," "Paragraphs," and "Forms of Composition." With much attention paid to the grammatical and mechanical correctness of written products and little paid to topical development, this text fits right into the realm of current-traditional rhetoric, reinforcing standards of English established by its native speakers. Despite its exclusive focus on the correctness of the written product, the book marks one of the early indigenous efforts to negotiate with the imported composition practice and to theorize English composition in the Chinese context.

After the devastating Anti-Japanese War, college students' impaired English proficiency led to less concern with teaching English composition. Subjects other than English started to be taught in Chinese in both state and mission colleges, leaving students fewer opportunities to use English. College English teaching, therefore, in the words of Miao Tingfu, shifted toward "a *thorough* review of the essentials of Grammar and Idioms, to be followed by a practical study of Sentence Revision and Composition" (Miao i). Gradually, writing instruction was reduced to helping students construct grammatically sound sentences and paragraphs rather than being structured according to the modes. For example, in the preface of Miao's composition textbook, *Daxue yingyu zuowen* 大學英語作文 (New College Composition with Exercises, 1949), the author explained the emerging views on composition instruction:

> The new trend in language studies has come to emphasize self-cultivation and free expression rather than to impart a set of rules pedagogically framed. In other words, this present volume is *functional* rather than formal. In so far as language is something organic, restrictions and fixed models are gradually breaking down. The teacher may thus make free use of whatever materials as subjects for composition, either from the readings he assigns to his students or from the experiences of our daily life. The students are to be given perfect freedom to express themselves according to the resources of their mind. (i)

Miao criticized the common use of rigid patterns and models when teaching writing, and he encouraged free expression among the students. The celebration of free expression needs to be understood contextually. The postwar students' low English proficiency upon entering college made composition at the discourse level seem virtually impossible and irrelevant. The theoretical perspective on free expression over rigid models conveniently lent support to this "paradigmatic" turn. Teachers would need to focus more on grammatical and mechanical concerns in their teaching, thus giving the students "freedom" to express whatever "the resources of their mind" would allow. It is not surprising that, as a "functional" text, its chapters covered the components and composition of sentences, capitalization and punctuation, sentence revision, and letter writing. By celebrating "self-cultivation and free expression," quite avant-garde terms, the author relegated the responsibility of teaching self-cultivation and free expression to the students themselves.

Some issues raised by these scholars were particularly keen for English composition in the Chinese context. They were raised again later in the People's Republic. For example, Faucett's scientific notion that oral composition should be conducted first to help the pupil form good language habits was revived in the early 1970s. Ge's argument that authorship was not the appropriate purpose for average students continues to be championed by many

English teachers in China even today. They conceived of English writing as a neutral, communicative tool that would benefit students' professional careers. Into the late 1940s, school subjects other than English were taught in Chinese; therefore English lost much of its previous service function. College English composition would continue to focus on grammatical concerns as proposed by Miao until the late 1980s. These early scholarly insights contributed to the ongoing nativization of English composition, recasting this foreign import to serve the Chinese needs.

Thus, the New Culture movement prompted intellectuals to consciously adopt elements of Anglo-American rhetoric and composition in the Chinese context. Adapting the Western modes of discourse, Chinese composition categorized writings according to their transcendental, psychological effects on the audience rather than their sociopolitical purposes. The modes downplayed the traditional moral-political function of writing as a vehicle to the Way and promoted writing as a technical means to effective communication. The modes also revitalized descriptive and narrative types of writing that had been suppressed by the *bagu-ce-lun* pedagogical system and infused in students the much-needed spirit of empirical investigation. The foreign imports also inspired theoretical and pedagogical explorations in English composition. Composition treatises by Lawrence Faucett, Ge Chuangui, and Miao Tingfu underscored students' situated needs and difficulties in various times, signaling the rise of English composition pedagogies sensitive to the Chinese context. The New Culture movement also encouraged students to practice Western-style oratory and writing, preparing them for a liberal democracy.

3

WRITING AND THE
PROLETARIAN REVOLUTION

1950–76

After Communists established the People's Republic in 1949, English was condemned as the Anglo-American imperialists' language for the next three decades. The Cold War created political and economic barriers between China and the West and weakened previous ties. As English fell out of use for average students, the teaching of it rapidly declined, and English composition as a college course vanished overnight except in Taiwan.[1] Only when Communist China returned to international political and economic arenas in the early 1960s and the 1970s did English make a noticeable comeback. Although despised as an enemy's tongue in public discourse, English continued to provide the most crucial bridge between China and the West.

Efforts to assimilate Anglo-American rhetoric and composition suddenly stopped after 1949. Influenced by structuralism in English teaching, writing was sidelined by a pedagogical focus on oral discourse. Chinese and English school writing were deeply altered and shaped by the transnational discourse of the Communist movement. Marxist dialectics came to be emphasized as the guiding heuristic in rhetorical invention. To participate in the transnational discourse, Chinese writers of English developed a revolutionary style of English particular to the Chinese context. The style was avidly studied and imitated by college English-majors. Increasingly, English writing, although little taught, was coated with Chinese political and educational colors.

The Decline of English Teaching

The rise of the People's Republic in 1949 ended a century of domestic upheaval and foreign exploitation. However, the nation continued to be challenged on both fronts. After numerous ravaging wars, the construction of a new China (*xin zhongguo* 新中國) had to start from almost complete ruins. Agriculture, industry, and services were all devastated. Militarily, the Nationalist troops led by Chiang Kai-shek, who had retreated to Taiwan, continued to harass the Communist government on the mainland. After the Korean War broke out in 1950, the threat of intervention by Western powers loomed large again.

After political and economic structures were rebuilt, the nation fell into a frenzy of so-called proletarian revolution in the 1960s. The Cold War created a great divide between the Communist and the capitalist blocs. Engulfed in domestic and international politics, the Chinese Communist Party (CCP) increasingly felt pressure to defend its socialist fruits against capitalist and foreign encroachment. Therefore, inside China, the CCP orchestrated a series of mass campaigns, culminating in the infamous Cultural Revolution (1967–76), to instill the Communist ideology among the people. Internationally, it joined hands with other third-world countries to promote decolonization and national independence; it also supported the civil rights movement in the United States.[2] In short, under Mao Zedong (1893–1976), China continued an unfinished battle against Western domination.

In the new People's Republic, students first and foremost faced the rapid decline of English teaching. Two political developments caused this decline. First, Russian replaced English as the dominant foreign language in school curricula. In the early 1950s, the Soviet and Chinese governments signed a series of treaties to rebuild China after the ravages of the recent wars. Thus, a nationwide impetus to learn science and technology from the Soviet Union rose quickly and frantically. Non-English-major college students dropped English and started studying Russian, and Russian language schools mushroomed all over the country. As the study of Russian replaced English in middle schools and colleges, many English teachers were forced to teach Russian. In 1949, roughly fifty universities offered an English language and literature program. The number dropped to only nine in 1953 (Li, Zhang, and Liu). For those Chinese who were anxious to learn advanced science and technology, Russian was *the* language.

Second, hostility between the Western industrialized countries and the Communist government also led to the shrinking of English teaching. The new China was isolated by the West. Mission colleges no longer received funding from abroad because diplomatic relations between Communist

China and the Western powers were not yet established. To survive, these colleges had to accept funding from the government and, therefore, became state universities. During 1952–53, institutions of higher education were restructured. English departments in mission colleges, together with those in state universities, were combined and integrated into nine state universities. In 1954, foreign language instruction stopped being offered in junior middle schools and only began in senior middle schools. Because there was little direct contact with English-speaking countries, the social demand for English plummeted.

The deterioration in English teaching saw no substantial change until the end of the 1950s. After a decade of intensive training, a sufficient number of professionals had become proficient in Russian. At the same time, ideological and military confrontations between China and the Soviet Union had heightened and turned them from friends into foes. In 1959, the Soviets terminated hundreds of contracted projects and withdrew their experts and consultants. In the early 1960s, the international political situation tilted more favorably to Communist China. In 1964, some Asian and African countries established diplomatic relations with the People's Republic, as did France, the first Western country to do so. The fluidity of international politics encouraged the teaching of other Western languages in college besides Russian.

However, the damage had already been done to English education following its drastic downsizing in the 1950s. Students entering college in the 1960s were certainly less prepared in English than those in the early 1950s. Take the writing section of college entrance exams as an example. In republican China, almost all college entrance exams required an English essay, but in Maoist China, essay writing was only required in three years: 1950, 1964, and 1965. A comparison of the writing tasks between 1950 and 1965 further reveals the sharp decrease in students' overall English ability. The 1950 prompts asked students planning to major in English to write a two-hundred-word essay and other students to write a one-hundred-word essay. In the 1965 test, students planning to major in English needed either to write a passage of seventy words or to answer two questions (Song and Tang). In timed essay writing, length is an important indicator of students' language proficiency. The reduced length requirements thus indicate high school graduates' rather low English proficiency before the Cultural Revolution.

The worst scenarios for English teaching developed during the Cultural Revolution. Mao Zedong believed that such a cultural revolution was necessary in order to completely uproot feudal and capitalist vices in people's minds and to replace those vices with a Communist consciousness. Feudalism, as represented by the Confucian school of thought, and capitalism, as represented by Britain and the United States, were both severely attacked. Universities and colleges stopped enrolling new students in 1966. College students instead took part in various Communist-oriented political and cultural activities. Many of them were sent to work on farms and in factories hundreds or thousands of miles away from home and school, where they were expected to reform their minds and to narrow the gap between educated elites and the working class. English teaching as a result experienced an unprecedented halt in both colleges and middle schools until the beginning of the 1970s, when Western countries headed by the United States became friendlier to Communist China.

During its revival in the early 1970s, however, English teaching was, in Tang Lixing's word, completely "distorted" (44). According to Tang, a middle school teacher at that time, the English textbooks did not deal with any foreign themes but only with Chinese political works published for foreign audiences. Without a basis in any linguistic or pedagogical theories, they were compiled solely according to instructions from school authorities. In middle schools, translating political jargon-ridden English texts into Chinese prevailed in the teaching of reading and writing. Writing exercises involved "copying the words and the text, doing grammar exercises, or translation" (45). Students of English generally were unmotivated because teachers were not supposed to give them any exams, a practice that allegedly symbolized the bourgeoisie's suppression of the masses. This particular pedagogy suited the political climate of the time. Learning English was part of the students' daily revolutionary work—to master, defend, and practice Mao's revolutionary thoughts in the fierce class struggle.

When the Cultural Revolution ended in 1976, its traumatic effects on English teaching were felt in all respects. College students started their first-year English by learning the alphabet. A severe shortage of qualified teachers plagued both colleges and middle schools. Teaching materials were scarce and outdated. Despite the devastating setbacks, English composition did survive in colleges. It lived, in a twisted path, with both old practices and new influences.

Old Practices and New Influences

The most striking feature in college English was the heavy-handed domestication of teaching materials. In republican China, most English texts were imported from the United States. After the People's Republic was founded, Communist reeducation programs were opened across university campuses, involving discussions and lectures on Marxist theories and the party's socialist agenda. To effect an ideological reorientation, English teaching materials were either rewritten or imported from the Soviet Union. Some universities compiled their own, taking source materials published in the Soviet Union (Li, Zhang, and Liu). These materials opened up a new contact zone for Chinese students, spaces where they would have to wrestle with transnational Communist rhetoric, Chinese revolutionary culture, and Anglo-American capitalism.

To get a sense of the texts published in the transitional period, consider Cao Weifeng's *Xinbian dayi yingwen* 新編大一英文 (New Freshman English, 1950), which went through several printings. Designed for intensive reading, it contains seventeen passages, ten of them on subjects related to the Soviet Union. Some deal with the Soviets' great achievements, such as "The Great Oath" (Stalin), "Trade Unions in the U.S.S.R.," and "The Stalin Five-Year Plans for the Socialist Industrialization of the U.S.S.R." Others deal with famous persons in the Communist world, such as Alexander Pushkin, Karl Marx, Ivan Michurin, Maxim Gorky, and Ivan Pavlov. There are four English essays that were originally written in Chinese by Communist or pro-Communist authors—Mao Zedong, Ke Lo, Guo Moruo, and Song Qingling. Besides those hailing the greatness of the Communist movement, two passages vent criticisms of American capitalism: "The Difference between Soviet and American Foreign Policies" (Song Qingling) and "The American Scene" (John W. Powell). As Cao's textbook reveals, students no longer read books from the American and British literary canons to develop their taste in English or a sympathetic understanding of Anglo-American cultures. English readings became a vehicle for moral/political education or for conveying the scientific, Communist Way. However, criticisms were also raised about the inauthentic language used in these Russian texts or translated Chinese works.[3]

Despite the new contact zone, as most college English teachers were trained in Republican China, writing pedagogy continued to be current-traditional rhetoric in the 1950s. With full attention devoted to form, hardly any pedagogical interest existed in helping students explore ideas. Composition meant getting rid of grammatical errors and forming good habits. Since the students' competency in English was low, if not lower than before 1949, this form-based pedagogy was well received by students. Gui Shichun, a professor of English, recollects his experience in learning English composition at Zhongshan University in the mid-1950s. To teach "correct and native-like English compositions" (Gui, "Yingyong" 354), his teacher devoted all his attention to students' grammatical errors and marked them with various symbols. Students were urged to heed different errors at different stages of their composing processes. The teacher's approach appealed to the students, particularly to those with low English proficiency. Once Gui became a college teacher and had the chance to teach English composition, he modeled his teacher's pedagogy. The teacher's devoted work, his systemic approach to teaching composition, and the students' appreciation of his effort perpetuated current-traditional rhetoric in the English classroom.[4]

The Russians also reinforced the current-traditional paradigm. In 1950, Joseph Stalin published several papers on language and Marxism, which quickly swept across Russian language-teaching circles. Chinese teachers were also exposed to Stalin's linguistic theories through his papers and a few English textbooks written in light of his theories. According to Stalin, as a medium of human communication, language does not belong to any particular social class, and thanks to grammar, human thoughts materialize through language. Therefore, grammar was the scientific key to mastering a foreign language. Through studying grammar, students would grasp the general rules of linguistic evolution, strengthen their abstract thinking, and cultivate their ability to observe linguistic phenomena. For Stalin, language was a rule-governed social phenomenon and, therefore, called for a Marxist, scientific attitude (Rakhmanov).

Stalin and other Soviet scholars celebrated a comparative method, one that unwittingly encouraged a nation-state consciousness in foreign language education. To implement the comparative method, scholars suggested translation to help students understand the form, logic, meaning, and thesis of any foreign-language passage. Therefore, grammar and translation were emphasized in teaching English reading in Chinese colleges. Teachers were interested in discussing grammatical structures and vocabulary. They asked students to translate English sentences into Chinese to test their understanding of both linguistic forms and their meanings. This grammar-and-translation approach to reading naturally directed students' attention to grammar and vocabulary in their English writing. In effect, the pedagogical emphasis on grammar and translation instilled an awareness of nation-states. As one of the texts imported from the Soviet Union claims, after studying the book, students should be able to "analyze both words and grammar in the sentence and translate all texts from English into his or her mother tongue, conforming to the structure and style of the mother tongue" (Purver 8). Translating between mother and foreign tongues, and between Chinese or Russian Communist and Anglo-American capitalist cultures, students were initiated into the ideology of nation-states in the Cold War.

Within a few years after the People's Republic was established, students experienced both old and new pedagogical practices in English writing. English majors no longer focused on Anglo-American literature but concentrated on general language skills. English textbooks were domesticated and featured a selection of passages dealing with Communist Party and Chinese matters.

Although English composition was no longer offered as a college course, its pedagogy virtually remained unchanged: it continued to focus on language forms rather than topical exploration. The infiltration of Russian linguistic theory reinforced this pedagogy by celebrating grammar and translation. The meshing of Stalinist linguistics and current-traditional rhetoric suggests that, like the Soviets and the Americans, the Chinese subconsciously employed linguistic forms to mark nation-states and their cultures in English teaching.

Structural Linguistics and Writing

In the late 1950s, Chinese scholars no longer scrambled to adopt Russian textbooks but produced texts grounded in the Chinese educational context. For example, Chen Lin and colleagues wrote *Daxue yingyu keben* 大學英語課本 (College English Textbook, 1957) for English majors in which they gathered readings by both Anglo-American and Chinese authors.[5] Xu Guozhang and colleagues wrote an eight-volume textbook *Yingyu* 英語 (English, 1962–64) for English majors.[6] The text progressed from the lower-intermediate to the advanced level, which accommodated students' low English proficiency upon entering college. The text was acclaimed by both teachers and students and was widely adopted by colleges until the 1990s. Some universities, such as Beijing Foreign Language Institute and Nanjing University, also wrote their own texts in the 1960s, featuring readings on current domestic and international affairs. Besides selecting readings that reflected China's political climate, texts such as those of Chen et al. and Xu et al. also developed a systematic way to teach college English.[7] As the eight-volume text *Yingyu* was the most influential, its pedagogical perspective deserves some attention.

The text is informed theoretically by structuralism in linguistics and language teaching.[8] Structural linguistics developed in North America and Europe in the first half of the twentieth century. Rather than studying archaic or artificial languages (such as Basic English and Esperanto), structural linguists were interested in spoken language data. They treated language as a system or structure to be studied analytically at various levels—phonological, morphological, and syntactical. Structural linguistics influenced language teaching during World War II and brought language teachers "the skills of isolating, closely observing, and analyzing specific linguistic patterns" (Stern 163). Emphasizing analytical methods, language teachers tended to focus on phonetics, lexicology, syntagmatic rules, and pattern drills in their teaching. It is in these areas that the textbook *Yingyu*, particularly the first four volumes, was structured.

As laid out in the text, the first two years of English teaching should focus on phonetics and grammar. As Xu Guozhang et al. declare, "The central tasks of first-year English teaching include both offering students rigorous training in phonemes, intonation, spelling, calligraphy, and basic sentence structures and cultivating their oral skills" (1:1). In the second year, teachers should "continue to help students build a solid foundation in phonetics and grammar and expand their vocabularies, and to teach them idiomatic English expressions" (3:1). With the announced pedagogical goals, each lesson usually consists of five sections—a text, a word list based on the text, phonetics, grammar, and exercises.[9] The exercises involve chiefly three types: "phonetics exercises," "grammar exercises," and "exercises to the text."[10] Thus, from the authorial announcements of the pedagogical goals to the design of each lesson, phonetics and grammar unfailingly occupy the central stage of freshman and sophomore English.

Because of structuralism's fascination with oral discourse and syntagmatic rules, writing is relegated to a lower status. Writing is never discussed in the sections of the text. It only appears marginally in the "exercises to the text" or in "oral and written work" (in vol. 3). In the first two years, writing serves to develop oral skills and to master language forms. As the authors explain: "Exercises to the text include answering questions about the text, writing dialogues following model sentences, translating phrases, sentences, and paragraphs, speaking about pictures, and talking on given topics. Through these lively and diverse exercises, students may further grasp sentence structures and develop their ability of connecting words into sentences" (1:2). In later volumes, additional oral and written exercises were added, including "retelling the text, outlining the text, translating paragraphs from Chinese into English, and composition" (3:iii). Translation prompts students to compare syntagmatic structures between English and their mother tongue; writing allows them to practice these structures in oral and written production.

Despite writing's marginal status in structuralism, students should find opportunities to practice writing, broadly conceived. As I suggested in chapter 2, translation was typically understood as a type of composition, requiring linguistic and rhetorical dexterity. The translator appropriates a text and re-creates it in a different language. Writing dialogues, retelling and outlining a text, and composing on given topics are also valuable forms of written work for students. As students enter their third and fourth years, they find phonetics and grammar exercises being significantly curtailed while translation and writing exercises are becoming more prominent. However, pedagogically, the service function of both translation and writing remain unchanged. They are supposed to facilitate students' mastering of sentence structures in the text and help them to connect their understanding of the text to their life experiences.

As the text examples are often politically charged, translation and writing exercises carry over and affirm the text's ideological undertone. Through the text and translation and writing exercises that follow, the textbook authors transpose mainstream discourse into pedagogical discourse. For example, a text called "A Sweet Potato Plot" in volume 3 tells a story about some Red Army troops who strictly follow army discipline when they run into a sweet potato plot during an engagement with the Nationalist Army.[11] After reading the passage, students are asked to answer the following questions in the "oral and written work" section:

1. What point of army discipline did Little Tsai forget?
2. Why did the old man insist that the Red Army men should stay in his home?
3. Why did the Red Army men feel puzzled when the old man invited them to his home?
4. What does the story show? (14)

If students understand the text, they will probably be expected to answer these questions as follows: (1) Little Tsai forgot that Red Army soldiers should not steal anything from the masses, even something as trivial as a needle or a thread. (2) Because the old man loved Red Army soldiers. (3) Because the place was recently liberated from the Nationalist control. (4) The story shows the importance of the army discipline in forging a harmonious relationship between the Communist army and the masses. Every "correct" answer is intended to evoke the CCP's glorious tradition in students' consciousness: the strengths of the Communist army are derived from the enactment of the army's discipline; the army serves and defends the masses' interests; and the masses should love the army. Thus, translation and writing were wedded intimately with the national discourse of the time.

Structuralism influenced not only college English in China but also U.S. composition instruction from the 1950s to the late 1970s. Sharon Crowley notes that linguistics brought democratic ideals into composition instruction by challenging American teachers' traditional notions of grammar as being static and pre-given. In this period, writing teachers developed syntactic exercises to help students avoid grammatical and mechanical errors. Among the exercises, sentence combining proved to be effective in enhancing syntactic maturity in students' texts. Structural linguistics played a limited role in American composition instruction on two major accounts. First, composition theorists focused on typical structures of spoken discourse rather than on more complicated ones used by professional writers, thus missing an opportunity to develop a useful stylistics for composition instruction.

Second, structural linguistics favored a rather narrow, arhetorical notion of language use and construed texts as though they were constructed in a cultural vacuum; thus linguistics became "insufficient as a comprehensive source of theoretical or practical assistance in composition instruction" ("Linguistics" 480).

The impact of structuralism differed in the two national contexts. First, while linguistics democratized American composition instruction by challenging the teacher's authority, it did not cause as much impact in China in this respect. Regardless of whether syntagmatic rules were derived from descriptive or prescriptive grammar, they were conscientiously taught, or imposed, by Chinese teachers to their students. In the process of teaching a foreign language, the Chinese teacher's first priority was to impart rules of spoken and written discourse to the students. Ideally, the students could use them deductively in various contexts. Second, while linguistics-oriented composition pedagogies focused on text editing and undercut U.S. humanistic education, structural linguistics did not limit Chinese students in their education. Essentially, they learned English as an additional language to participate in transnational proletarian discourse and to enrich modern Chinese culture. Moreover, they practiced translation and writing on ideologically charged topics, which constituted part of the civic discourse of the time.

Embedded in various political movements, as the above oral and written exercise illustrates, students' use of English was shaped by concurrent political discourses that affected not only the topics but also other rhetorical aspects of students' written work, including truth, epistemology, invention, and style. I call the novel constellation of rhetorical assumptions and practices that emerged from the political movements "Chinese proletarian rhetoric," which shares a significant overlap with socialist realism in literary and artistic practices in other socialist countries.[12] Students were inculcated to a distinct rhetoric on a daily basis through the mass media, political study sessions, and their politics class. In fact, most of them were formally inducted into this rhetoric in their Chinese writing class.

Chinese Proletarian Rhetoric

As soon as the Communists came to state power, they popularized proletarian rhetoric. After the CCP was founded in 1921, it developed its own communication theory for the Communist movement in China. Chinese Communists heavily referred to Lenin and Stalin in their theory building. The theory synthesized Russian thoughts on class struggle and inherited Confucian emphasis on self-cultivation. It matured during the Anti-Japanese War period and served as a guide for fighting feudalism and imperialism not only in China but also in other colonial countries.[13] From the very beginning, this particular rhetoric was deeply concerned with national liberation and independence. Therefore, the day the People's Republic was conceived, the new rhetoric was quickly taken up by the masses.

In proletarian rhetoric, the self turns into a disciplined cultural combatant. In rhetorical transactions, the proletarian self needs to be conscious of the correct rhetorical goal, to take an unambiguous standpoint, and to understand the audience. Speaking to his fellow comrades working in art and literature, Mao Zedong articulated an overarching goal for proletarian rhetoric in 1942: "to fit art and literature properly into the whole revolutionary machine as one of its component parts, to make them a powerful weapon for uniting and educating the people and for attacking and annihilating the enemy, and to help the people to fight the enemy with one heart and one mind" (Mao, "Talks at the Yenan Forum" 243). While Communist soldiers fought with Japanese invaders on the military front, Communist artists and writers fought on the cultural front with representatives of feudalism, imperialism, and bureaucratic capitalism. Drastically departing from Confucian rhetoric, which strives for social harmony through peaceful negotiation of rituals across social classes, proletarian rhetoric wanted to eradicate social inequality by disturbing the social hierarchy—by educating and uniting the oppressed and attacking the oppressor.

Taking such an ideological position, Mao argued that the Communist self needs to differentiate friends from foes and to treat them according to their nature. With regard to the enemies, Mao instructed that artists and writers should "expose their cruelty and chicanery, point out the tendency of their inevitable defeat," and encourage the people to fight them with a united resolution (243). In terms of allies and friends, cultural workers should promote the unity and criticize them if they fail to put up an active resistance against the enemy. In relating to the broad masses that the Communists vowed to serve, cultural workers should praise and educate them in their own efforts to forsake backward ideas. In ideological combats, where one stands determines the rhetorical tactics he or she deploys, including exposing, uniting, criticizing, praising, or educating. Never before had an emphasis on audience awareness based on social classes been raised in Chinese rhetorical treatises. While classical Chinese rhetoric mainly served a small group of social elites and silenced the masses, proletarian rhetoric claimed to do exactly the opposite.

The new rhetoric stressed that artists and writers must be empathetic with their audiences. They need to understand the experiences of the people, speak their language, and sympathize with their ideas and feelings. In their creative work, their ideas and feelings need to be fused with those of the broad masses. They have to remold their thoughts and feelings through working and living together with the workers, peasants, and soldiers. Only after the cultural workers have mingled with the masses can the people understand their creative work and thereafter be educated in Communism and the Communist Party's policies. Therefore, to establish *ethos*, one has to undergo a painful transformation, ridding the self of feudal or petty bourgeois thoughts. A true proletarian rhetorician is thus conceived of as a person reborn.

As part of the rebirth, the cultural worker should never stop seeking ideological self-cultivation. According to Liu Shaoqi (1898–1969), a disciple of Leninism and a mastermind of Chinese Communism, Communists need "to make constant progress and serve as examples for others" (Liu 97). The self should develop a Communist worldview and a firm party and proletarian-class standpoint through study and revolutionary struggle. The self needs to examine its thinking and behaviors and to correct all erroneous ideas. The self should take firm control over itself in thought, speech, and action, making sure that these things adhere to correct Communist Party principles. Ultimately, in Mao's words, the Communist self was a disciplined fighter "looking upon the interests of the revolution as his very life and subordinating his personal interests to those of the revolution" ("Combat Liberalism" 199). In their deliberations on how to nurture a good Communist, Liu and Mao have clearly inherited the Confucian notion of ritualization, that is, seeking an intimate coordination between one's thoughts, speech, and actions. Ultimately, they envisioned a good, or ritualized, Communist who would radiate endless inspiration for others.

After 1949, proletarian rhetoric prevailed in Chinese composition, becoming particularly noticeable in the aspect of invention, or the treatment of theme (*zhuti* 主题). In terms of invention, or seeking "the available means of persuasion in each case" (Aristotle 36), school writing was assigned a new, overriding purpose, namely, "to cultivate in the students revolutionary thoughts and morality through the study of the Chinese language" (Dong 5). The function of writing was apparently twofold. One was to nurture Communist cultural workers to promote the socialist course; the other was to educate the students who would be future workers of socialist China and to equip them with a progressive consciousness. With cultivating revolutionary thoughts and morality set as the cardinal rhetorical purpose, aesthetic, pragmatic, and emotional purposes came to play subservient roles in the writing class. To help students cultivate revolutionary thoughts and morality through writing, composition scholars developed some invention heuristics. A peek into *Zuowen zhidao* 作文指導 (Composition Guide, 1951), by Zhu

Dexi, an influential text published in China for college students, unveils some of these invention strategies.

The text first defines the scope and nature of rhetorical invention for a cultural worker. The book is organized into six chapters: theme, structure, presentation, diction, sentence, and punctuation. In the chapter on "theme," the author Zhu Dexi (1920–92) lays out the "scientific," or Marxist, approach to observing and analyzing subject matter. First, he admonishes his students to focus on correct, constructive, and educational themes in their writing, thus "offering the readers nutrients rather than poison or drugs" (2). By positioning writers as cultural workers who could furnish positive, educational inspiration to the people, Zhu entrusts them with great rhetorical agency and responsibility.

Next, Zhu promotes Marxist dialectics as the guiding heuristic in theme development. Marxist dialectics embody a particular perspective on how nature and human society evolve as well as how humans reason. Marxists view natural and social phenomena as being interconnected, in constant motion and change. Furthermore, they believe that the evolution of nature and human society is driven by interaction and struggle between various opposing forces. Human reasoning is a reflection of nature and human society in motion and change and of the interaction of various opposing forces. Therefore, the dialectic principles suggested by Zhu include avoiding overgeneralization, acknowledging both unities and conflicts of the subject matter, taking a developmental perspective, and differentiating between the appearance and the essence of subject matter. Marxist dialectics are congruent with traditional Chinese ontology, which perceives the world in a holistic, evolving, and interconnected fashion. In the chapters on "structure" and "presentation," Zhu emphasizes that the selection, organization, and presentation of materials all need to center on a chosen theme. Thus, while the emphasis on empirical, "correct" writing could still be seen as a current-traditional hangover and a limitation, Chinese proletarian rhetoric transcended current-traditional rhetoric by locating invention at the center of rhetorical practices.

However, adhering to proletarian rhetoric was never easy for students who received much of their education in republican China. The Communist cultural turn entailed that they alter their rhetorical views and practices. Their struggles were captured in many student essays quoted in Zhu's book. In the chapter on "theme," for instance, Zhu stresses that the writer should take the right stand and cultivate correct opinions in the reader. He quotes a student essay to illustrate "the right stand," or the celebrated position of the masses. The essay describes a widow whom the student writer encountered while participating in the Land Reform movement in the late 1940s. In the movement, arable land was seized from landlords and redistributed among peasants. Zhu comments at the end of the essay:

> The student described the figure [the widow] vividly and used the peasant's language quite skillfully. However, in terms of the selection of theme, this essay is problematic. A suppressed woman typical in the old society, Mrs. Zhuwang is perseverant, industrious, and kind. She struggled in her miserable life with little resistance, submitting everything in her life to fate. Such a figure and such a story cater exactly to the taste of petty bourgeoisie. Therefore, the author expressed his sympathy, unconsciously celebrating her loyalty to her deceased husband and her filial obedience to her parents. (5)

Rather than catering to the taste of the petty bourgeoisie, who clung to the traditional Confucian values of fate, loyalty, and filial obedience, Zhu suggests that the author should have taken the position of the masses. He should have focused on the great achievements of the Land Reform movement in which, under the Communist Party's leadership, peasants were liberated from the exploitation of landlords. Although the story might be true, Zhu censures it, saying that it neglected or downplayed the great achievements of the liberated peasants. Therefore "partial truth might turn out to be complete untruth" (6). In light of Marxist dialectic, the student had failed to take a developmental perspective, nor had he identified the essence of the Land Reform movement behind the widow's miserable life. Without grasping the essence of the theme, the student's writing simply warped the "truth" and misled the reader. The student's inability to fully grasp the essence of proletarian rhetoric was not an insolated case, but mirrored the struggle of most students shifting from an old rhetorical frame to a new one.

Zhu's emphasis on choosing correct, constructive, and educational themes echoed Mao Zedong's renowned speech, "Against the Eight-Legged Style of Writing within the Party" (1942). In this speech, Mao warned party members against writing without a clear theme, an honest and scientific attitude, an awareness of the audience, or the use of the people's common language. Clearly, the Marxist invention heuristics were a mixture of Western scientific rhetoric and Confucian ritualization. On one hand, Zhu and Mao both perceived the natural world and human society as observable, materialistic objects, where truth primarily resides. They evolved along certain trajectories that resulted from their internal unities and conflicts. On the other hand, Zhu and Mao urged the writer to take responsibility to educate the masses in their own language. The writer's primary task was discerning the essence of a subject, or the truth, under the direction of a Marxist world-view, and exposing it "objectively" to the masses. The writer's ideological standpoint ultimately determined what was truth, partial truth, or untruth. Historically, Western scientific rhetoric took a positivist position towards truth that served the capitalist democracy. In contrast, Chinese proletarian rhetoric conceived truth in a dialectic, materialistic fashion—truth means objectivity through the masses' lens, or the terministic screens of the "Party spirit" (Chung xv.). Thus, proletarian rhetoric inherited, but also transcended, Western scientific rhetoric. However, what both Zhu and Mao preached as desirable heuristics and guidelines in writing was soon swept away by extremely leftist discourse during the Great Leap Forward (GLF) movement and the Cultural Revolution.[14]

Writing in the Party Spirit

At the end of the 1950s, students were confronted with a new rhetorical situation brought on by the GLF movement. After the first Five-Year Plan (1953–57), a relatively comprehensive industrial infrastructure was established in the country. Overzealous for economic achievements, Mao Zedong and his fellow Communists launched the GLF movement (1958–59) during the second Five-Year Plan (1958–62). The movement aimed to achieve a higher economic growth rate and to develop a socialist economic model more suited to Chinese conditions. During the movement, the Communists mobilized the masses by appealing to their enthusiasm for Communist ideals, which led to an overflow of extremely leftist rhetoric. With unrealistic expectations among the party cadres, the second Five-Year Plan was implemented rather unscientifically and hastily at various levels. For example, to fulfill the required quota in industry, workers often sacrificed quality for quantity. Quality in agricultural production also suffered from the lack of technical know-how among farmers. Often statistics for both industrial and agricultural production at grassroots levels were reported with sheer exaggeration. Then the twisted figures were used by the party's propaganda machine to celebrate "the great achievements" of the people under the party's leadership. The "great" news further propelled the masses to work harder and led to even higher expectations for economic production.

The GLF spirit also pervaded college English teaching. Under the Communist Party's direction of combining education and labor, English majors spent many days working on farms or in factories. In the fall of 1959, for example, sophomores at Nanjing University spent 38 days on labor work, 17 days on educational reform activities, 17 days on political rallies, and 65 days on English studies. Quantity rather than quality was actively sought in teaching and learning. Within two weeks, students studied thirty-two English passages on current politics and learned two thousand new words. By the end of the semester, students and teachers jointly edited an anthology of political essays and a textbook on English conversation. The students boasted cheerfully, "Compared with the past, our speed in mastering English vocabulary and grammar and improving our reading, writing, and translation abilities has more than doubled, but has increased by at least seven times" (Nanjing daxue, "Yingyu jiaoxue" 17). Thus, it is clear that the GLF movement took place in every sector of Chinese society and created an extremely leftist discourse.

Students formally studied this leftist discourse as part of the transnational Communist rhetoric. Under the slogan "To serve politics; to serve production," students read exaggerated reports about agricultural production, steel production, and irrigation. For example, juniors at Nanjing University read a commentary written by R. Page Arnot, a British reporter, in their English textbook. Originally published in the British *Labour Monthly,* the commentary alerted the British Labor Party to the achievements made in socialist countries, particularly China. The author was deeply impressed by the speed of revolution in the GLF movement. In one place, he declared, "That aeroplanes and cyclotrons and a planetarium are being built in China may seem a marvel: but it is already commonplace compared to the cornucopia of agriculture, from which this year's [1958] yield of food crops is already *double the harvest of 1957*" (emphasis original, 6). Even a foreign reporter was not shielded from the leftist exaggerations. Arnot's report effectively turned the GLF discourse into part of the transnational Communist rhetoric. Reading the report in the class engaged Chinese students in global cultural flows.

Translation work that came after the passage further perpetuated the celebratory discourse of the GLF. After reading Arnot's commentary, for example, students were asked to translate two English passages into Chinese and a Chinese passage into English. The translation work expressed joy, excitement, and pride for the people's "achievements," thus legitimizing the party's leadership. The Chinese passage was a speech script, and many students reading it would empathize with the speaker's revolutionary spirit:

> Look, how many workers make technical innovations and break production quota day and night; how many experts make inventions and design new plans while forgetting sleeping and eating; how many peasant brothers work hard throughout the year for a good harvest of cotton and grain; and how many business workers rack their brains for keys that will guarantee abundant market supply. . . . Ah, just like this, they are working untiringly. Yesterday, the wall was crowded by pledges to

offer presents to our People's Republic on its tenth birthday. Today, there are already production reports and bulletins of glad tidings in various colors. All of these are intended for greater, faster, better and more economical results in our socialist construction. (Nanjing daxue waiyuxi sannianji 278)

Using parallelisms and contrasting "yesterday" and "today," the passage was intended to stir up the readers' feelings and make them identify with the grand Communist course. As students pondered about how to transpose the passage into English, the glorious images, spirited words, and leftist logic would emerge and be further ingrained in their minds. Seemingly, they did the translation for an English-speaking audience. In fact, they did it much like they would write an eight-legged essay; they could not really inform or persuade the intended but nonexistent audience. Instead, they displayed their revolutionary morale and allegiance to the Communist Party through skilled or unskilled English writing. Simply put, translation constituted part of their Communist ritualization. Consequently, the students' minds were revolutionarily reengineered, and they made ideological leaps forward as well.

While abiding by the Communist Party spirit, students were not unreflective of what they experienced in the GLF movement. Written work, for example, offered them some deliberative space to come to terms with the party's educational stipulations. In an English essay, "Our Factory," two students from Beijing Foreign Language Institute accounted their experiences working in a chemical tile factory operated by their school. In the first part of the essay, they explained how they had overcome difficulties while producing chemical tiles as untrained student workers. Next, they revealed their confusion over and struggle with the notion of "combining education with productive labor," a slogan that prevailed in Maoist China:

Why should we students in the Foreign Language Institute set up factories? Why must schools follow the principle of combining education with productive labour? Might it not have bad effect on the quality of education? And so on.

We came to realize that setting up factories in schools was one of the basic ways to combine education with productive labour. Everybody should be able to do both mental and manual work. This is the demand of socialist and communist society. We do not think that setting up factories by schools will lower the quality of education, for it's in the factories that we learn a lot of things which we connot [sic] learn from the books. And we know that when we are working we are also reforming ourselves. (Pi and Lu 27–28)

This confessional account showcases the process of proletarian subject formation, which is quasi-religious. The students doubted the necessity of the Communist Party's educational stipulations. They sought answers to their doubts not from elsewhere but from the party spirit, or both the Communist worldview and the party's policies. Kenneth Burke's notion of "scene-act ratio" is particularly suited to explicate the students' language use here. The nationwide GLF movement and its frantic discourse (*scene*) prompted students to use the party's vocabulary to resolve their puzzlements over its educational policy (*act*). In their rhetorical act, the party spirit ascended as the unquestionable truth, or the Way.

Ironically, the students used the enemy's language unapologetically to actuate their proletarian subject formation. As conceived in the leftist discourse, English was a language of Anglo-American capitalists. Chinese students were supposed to master the language to fight against capitalism externally. However, the two students adopted it internally to develop their proletarian subject positions. When doing so, they made use of multiple rhetorical resources. First, like traditional Chinese literati, they performed self-examination by reflecting upon personal issues in relation to the state. They wanted to understand an educational policy that had deeply affected every Chinese youth. Second, they persuaded themselves by asking rhetorical questions and adopting an expository mode. Third, as I have mentioned, they resorted to the party's political terms to reason with themselves. In an era dominated by an extremely leftist discourse, using an enemy's language to reconcile with personal issues in effect undermined the leftist rhetoric, which was negative about and hostile to English in Chinese society.

Intriguingly, a similar party spirit also saturated students' English writing in Taiwan, though perpetuating a different ideology. After the Nationalist Party retreated to the island, it endeavored to cultivate Chinese nationalism among the islanders and vowed to retake the mainland. Such a party spirit was pervasive on college campuses, as manifest in the following student essay "The Labor Program." Some colleges established labor programs in the 1950s to democratize higher education. Doing menial work on campus, poor students could pay for their tuition, board, and lodging; students in general learned "to take care of public property, to become part of a team, to be efficient, responsible, and punctual" (Speidel 31). Three students of Tunghai University, a Protestant mission school, reflected upon the transforming power of labor work in the early 1960s:

> In traditional Chinese thought physical labor was not the business of educated men. They let illiterate people do such trivial things. Although that time has gone by, the hackneyed idea still permeates many people's

minds. We also have the duty to wipe out this kind of prejudice. So the purpose of setting up the Labor Program is "To train the students in good habits of mental and physical exercise, and to develope [*sic*] a sense of responsibility, cooperation and loyalty to the institution or group." . . .

The program has made remarkable progress during the past eight years. Students also can expend the spirit on other tasks. For example, during leisure time many students voluntarily organized work camps to help poor farmers in the neighboring villages. This is a proof that Chinese will never be looked upon as a handful of sand as before. Co-operation and responsibility will produce strong power which leads us to victory. (Chou, Shen, and Lu)

Compared with the Communist stipulations of combining education with productive labor on the mainland, the labor program seems to have produced a similar effect: labor altered intellectuals' traditional prejudice against menial jobs and brought them closer to factory workers and farmers, which, thus, democratized education. However, the ultimate goal of the labor program, according to the three students, was to encourage "cooperation and respon-sibility" among people, to alter the old image of the Chinese as "a handful of sand." Decades before, Sun Yet-sen had chided the Chinese with a similar metaphor ("a sheet of loose sand"), criticizing them for being loyal to their family and clan but not to the nation when it faced foreign aggression. These Tunghai students believed that the labor program would strengthen the Chinese nation and eventually lead to "victory over the Communists" (Benda 10), which represents precisely the spirit of the Nationalist Party at that time.

In the process of writing for advancing the party spirit and for personal cultivation, Chinese students developed their own writing style. During the GLF movement, quantity was valued more than quality, a factor that often rendered students' writing style rather hollow. To hurry through a large number of writing assignments, students tended to imitate or plagiarize ideas from others' writings. They repeated political slogans that they had learned from various political movements. Not required (or uninspired) to express their individual thoughts, through these writing assignments, they developed a fabricated, exaggerated, and empty style (*jia da kong* 假、大、空) in both their Chinese and English writing. Their style clearly betrayed Marx-ist heuristics in writing; that is, the writer needed to write with an honest, scientific attitude and to avoid overgeneralizations. The style became part of the way English was used in Communist China, a style that some dubbed "bastardized" English.

Writing in "Bastardized" English

Students were exposed to a hybridized English style with rich Chinese cultural references in their readings. The hybridized style arose in the contact zone of the transnational Communist movement. Infused with socialist zeal, the country was haunted by a growing sense of national pride and an urge to introduce the Chinese socialist experience to the rest of the world. Chinese writers translated Chinese concepts and words literally when they wrote English news reports or translated Mao Zedong's works into English. They believed that literal translations conveyed Chinese meanings more effectively. The following passage, translated from one of Mao Zedong's speeches, "Imperialism and All Reactionaries Are Paper Tigers" (1946), exemplifies the rhetorical effects of literal translation in English[15]:

> Chiang Kai-shek and his supporters, the U.S. reactionaries, are all paper tigers too. Speaking of U.S. imperialism, people seem to feel that it is terrifically strong. Chinese reactionaries are using the "strength" of United States to frighten the Chinese people. But it will be proved that the U.S. reactionaries, like all the reactionaries in history, do not have much strength. In the United States there are others who are really strong—the American people.
>
> Take the case of China. We have only millet plus rifles to rely on, but history will finally prove that our millet plus rifles is more powerful than Chiang Kai-shek's aeroplanes plus tanks. Although the Chinese people still face many difficulties and will long suffer hardships from the joint attacks of U.S. imperialism and the Chinese reactionaries, the day will come when these reactionaries are defeated and we are victorious. The reason is simply this: the reactionaries represent reaction, we represent progress. (Beijing waiguoyu xueyuan 104–105)

First of all, the English translation of the title "Imperialism and All Reactionaries Are Paper Tigers" was uniquely Chinese: Chinese abstract nouns can be combined with concrete ones in a way that is not usually done in Anglo-American English. In this passage, Mao Zedong described Chiang Kai-Shek and the United States metaphorically as "paper tigers" (*zhi laohu* 紙老虎), who appear to be superficially powerful but tend to overextend themselves in reality. To support his assertion, Mao evokes the seemingly miraculous fact that the Communist troops, armed with only "millet plus rifles" (*xiaomi jia buqiang* 小米加步槍), defeated the seemingly more powerful Nationalist troops, who were equipped with airplanes and tanks by the U.S. government in the late 1940s. In this passage, the literal translation of "Imperialism and

All Reactionaries Are Paper Tigers" (animalification and metaphor) and "millet plus rifles" (metonymy) vividly retain these expressions' historical, cultural references.

For a native speaker, English texts dotted with such literal translations might be odd, confusing, and frustrating and, thus, regretfully considered a "bastardized version of his own language" (Lary 4). This native-speaker perspective was considered inherently hegemonic and suppressive due to the worldwide dominance of Anglo-American culture. Through loaned translations and coined phrases and structures as in the above passage, Chinese translators used English to convey the unique local political culture and to subvert imperialist discourse. In global contact zones, English translations became what Mary Louise Pratt has called auto-ethnographic texts; they were "merged or infiltrated to varying degrees with indigenous [here, Communist Chinese] idioms to create self-representations intended to intervene in metropolitan [capitalist Western] modes of understanding" (35). In fact, the notion that "Imperialism and All Reactionaries Are Paper Tigers" was so resoundingly clear and inspiring to the Third World people that usage has established this uniquely Chinese expression in the English language. The Communist flavor emitted by the hybrid, or "bastardized," language thus disrupted the colonial and capitalist discourses performed globally through English. These translations, through their domestic circulation, also engaged translators, students, and other readers to reason and to imagine within a Chinese nation-community. It was exactly those "bastardized" English texts that students read and modeled in their translation and writing exercises.

Hybridized English was internalized in students' discourse through a politicized process of textual production. Soon after the GLF movement started in 1958, both Chinese and foreign language textbooks were recompiled for "healthy" language. The new texts excluded anything deemed antisocialist or unsocialist. Remaining were passages from the works of Karl Marx, Vladimir Lenin, and Mao Zedong and translations of recent articles published in the *People's Daily*, one of the Communist Party's publications. English majors all studied English translations of Mao's three time-honored texts: "Serve the People," "In Memory of Norman Bethune," and "The Foolish Old Man Who Removed the Mountains."[16] These texts emphasized cultivating unselfish, noble-minded Communist workers for the socialist course. The "paper tiger" speech by Mao, for instance, was quoted from a textbook compiled by the Beijing Foreign Language Institute in the early 1960s. Diana Lary, who taught English at this institute during the same period, says the process of course material compilation was "in fact for the political department to send out a text in Chinese, which will be translated into different foreign languages by the various departments, checked by the foreign teachers for accuracy in the language, rechecked by the political department for purity, and finally given to the students" (4). Lary's account typified the process of textual production in foreign language programs. School authorities, foreign language departments, and political departments took good care of textual production and circulation in which they hybridized the text with Communist thoughts and coined expressions. And the students, through reading, translating, and writing about these texts, consumed the Communist discourse of revolution and socialist construction.

In the textual circulation process, students devoted their attention to the political meanings of texts. Throughout the 1960s and the 1970s, rather than dealing with petty and "bourgeois" issues in life, writing in both high schools and colleges was geared toward collective life in communes and factories. Students were asked to write about activities or issues in those places, and sometimes their compositions were assessed by their fellow peers rather than by their teachers. David Crook (1910–2000), who taught English at Beijing Foreign Language Institute in Maoist China, observed the students' Chinese composition exams: "The students read their pieces to a gathering of commune members and cadres, including the Party branch secretary and a number of educated young people who had settled in the villages (as these students would do in their turn). Each piece was discussed and appraised both for its writing technique and its content and ideology, separate marks being given for each" (25–26). Writing for proletarian audiences and inviting them for evaluation achieved the goal of disrupting the elitist educational tradition. Public reading of a student's composition created a forum for the masses to deliberate upon the subject matter and to gauge it against the mainstream discourse and their own life experiences. Thus, as with the eight-legged essay, the performative aspect of composition gave rise to an epideictic moment in which both the writer and the audience were ritualized into the Way, or the Communist worldview.

However, to be ritualized into the Communist Way and to abide by the party spirit, students sometimes had to sacrifice their individual voices and styles, adopting a fabricated, exaggerated, and empty style. This feature of language use was exacerbated during the Cultural Revolution. Students participated in political study sessions and public rallies, wrote wall posters, and recited Mao's works. On a daily basis, they were besieged by obscure, simple, and agitating slogans invented by the party's propaganda organs. Therefore, slogan-ridden, formalized language seeped into pedagogical discourse as manifested in students' reading and writing. For example, in a freshman English lesson, students of Shanghai Foreign Language Institute studied a conversation between a worker and his son. The father encouraged his son to face difficulties boldly when learning English in college. He explained, "Chairman Mao has sent you to college. You must work hard for socialist revolution and socialist construction. You must win honor for Chairman Mao" (Shanghai waiguoyu 224). After studying the lesson, students were asked to translate a Chinese conversation into English. Here is part of the conversation:

> A: After liberation, my mom continued to work in the same plant, but her life completely changed. She learned to read and write. She began studying Chairman Mao's works and understood that we must do revolution. Our family is living a very happy life.
> B: We should not forget our miserable lives in the past. We should always listen to Chairman Mao and follow the Party. (233–34, my translation)

In this short passage, there are at least four slogans: "work hard for socialist revolution and social construction," "win honor for Chairman Mao," "do revolution," and "always listen to Chairman Mao and follow the Party." Finally, students were asked to compose an essay titled "Study English for the Revolution"; apparently the students were expected to borrow ideas from their reading and translation and to use similar phrases and slogans in their essays. As a reaction to bourgeois individualism, thus, the insistence on Marxist correspondence between language and reality conditioned individuals' subjectivity, placing limitations on invention within the proletarian rhetorical system.

Students' daily political activities had prepared them for this type of writing in which they virtually translated their daily discourse into school writing. Xing Lu found much truth in her observation of the rhetoric of the Cultural Revolution: "As the formal language was plagiarized in every political speech, it deteriorated into dry and cumbersome clichés, which led to linguistic impoverishment and thought-deprivation" (*Rhetoric of the Chinese* 43). As was required in writing exam essays in the Qing dynasty, students were confined to orthodox thinking and to speaking in an impersonal or inauthentic voice (often in the vicarious voice of Confucius or other sages). As the overriding function of language teaching was to ritualize students into the Communist Way, this hybridized English writing served that purpose.

English Pedagogy for Proletarian Revolution

While students promoted the Communist Way in translation and writing, Chinese scholars explored theoretical issues in foreign language teaching to advance the proletarian movement. In the late 1950s, a scholarly interest in developing a new and "scientific" foreign language teaching and research system was kindled by the redefinition of education in a socialist country. As promulgated by the CCP, education needed to serve the proletarian class and be combined with productive labor. Accordingly, foreign language teaching was not class neutral but part of the class struggle. A new and "scientific" system needed to be established to serve the proletarian class, or the Chinese masses. Scholars critically examined foreign language pedagogies developed in ancient China, republican China, and Western countries. Their criticisms of those pedagogies theoretically refigured the teaching of English writing for the proletarian revolution.

First, scholars criticized the direct method and celebrated the translation approach to foreign language teaching. On the one hand, as some pointed out, the direct method had served Western colonial interests in both the late Qing dynasty and republican China. In order to produce bilingual individuals, students were disconnected from their mother-tongue environment and brainwashed with Western capitalist culture. As Li Zhenlin explained, "Historically bilingualism was always tied with ethnic suppression and forced language assimilation. Bilingualism in old China was also connected with national suppression" (Li 14). On the other hand, during the past thousand years, Chinese scholars had been engaged in translating Buddhist scripts from Sanskrit into Chinese. They succeeded in learning Sanskrit through textual analysis and translation, which meant that both methods were proven effective for Chinese students trying to learn a foreign language. Therefore, translation was recommended by these scholars as a strategy for improving students' English writing (Ding, "Lue Tan"; Wang Zuoliang). The scholarly attention to translation coincided with the Russian influence, which had already penetrated reading classes.

Despite being grounded in history, discussions about the direct method and translation unveiled Chinese scholars' anxiety and their mechanistic view of language and culture in intercultural exchanges. Underneath their arguments was an assumption that foreign languages would be best learned within the geographic and cultural confines of the Chinese nation-state. They feared that students would lose their cultural purity and authenticity as they became engaged with and adopted values of other cultures through foreign language studies. Scholars conceived of translation as the best pedagogical choice because it could minimize direct cultural contact, restricting it to the textual level. Apparently, their intercultural anxiety and narrow-mindedness was derived from the political and cultural insularity that Communist China experienced in the 1950s. Average Chinese found few opportunities to interact with Anglo-American people or to consume their cultural products.

The mechanistic view of language and culture that assumed they were easily separable was clearly a vestige of the *ti-yong* dualist mentality.

Second, the Communist scholars criticized the reading of Anglo-American literature and advocated the study of Mao's translated works. In the past, as a few scholars claimed, English textbooks were loaded with Anglo-American literary pieces that reflected a capitalist lifestyle and bourgeois sentiments. They "poisoned" students' minds. Now, English became a weapon for proletarian struggles in the international arena. The reasons for mastering foreign languages were, as Chen Zhongsheng explained, "to help spread Chairman Mao's thoughts, to introduce to the rest of the world the theories and experiences derived from our revolution and construction work, and to unite and encourage the suppressed in the world to fight against imperialism, colonialism, revisionism, and any counter revolutionaries" (Chen 6). As users of the weapon, students were expected to master Mao's thoughts thoroughly and to express them fluently in foreign languages. Through oral and written exercises, teachers could discuss Mao's thoughts and help students enhance their political consciousness. Mao's translated works also provided students with good examples for studying English grammar, vocabulary, sentence structure, and rhetorical strategies. Voices were raised in the early 1960s against the use of translated works; however, those critics were condemned as representing a counterrevolutionary standpoint.[17]

Third, the Communist scholars criticized the lack of attention to the systematic teaching of English writing. As Ding Wangdao pointed out, no writing courses were offered in English departments. Writing was supposed to be taught in intensive reading classes, but teachers there tended to spend little time on it. Even if they addressed writing issues in class, they tended to focus on grammar and diction errors. Although topical exploration, textual arrangement, genre, and rhetoric could be discussed in analytical reading classes, Ding argued that they should be systematically treated in a separate writing class. Quite insightfully, Ding emphasized the importance of teaching grammar within rhetorical contexts:

> The so-called misuse of language means a certain structure, a tense, or a mood being used inappropriately for a certain context. To deal with these issues, passage- or paragraph-based exercises excel markedly over single sentence-based exercises. To address grammatical issues together with the structure and rhetoric of an essay can help the students achieve a firmer grip of the grammar. It helps them to conceive grammar as a lively being rather than some mechanical rules. Therefore writing instruction and grammar instruction can complement each other. ("Lue Tan" 214).

Ding's promotion of teaching writing and rhetoric was an indirect criticism of the decontextualized treatment of grammar during the grammar-translation pedagogy. His criticism echoed American scholars' rebuttals of linguistics-oriented U.S. composition pedagogies in the same period (see Crowley, "Linguistics"). Therefore, Ding suggested that a separate writing course should be offered to students after they completed a grammar course in an English-major program.

Fourth, the Communist scholars also criticized the pedagogical focus on expository argumentation essays. Dai Liuling observed that students most frequently wrote this type of essay on political and economic topics. However, he argued, focusing on a narrow scope of subject matters performed a disservice to the students' writing development: "For many writers, their essays tend to be shallow and superficial with abstract words and sentences all lumped together" (Dai 11). Therefore, Dai suggested that students should practice more narrative and descriptive writing, which would allow them to use their own words to describe what they had heard and seen, and would please the reader by presenting events and objects in more concrete and sensual terms. These types of writings could help students develop the good habit of seeking truth from facts. As Dai's suggestion for more narrative and descriptive writing was made soon after the GLF movement, he prescribed an antidote to the fabricated, exaggerated, and empty style prevalent at the time. His suggestion also echoed Liang Qichao's argument for having students practice narrative and descriptive writing in Chinese composition in the 1920s (see chapter 2). As part of Confucian rhetorical tradition, the Chinese inclination for expository argumentation appeared to continually shadow both Chinese and English composition. It would remain a shadow in the test-driven English writing instruction of the 1990s (see chapter 5).

In a concerted effort to seek effective foreign language pedagogies, these professionals examined Chinese educational tradition very closely. They reviewed how Chinese had learned foreign languages in the past and, with a stint of intercultural anxiety, identified textual analysis and translation as treasured pedagogical choices in modern China. They critiqued the Chinese inclination for expository argumentation essays and suggested that narrative and descriptive writing should receive more attention in English writing classes. With foreign languages being conceived of as a weapon for international proletarian struggles, they recommended including Mao's translated works in English textbooks. With their theoretical endeavor grounded in Chinese tradition and the current political situation, the field of foreign language teaching and research made big strides toward forming pedagogical theories with Chinese characteristics. Unfortunately, discussions of these matters died down in the late 1960s and were not revived until the end of the Cultural Revolution in the late 1970s.

During the three decades of the Maoist government, the most striking developments in composition instruction were the rise of Chinese proletarian rhetoric and the domestication of English composition. Derived from decades of struggle with feudalism and Western imperialism, proletarian rhetoric emerged as an archetypical contact zone product mixed with orthodox Marxism, Russian Communist thought, and Confucian rhetoric. In the new discursive theory, the rhetor was an enlightened, disciplined cultural worker engaged in the proletarian revolution. He or she worked to educate and unite the masses so that they could fight the enemy with one giant fist. In composition instruction, proletarian rhetoric inherited current-traditional rhetoric, but transcended it by promoting Marxist dialectics as the cardinal invention heuristic. In the international proletarian movement, English was localized to capture Chinese thought and experience and then used to introduce Chinese socialism to the world. Reading and writing in this sinonized English style, students participated in and, thus were ritualized through, Chinese socialist discourse. In the late 1950s and early 1960s, Chinese Communist scholars also explored how to develop a "scientific" system of foreign language teaching and research to facilitate the proletarian revolution.

4

WRITING AND THE FOUR MODERNIZATIONS

1977–90

When China reopened itself to the outside world in the late 1970s, public attitudes toward English changed overnight. Although it was still regarded as a foreign tongue, English was no longer demonized. The Cultural Revolution had severely interfered with and thus degraded the national economy, scientific research, and education. To boost developments in these areas, the Communist Party decided to reopen the country to foreign investments and to acquire advanced Western science and technology. As it had done after the Opium Wars, English again became a vital medium for the Chinese who desired to fully participate in global affairs. However, learning English became a voluntary national choice rather than the forced one that it had been in the colonial years.

The open-door policy jump-started a nationwide frenzy toward the teaching of English and other foreign languages. English teachers were exposed to new applied-linguistics theories and Anglo-American composition pedagogies. The most significant borrowings from the West were communicative English teaching theory and process writing pedagogy. Composition became a separate course in English-major programs again; writing was studied for its own sake rather than serving to develop other language skills as in structuralism-informed language pedagogies. After the Cultural Revolution, proletarian rhetoric gradually atrophied, but Marxist heuristics stayed in Chinese composition instruction, a development that in turn affected English composition. Composition no longer served the proletarian revolution but instead helped to define the new direction of Chinese modernization.

The Return of Anglo-American Teachers

Chinese education turned a corner in 1976, the year Mao Zedong died. After his death, Mao's leftist party loyalists lost their grip on state power and were superseded by pragmatists. In 1977, college entrance exams were restored; high school graduates of that year and those who had lost the opportunity to go to college during the Cultural Revolution were able to take the exam. In December of 1978, the Communist Party declared that class struggle as the totalizing scheme of social activities was no longer the cardinal principle in Chinese political life. Instead, the nation would move on to construct a socialist power emphasizing modern industry, agriculture, national defense, and science and technology, which were known as the Four Modernizations. The new CCP leaders steered the party toward an open-door policy to encourage foreign investment and to import Western science and technology. To adopt the world's advanced technologies, scientific and educational work was reemphasized. Thus, China changed its modernization program from a revolutionary mass-mobilization model to a professional and orderly development model.

The open-door policy generated an increasing demand for English in Chinese society. By the end of the 1970s, the People's Republic had established diplomatic relations with over one hundred nations, including Britain and the United States. Foreign investments also surged significantly. Chinese students and scholars were sent selectively to study in Western countries by the government. Zeal for learning English grew among students and workers. The English-teaching TV program "Follow Me!" produced by the BBC and the Voice of America (VOA) radio program "English 900" became great hits, indicating the historic reentry of Anglo-American cultural forces in mainstream Chinese society. By the mid-1980s, more than three hundred higher education institutions had established undergraduate English-major programs (Li, Zhang, and Liu), and English became a compulsory course for most college students.

Once the Chinese door to the outside world reopened, foreign educators were invited into the country. They fell into three groups based on how they made their way into China. The first group consisted of experts and teachers sent by government agencies, such as the British Council and the Fulbright Foundation of the United States. The second group was made up of teachers who came through intercollegiate exchange programs. The third group was comprised of teachers sponsored by church organizations.

British and American teachers played a pivotal role in English-teacher training, though with different focuses. After the Cultural Revolution, an urgent demand rose for quality English teachers all over the country. Some universities, such as Beijing University, Beijing Foreign Language Institute, Shanghai Foreign Language Institute, and Wuhan University, established English-teacher training programs. From 1980 to 1983, these programs produced 5,771 teachers with master's-equivalent certificates, adding 40 percent more teachers to the college English teaching staff as of 1980 (Li, Zhang, and Liu). Chinese and Anglo-American teachers co-taught in these programs. Courses often varied depending on where the foreign teachers came from. For example, teachers dispatched by the British Council taught at Beijing Foreign Language Institute. They offered courses in Anglo-American literature, Anglo-American societies and cultures, and linguistics and teaching methodology, but offered no courses related to English rhetoric and composition. In contrast, the program at Shanghai Foreign Language Institute, staffed by Fulbright scholars, featured a half year of advanced training in listening, speaking, reading, and writing. As was true in republican China, American scholars were keen to teach writing.

In their teaching, American scholars called Chinese teachers' attention to discursive issues in composition, an area where they had lacked training in Maoist China. At Shanghai Foreign Language Institute, Ann Johns noted that most of the students, despite all being experienced English teachers, "had had little practice in producing text beyond the sentence" (69). Therefore, American scholars set clear goals for teaching composition: "to develop the students' writing skills and to teach the basic formats of English essays—from the basic knowledge about paragraph writing to paper writing for college courses" (qtd. in Li, Zhang, and Liu 513). When they graded student papers, they paid much more attention to the development of thoughts, discourse structure, transition between paragraphs, and logical connections than to grammar and vocabulary (Gao Junhua). Thanks to such international educational exchanges, the dreadful situation of teaching English writing would gradually improve in Chinese colleges.

However, in contrast to the colonial period, the government exercised full institutional control over foreign educators' work. For instance, foreign church organizations, instead of claiming to salvage the "hopelessly weak and corrupt" government and the "poor and ignorant" people, were aware of ideological complexities of the new mission and had to set a different goal for their reentry. The United Board for Christian Higher Education in Asia (UBCHEA), the coordinator for American mission colleges in Republican China, returned in 1980. Invited by the Chinese Society for Education, a delegation headed by president of the UBCHEA and former Harvard president Nathan Pusey visited China and signed an agreement with the Society for educational exchanges and cooperation. In a statement, UBCHEA announced its aim "to help provide a Christian presence in secular academic communities" (United Board 1). Further, it declared: "All education in China is under the guidance of the Communist Party and is offered within the context of Marxism, with its particular views of religion. . . . However, there is an opportunity for effective Christian witness in serving Chinese scholars and students in their search for truth and professional skills" (2). Under the suspicious gaze of the Chinese, UBCHEA had to agree to adhere to its original purposes. After acknowledging the Communist leadership and using moderate and vague terms, such as "a Christian presence" and "effective Christian witness," UBCHEA was cautiously welcomed by the Chinese again. As a mission strategy, adapting its proselytizing work to local ideological, cultural currents was not new. The strategy had been repeatedly used since the first day missionaries stepped on Chinese soil.[1] Only after the nation had broken away from the shackles of its past colonial masters might foreign educators truly serve the Chinese needs.

Despite the governmental control, foreign teachers found ways to circumvent it. For example, they were forbidden to teach religion. However, like evangelist educators at Tong Wen Guan in the nineteenth century, many of them spread Christianity covertly, chiefly through private interactions with students. In Anglo-American literature and culture classes, they engaged students in discussions of Western democracy and life styles through oral and written work. How to shield English teaching from undesirable Anglo-American cultural influences was always a contested, challenging issue for Chinese authorities.

In a time of drastic social transition, students continued to find English composition a liberating force in their personal lives and a vehicle for intercultural communication. English satisfied their yearnings to share with an audience imagined or real, domestic or international; it created a distance for them to examine Chinese society critically. Michael Yetman, a Fulbright scholar who taught at Beijing University in the early 1980s, gave a reflective account of how his students came to terms with their painful experience in the Cultural Revolution:

> Like "the Bard" Mr. Huang's tale of separated lovers, by far the greatest number of themes in my composition classes focused, sentimentally or unsentimentally, on the emotional suffering and physical dislocation of the participants during the Cultural Revolution. But there was surprisingly little of the sensational stuff one had already read about in

professional accounts: accusations by lifelong friends, criticism sessions, public humiliations, forced confessions, physical torture, death by beating, suicides. Mostly the accounts I received were of scared young men and women sent away from families, sweethearts, towns of upbringing, often to distant places hitherto known only by name, there to work with their hands and backs for the first time by learning how to plant rice, harness a water buffalo, lay railroad tracks, slaughter pigs, fire a brick kiln—even eat rats, on occasion, when nothing else was available. It was simply and accurately Chinese survival literature. What struck me again and again as I read these accounts was the absence of personal bitterness, the muted, understated stoicism of the writers; but even more their sense of gratitude that it was over, finally, and that things had not gone nearly so badly for them as for countless others they knew, both the many who died and the many who hadn't. (170–71)

In retrospect, the Cultural Revolution was revealed as a devastating faux pas in the national modernization project. Due to leftist educational policy, students were sent to remote areas to work on jobs marginally related to what they had learned in school. When it was over, "the absence of personal bitterness" and "the muted, understated stoicism" marked a prevailing ambivalence among the students about their ideal "New China." English writing offered students a safe space for public memory and deliberation. Writing about their miserable life experiences, the students went through a therapeutic treatment. They also offered their foreign teachers glimpses of the ordinary Chinese people's lived experiences.

While students found English composition a haven for their lived experiences, they were challenged by a series of institutional, pedagogical, and rhetorical changes in relation to composition instruction. English composition was redefined in alignment with the Four Modernizations and was offered as a separate course for English majors; the "Intensive English Reading" course deeply impacted writing instruction; and teaching communicative English was an innovative move in composition pedagogy. Besides these new aspects of English composition, students also experienced an overhaul in Chinese composition instruction, which reasserted the Marxist heuristics as advocated by both Mao Zedong and Zhu Dexi in the 1940s and 1950s. In turn, the Marxist heuristics affected students' English writing.

The Marxist Style of Writing

The rejection of proletarian rhetoric breathed new life into Chinese composition. Starting in May 1978, a nationwide debate on the meaning of truth led people to reconsider Mao's thoughts in relation to the future course of

Chinese socialism. The debate resulted in a consensus within the Communist Party that truth, including Mao's thought and the party's policies, must be tested by practice. The new leadership agreed that the time had come for the people to "emancipate their thinking, dedicate themselves to the study of new circumstances, things, and questions, and uphold the principles of seeking truth from facts" ("Communiqué" 14–15). The emphases on examining new circumstances and on seeking truth from facts dethroned extremely leftist ideology and legitimized a pragmatic reorientation for national modernization. The ideological and epistemological adjustments were clearly reflected in several new Chinese composition texts published in the late 1970s.

These texts tried to remedy the extremely leftist rhetoric derived from the GLF and the Cultural Revolution. *Xiezuo jichu zhishi* 寫作基礎知識 (Essentials in Writing, 1979), written under the auspices of the Beijing Normal University Chinese Department, represented the works of the time. The text was written primarily for college students who would become secondary-school teachers. Compared with Zhu Dexi's *Zuowen zhidao* (1951), the new text elaborates on the nature of writing, materials, and style, which were only briefly touched upon in the former.[2] These topics were crucial to bringing back the Marxist style of writing, which had been distorted during the previous political movements.

What is the nature of writing? The authors of *Xiezuo jichu zhishi* emphasize the dialectic process of representation in writing. They first invoke Mao's words from 1942: "Writing is a representation of objective matters" (Beijing shifan daxue 1). However, writing is not a process of mechanical copying but rather a dialectical, transactional process with full human agency. To understand objective matters thoroughly and correctly, the authors suggest, "We must participate in the praxis of transforming objective matters. In our praxis, we must mobilize our eyes, ears, noses, tongues, and bodies and take detailed notes of the materials [for writing]"(4). Defining writing in connection with the praxis of transforming objective matters, the authors envision a self with critical consciousness. This person does not subscribe to orthodox precepts but rather constantly negotiates between theory and practice. An emphasis on the dialectical process of representation thus rebuked the clichéd, jargon-ridden writing from the Cultural Revolution, which simply parroted the ongoing political discourse without critically examining Chinese social life. Although Mao's leftist rhetoric was accused of causing the Cultural Revolution, the authors invoke Mao's definition of writing because it embodies the Marxist dialectic, materialistic approach to knowing and presentation. Mao's definition is also reminiscent of the Confucian conception of writing as both patterns of the universe and a means to the Way. The difference is that Mao underscores the individual's critical agency in the dialectic process of representation.

The authors insist that materials (*cailiao* 材料) be gathered and evaluated in sync with Marxist heuristics. They first define *material* in general terms as "facts or evidence that the writer collects from everyday life, absorbs, and expresses in his or her writing" (23). Then, quoting Mao's comment that "people's lives contain the mineral treasure for both literature and arts" (27), they urge readers to observe life closely and to conduct systematic investigation. After the materials are collected, one should carefully evaluate them. The writer should identify their nature, determine whether they are true or false, evaluate their meanings, and weigh their functions. Centering on a particular theme, the writer moves on to select the most appropriate materials. The materials not only need to be truthful and accurate but also represent or reveal the essence of the subject matter under discussion; further, they need to be lively and fresh so that they can appeal to the reader. Both truthful representation and the essence of the subject matter are key elements of Marxist dialects. The emphasis on gathering materials from one's everyday life also clearly carried forward the empiricist tradition of Western scientific rhetoric.

Indeed, empiricist rhetorical practice was conducive to the national modernization project. When explicating the import of fresh materials, the authors connected writing to the Four Modernizations: "For new facts, new experiences, new issues, and new situations that constantly emerge in our praxis, we should capture them quickly, summarize them skillfully, and be bold to draw new generalizations. In our new long march[3] toward the Four Modernizations, we should show our high spirits, liberate our minds, and write more with fresh materials and profound thoughts" (49). The authors encourage students to gather fresh materials by taking note of new facts, experiences, issues, and situations in their lives. While making the point, they mobilize political slogans, such as "new long march toward the Four Modernizations," "show our high spirits," and "liberate our minds." Metadiscursively, the authors' emphasis on fresh materials reflects the essence of the time, or the Way of Chinese society as perceived by the ruling class; that is, a concerted national effort toward the Four Modernizations.

The authors devote one chapter to the Marxist style of writing (*wenfeng*). The word *wenfeng* 文風 first appeared in Liu Hsieh's *The Literary Mind and the Carving of Dragons* (501 C.E.), referring to the power of one's writing to influence and move readers like the wind (*feng*), reminiscent of a Confucian gentleman's ritualizing power. However, for the Marxists, its contemporary use emphasizes a politically charged meaning. The authors define *wenfeng* as "a general and trendy phenomenon of writing during a certain historical period"

(268). As a social phenomenon, a style of writing reflects the worldview and reasoning style of a certain social class, a party, or an individual. Therefore, for the authors, a style of writing is inherently political in nature.

The Marxist style of writing was characterized as being accurate, clear-cut, and lively. Being accurate meant that the writing needed to have "correct" opinions and precise materials for support. To be clear-cut, the writer needed to take his or her position and express it without any reservation. However, the authors warned that "unreserved fighting spirits needed to be combined with serious scientific attitude; clear-cut opinions needed to be established on the basis of sober analysis of evidence; and the writer's love and hate must be interweaved with sound evidence and be instilled into words and expressions" (293). The warning apparently serves as an antidote to the fabricated, exaggerated, and empty style that lingered in students' writings. To write lively, one needed to bring out new observations and new opinions after careful investigation of the subject matter and to make skillful use of vocabulary, syntactic structures, and rhetorical devices. Ultimately, according to the authors, the Marxist style requires the writer to reform his or her old thoughts, replace them with the Communist worldview, and write for revolutionary work—a remarkable residual of proletarian rhetoric. In their discussions, the authors singled out the eight-legged essay and the fabricated, exaggerated, and empty style for criticism. However, in a sense, the Marxist style is no different from the other two in that all of them are ritualistic measures to gear both the writer and the reader toward a certain way of seeing and being.

The Marxist style encouraged an honest expression of the self in school writing. Chinese language teachers urged students to observe life closely and to focus more on narrative and descriptive types of writing, as advocated by Liang Qichao in the early 1920s. Practice in expository argumentation was postponed to senior middle schools. Of the kinds of writing taught in middle schools, one genre, *sanwen* 散文 (scattered writing), gained particular favor among both teachers and students. As a traditional genre, *sanwen* dated back to the Spring and Autumn period (770–476 B.C.E.) in which philosophers and politicians wrote *sanwen* to engage debates and to spread their thoughts. Historically, it referred to any unrhymed essay. In the early twentieth century, Chinese writers consciously imitated Western essays in their *sanwen* writing, thus enriching this ancient genre by incorporating such features as skepticism, antischolasticism, and unrestrained textual organization from Western essay traditions.[4]

Sanwen was a pedagogical favorite because its unrestrained form gave students a sense of freedom that was unavailable in the old civil exam essays or in any of the Western modes of discourse. The genre allows for the interweaving of narration, description, commentary, and personal feelings. It is called scattered writing because there is no restriction on topics, which can involve either the past, present, or future, serious political issues or trivial daily events, and natural objects or social phenomena. There is no structural or stylistic constraint either; writers are allowed a great deal of stylistic creativity to accommodate their various topics. However, despite the topical, structural, and stylistic liberty, the essay should maintain a spirit (*shen* 神), or a focused theme, which unifies the seemingly scattered thoughts and form.

To gain a better sense of how *sanwen* boosted the honest expression of the individual in school writing, we will look at a student essay that I read as a child. Quintessentially, the essay reflected the worldview of a middle school student in the early 1980s, which blended both Chinese Communist teachings and modern technological visions. The following is the first part of a *sanwen*, "Tomorrow," from a collection of model essays for middle school students. Editors praised this essay for its success in intermingling narration, commentary, and personal feelings:

> When I was little, I was a story-lover. I begged my grandma to tell me stories every evening. Once she finished a story, I always pleaded to her, "one more," "one more." But she always said to me sleepily, "You go to sleep now. I will tell you stories again tomorrow." Satisfied, soon I fell into tight sleep. In my tender heart, I always felt that tomorrow is a jolly, interesting "thing."
>
> I started going to school. When I reviewed my lessons every evening, I thought, "If I don't do my homework well, I will not be able to answer the teacher's questions tomorrow . . ."
>
> As I age, I understand more about tomorrow. I know that my hard work today is the key to success tomorrow.
>
> We sing The Internationale loudly, "And the last fight let us face / The Internationale unites the human race." Alas, this is the tomorrow dreamed of by countless revolutionaries.
>
> That's right. How many of our revolutionary forefathers sacrificed their lives for the beautiful tomorrow. Our good elder sister Liu Hulan wasn't scared of the enemy's handheld hay cutter. She was martyred for the beautiful tomorrow. Look, Dong Cunrui, Huang Jiguang, Jiang Zhujun, Lei Feng . . . For the revolutionary course, they dedicated their lives to tomorrow. (Shaonian wenyi 8–9)

The student writer started the essay with one of his childhood experiences. Then his mind drifted to the present and then to the past again, pondering the idea of "tomorrow" in the song "The Internationale" and those Communist fighters who had been martyrs for an ideal tomorrow. Rather than adopting formal logic or any prescribed structure like that of the eight-legged essay, the writer followed what Paul Heilker calls "chrono-logic," according to which an essayist structures his or her thoughts rigorously as they occurred associatively over time. Despite the informal logic, if one reads between the lines, the student's strong feelings can easily be sensed. Later in the essay, the writer recalls the setbacks caused by the Cultural Revolution and praises the CCP for correcting its own mistakes. He envisions various scenes of China in the future and concludes the essay:

> At that time, we can call the moon palace through telephone, travel in the outer space in spaceship, and take rocket-propelled shuttles to go to other planets for vacation.
>
> It is for this magic, wonderful tomorrow that today we, in our flower-blossoming school, must study hard, research painstakingly, study science, study culture, uncover the treasure trove of knowledge, and climb the scientific mountain. We will contribute our wisdom and youth completely to tomorrow.
>
> Were there thousands of risks in our course, they could never stop our steps moving toward tomorrow, nor could they put out the youth's fierce fire in our hearts. Because there is a beautiful word in our hearts— "tomorrow." Let's continue our long march following the Communist Party's leadership, and stride toward tomorrow! (10)

The writer's modern scientific and technological visions are impressively romantic and optimistic. He lets his imagination fly and suggests that students should study hard and follow the Communist Party closely in the Four Modernizations. In this essay, the author successfully blended his personal experience, his imaginative rendering, and his feelings, which justified the editors' selecting it as a model *sanwen* for middle school students. This piece also reflected the Marxist style of writing—using accurate details, taking a clear-cut ideological position, and speaking with lively language. However, even such a successful *sanwen* could not avoid concluding with two paragraphs of slogans. *Sanwen* allowed the author great structural and stylistic freedom, but he still chose a clichéd ending, which indicates that the leftist rhetoric continued to haunt school writing. In fact, as we shall see, political rhetoric also undergirded college English writing in the 1980s.

Redefining English Composition

Like Chinese composition, English composition also underwent an overhaul both institutionally and pedagogically. However, rather than emphasizing any explicitly political, ideological intents like in Maoist China, the major in-stitutional change reoriented English composition instruction in functional terms. In the 1980s, the Ministry of Education issued several national syllabi for both English and non-English majors. In these syllabi, English teaching at the foundation stage (the first and the second year) took on a rather broad and pragmatic goal: to develop students' ability in the actual use of English for communicative purposes. The pragmatic, communicative turn suggests that, first, the *ti-yong* dualism continued to shadow the Chinese discourse of English teaching and, second, in an open-door era the Chinese became proactive and confident in intercultural exchanges.

For English majors, the syllabi did not prescribe any specific commu-nicative circumstances but rather communicative competence in abstract and open terms. For example, in "English Syllabus for Foundation Stage Instruction for English-Major Programs in Higher Educational Institutions" (1980), the goals were laid out as follows: "to provide students comprehensive, strict training in basic English knowledge and skills; to cultivate in them the genuine capacity for using the language; and to build a solid foundation for studying the language at the advanced stage" (qtd. in Li, Zhang, and Liu 456). General terms were also used to prescribe the goals for English teaching at the advanced stage, and the primary emphasis was invariably placed on communicative competence—"to cultivate their [students'] comprehensive English skills, enrich their [Anglo-American] cultural knowledge, and en-hance their communicative competence" (Gaoxiao yingyu 1). Thus, writing became part of an English major's communicative competence.

The syllabi for English majors provided specific requirements that drew a general picture of what communicative competence meant in terms of writing. For example, in "English Syllabus for Foundation Stage Instruction for English-Major Programs in Higher Educational Institutions (Draft)" (1979), a sophomore was expected to "be able to write a summary of or to retell in standard written language what the student has understood from the listening or the reading materials" and "be able to write a short passage of 300–400 words with logic and coherence, such as a sketch, a journal entry, or a letter, after the material has been studied" (qtd. in Li, Zhang, and Liu 453). Apparently the requirements were low-level, and the students were expected to write highly controlled compositions in the academic context. However, the syllabus did not specify the subject areas in which students would use writing. As English writing had not been taught in most colleges for three decades, these specific requirements were intended to be experi-mental. They were revised in more realistic terms in later years. Defining the expected writing competence, these new requirements were revolutionary for their time because they reasserted the importance of English writing in college.

Communicative competence, the central concept in communicative language teaching (CLT), was first introduced into discussions about language use and second language teaching in the West in the early 1970s. In Europe, the Council of Europe developed a notional-functional syllabus for foreign immigrants and workers to learn European languages.[5] The syllabus reflected British functional linguists J. R. Firth's and Michael K. Halliday's views of language as "meaning potential" and the "context of situation" as central to understanding language systems and how they work. This syllabus emphasized assessing the communicative needs of the learners and enabling them to actually function in a target language. In the United States, departing from Noam Chomsky's notion of "linguistic competence," used to describe an ideal native speaker, Dell Hymes proposed "communicative competence" in 1971 to describe an individual's ability to use language in social contexts. In the same year, Sandra Savignon published a seminal study that examined "the ability of classroom language learners to interact with other speakers, to make meaning, as distinct from their ability to recite dialogues or perform on discrete-point tests of grammatical knowledge" (3). Later the concept of "communicative competence" was expanded to include competence in grammatical, discursive, sociolinguistic, and strategic aspects.

Framing English teaching in communicative terms, Chinese scholars entered the international contact zone of teaching English as a second language. After the Cultural Revolution, Chinese scholars were sent to study abroad, and foreign professionals in English language teaching were invited to work in China. At Guangdong Foreign Language Institute, for example, teachers worked with Canadian language experts to develop CLT materials suitable for the Chinese context. They wrote an influential college English textbook, *Jiaoji yingyu jiaocheng* 交際英語教程 (Communicative English for Chinese Learners, 1987), with CLT as the overarching frame. Several other texts published in the 1980s also featured the CLT approach, which will be discussed shortly. By bringing in the notion-functional syllabus and the concept of communicative competence, China rejoined Western discourse on second language teaching, which, by then, had been largely informed by developments in linguistic and applied linguistic studies in the West.

The Chinese fascination with communicative competence and English syllabi was motivated by a scientistic attitude valued in the Four Modernizations. On various occasions, scholars advocated for scientism to strengthen the English language teaching profession in China. For example, Hu Wenzhong criticized previous English syllabi for lacking scientific support and objective assessment. They were frequently revised following the changes in the political climate. Therefore, Hu suggested that syllabus design be treated as a scientific investigation. Only through repeated tests may a syllabus prove to be effective and, thus, acceptable among English-language teaching professionals ("Kexue"). Along the same line, Gui Shichun emphasized the importance of invigorating assessment in English teaching: "From the perspective of scientific experiment, all instructional principles and measures formulated according to the Party's educational policy and the need to train professionals for the Four Modernizations, should be tested to see whether they reflect the objective reality" (Gui, "Kaizhan" 1). He suggested that, to improve educational accountability, China should establish systems of examination, adopt standardized tests, and enhance the professionalism of those involved in administering and designing tests. In these scholarly discussions, scientific investigation was portrayed in alignment with the Four Modernizations, thus furnishing much-needed *ethos* to the thriving English language teaching profession.

Syllabus design was indeed supported by empirical research. Field investigations of English teaching provided information for the revision of the college English syllabi. For example, as time elapsed, the social demands for English writing ability increased, as indicated in a survey conducted in 1983 on the need for foreign languages among workers and college graduates working in science and technology (Chen, Yang, and Huang). Once the survey results became available, writing requirements for both English and non-English majors were increased. When we compare a 1979 syllabus with a 1986 syllabus for English majors, we see that the writing requirements for sophomores became more rigorous over time. In addition to writing summaries for what they had read or listened to, students were also expected to write outlines and take notes in English. For daily applications of writing, students were expected to "be able to write letters, notices, notes, and invitations for general purposes and to fill out simple forms" (Gaodeng xuexiao 11), which were not specified in the 1979 syllabus. The increasing demands for English in Chinese society, through field investigations, were quickly translated into pedagogical terms.

In broad terms, the attention to syllabus design with an emphasis on scientific research supported the government's social engineering. The goal of an effective syllabus was defined as reflecting the current needs of society, students' language acquisition processes, and a repertoire of proven pedagogical methods. By prescribing the procedure and the content for teaching and learning, a syllabus helped students achieve language goals in an economical and efficient manner, which was, thus, conducive to the Four Modernizations. For example, the CLT syllabus streamlined language learning in a technological fashion. Grounded in linguistic science, it dissected language use into several communicative competences and then created an artificial community for students to negotiate meaning and to achieve these objectified competences. However, prescribed procedure and content also meant ideological control and regimentation. The design and refinement of English syllabi was meant to rationalize communication as information exchanges, downplaying historical, contextual, and human factors. Students were encouraged to acquire English competence as a value-free tool without questioning its ideological repercussions at both individual and societal levels. The syllabi spread out like grids that overshadowed and sometimes even suffocated students, as will be shown in chapter 5. In short, syllabus design corroborated the socialist blueprint for constructing an orderly and efficient China through science and technology.

Teaching Writing to English Majors

Writing was taught with different foci for English majors and non-English majors. After the Cultural Revolution, English composition returned as a separate course in English major programs. Students could study English writing systematically, as Ding Wangdao had advocated in the late 1950s (Ding, "Lue tan"). In contrast, before 1986, non-English majors learned English writing at a rather rudimentary level, namely constructing sentences with correct words and grammar. Writing was taught as one of several language skills in the intensive reading class. After a nationwide college English test (CET) was launched for non-English majors in 1987, they started composing beyond the paragraph level (see chapter 5).

The writing pedagogy for English majors was similar across the country in the 1980s. The pedagogical uniformity derived from two major causes. First, English-major programs all worked under the guidance of the national syllabi. Second, very few textbooks before 1986 were written for developing general writing abilities.[6] These texts included *Yingwen xiezuo yu xiuci* (English Composition and Rhetoric, 1984) by Yang Xiahua; *Yingyu xiezuo shouce* (A College Handbook of Composition, 1984) by Ding Wangdao et al.; *Yingyu xiezuo* (The Writing of English, 1985) by Ge Chuangui; *Yingyu xiezuo zhidao: Yufa yu xiuci* (A Guide to English Writing: Grammar and Rhetoric, 1986) by Xu Ming and Zheng Zhining; *Yingyu xiezuo jiaocheng* (An English Writing Course, 1986) by Wu Jinye and Qiao Xizhong; and *Daxue yingyu xiezuo* (Writing in English for College Students, 1986) by Jiang Jinzhi. These texts were all written under the clear influence of current-traditional rhetoric. As a majority of the English teachers were educated in the People's Republic, they received little training in English writing when they were in college. They had to rely on textbooks to teach themselves while they taught their students. The unified syllabi and the limited number of texts thus made the writing pedagogy for English majors similar across the board.

To understand the uniform writing pedagogy, we may examine a very popular text and its classroom use. *Yingyu xiezuo shouce* was written by Ding Wangdao and his colleagues at Beijing Foreign Language Institute. Ever since its first release, it has become the most widely adopted composition text in colleges.[7] The writing course offered at Beijing Foreign Language Institute also deserves some attention because it reveals how the text was actually used in the classroom. According to Zhang Zhongzai, the institute offered its first English composition class in 1980 after the Cultural Revolution, and the course materials were published as the textbook that we examine here. Together, the textbook and Zhang's account shed some light on how English writing was taught at the institute in the early 1980s.

Like composition texts published in republican China, the text was structured according to current-traditional rhetoric. The first four parts of the book form a hierarchy of linguistic layers, starting with words and ending with passages:

Part One: Diction
    I. The appropriate word
    II. The exact word
    III. The dictionary
Part Two: The Sentence
    I. Sentence sense
        1. Elements of a sentence
        2. Sentence fragments
        3. The comma fault and run-on sentences
    II. Types of sentences
    III. Effective sentences
        1. Unity
        2. Coherence
        3. Conciseness
        4. Emphasis
        5. Variety
Part Three: The Paragraph
    I. General remarks
    II. Ways of developing paragraphs

Part Four: The Whole Composition
    I. Steps in writing a composition
        1. Planning a composition
        2. Types of outlines
        3. Writing the first draft
        4. Revising the first draft
        5. Making the final copy
    II. Organization
    III. Types of writing
        1. Description
        2. Narration
        3. Exposition
        4. Argumentation (i–iv)

Clearly, this structure reflects strong traces of current-traditional rhetoric. Writing is taught as a scientific subject and analyzed at different levels of language structure. Discourse is classified into the familiar modes. One can note recent Anglo-American influences in the ten references listed, seven of which are rhetoric and composition texts published in the United States and the rest in Britain.[8]

The writing course at the institute was taught following the modes of discourse. Students started by writing summaries and then moved on to writing descriptive, narrative, expository, and argumentative essays. At least three essays were written in each mode in this two-semester course. For each mode of writing, the instruction involved similar steps: the teacher lecturing on the rhetorical features of the mode and introducing writing samples; students writing imitations of the samples; classroom discussions; revisions; and the teacher commenting on the students' writing in class.

However, elements of the process approach were articulated in the textbook and emphatically practiced in the classroom. The text states, "Nearly all good writing is the result of much revision. In revising a composition, [the student] should read and reread it several times, for it is impossible to notice all the errors and things that need changing in one or two hasty readings" (88). In two hours of class time, according to Zhang, the students spent half an hour on prewriting activities, such as collecting data (formulating ideas in their minds) and organizing the ideas into different paragraphs. Then, they spent another half-hour writing the first draft. Next, the class divided into small groups of three to evaluate each other's first drafts. They discussed the drafts and made suggestions on the aspects of content, language, and paragraphing. Using peer feedback, the students revised their first drafts and handed them to the teacher. After taking a quick look at a few students' drafts, the teacher would make some general comments and then return the drafts to the students, who would polish them after class.

The peer-reviewing and multidrafting activities affirmed and perpetuated the spirit of the process approach; that is, the writer negotiated meaning with both the self and the intended audience through recursive processes. On one hand, such community-based writing inherited the communal practice of writing during the Cultural Revolution (see chapter 3). On the other hand, it adopted the social-constructivist epistemology in composition instruction in the United States through international exchanges of writing pedagogies. Valuing community-based writing practices thus presented an excellent example of cultural negotiation and convergence in a contact zone space.

The epistemic function of writing was also highlighted in the text. The authors devote a large section to "The Research Paper." This quite unprecedented highlight can be attributed to the new syllabus for English majors, who were expected to produce an English thesis for graduation. When the authors explain the benefits of research papers, they focus particularly on the opportunities that these papers afford the students to learn something new: "We learn more about a subject and learn it more thoroughly if we have to sift evidence, organize various kinds of material, and then explain it to others by means of written exposition. It is always pleasant to discover that we have become somewhat expert on a subject about which we previously knew little" (Ding et al. 131). Learning about a subject through college English writing had also been practiced in republican China; however, the epistemic potential of writing had not been so heavily emphasized before.

The rationale for the research paper and its pedagogical practice was, again, influenced by Anglo-American composition instruction of the time. First, the epistemic function of writing was popularized in the United States in the 1970s and the 1980s, at a time when the disciplinary formation of American composition studies was taking place. Second, like their American counterparts, Chinese students were warned against plagiarism in a stern tone by the authors: "For your own safety and self-respect, remember the following rules—not guidelines, *rules*" (151, italics original). One of the rules states, "Changing a few words or phrases from another writer's work is not enough to make the writing 'your own.' . . . The writing is either your own or the other person's; there are no in-betweens" (152). Connecting plagiarism to personal safety, self-respect, and honesty, the authors employ a rather (de)moralizing language, echoing that used at American mission colleges before 1950 (see chapter 2). Third, as in U.S. English departments, only the MLA documentation style was taught for research papers, implying that the authors supposed that English majors would research largely humanities topics.

Despite these hegemonic American practices in academic writing and global circulation of knowledge, the writing teacher was assigned the traditional role of a moral guardian. As a mastermind of the composition course at the institute, Ding Wangdao emphasized that the teacher should also be a caring person. "Whether the student is conscientious with his study, whether his thinking is active, whether he has extensive knowledge, whether he analyzes things in a sophisticated manner, or whether he holds a positive attitude toward life and the current affairs, could all be reflected in his writing" (Ding, "Guanyu" 254). Therefore, the writing teacher should understand the student better than teachers of other courses do. With this advantage, the teacher ought to show greater care for the student's well-being, which, according to Ding, has proved to be an effective measure in improving students' writing.

Ding's conviction that writing teachers should take responsibility for their students' well-being reflects the humanistic tradition of Chinese education. Since ancient times, Chinese teachers, or masters as they were called, were held responsible for cultivating virtuous gentlemen by transmitting the transcendental truth (the Way), imparting knowledge, and resolving doubts. In the Confucian tradition, students were encouraged to explore their moral being through reflection, discussion, and writing. In republican China, where scientific rhetoric came to supersede Confucian rhetoric, some Chinese scholars insisted that the writer should seek to express the self and reality in his or her honest voice (Chen Wangdao; Liang, "Weishenme"; Ye Shaojun). Ding's argument sustained the humanistic lineage in writing instruction, underscoring that education bears high stakes in a student's moral growth and that a teacher plays a crucial part in the process.

The combination of the modes, elements of the process approach, and research papers was only seen in writing courses for English majors. In some universities, the writing course was watered down to only teaching the modes. More commonly, students wrote in another English course called Intensive Reading, which grew out of structuralism-oriented English teaching. This course became so widespread and influential that it continues to shape how writing is taught to both English and non-English majors even today.

Intensive Reading and Writing

According to common lore in English language teaching circles in China, intensive reading could be traced to college English reading courses offered in the 1950s.[9] As a pedagogical approach, intensive reading has been commonly attributed to Harold Palmer, who first proposed it in the early 1920s.[10] Some have considered the wide use of grammar and translation in teaching English in republican China as an intensive reading approach[11] and, thus, as a precursor to intensive reading as a college course in the People's Republic. In the 1950s, due to the Russian influences in foreign language pedagogy, college English reading was taught less for literary appreciation and more for developing analytical reading skills at both the grammatical and stylistic levels. The wide circulation of structuralism-oriented English textbooks after the late 1950s finally set a conceptual frame for this college course.

The original intent of intensive reading was to develop students' analytical reading capacities. According to Li Funing (1917–2004), an English professor at Beijing University, because a text consists of content and form, both areas need to be analyzed in the intensive reading class. The ultimate goal was that, through meticulous but accurate analysis of the language, students would understand the author's thoughts, attitudes, and feelings. A text could be analyzed in terms of vocabulary, grammar, and rhetorical devices. Li suggested that analyzing key words could sometimes be vital to the comprehension of a whole text. To do so, the teacher could introduce not only the basic, denotative meanings of a word but also its connotative meanings. For each of these meanings, the teacher could give exemplary sentences for illustration. Attention also needs to be paid to rhetorical effects that are achieved through discursive structures and to how those rhetorical effects are related to the author's thoughts and feelings (Li, "Tantan"). In intensive reading, a student needs to mobilize both analytical and synthetic skills to achieve a correct understanding of a text. Therefore, Li claims, "the other function of the Intensive Reading class is to nurture in students a basic ability in scientific research" (47).

I suggest that, besides its shared rationale with Russian reading pedagogy, intensive reading drew upon a local intellectual tradition. Since ancient times, Chinese scholars had developed ways of reading Confucian classics similar to that delineated by Li Funing. One of these traditional ways is called *zhangju* 章句 ("paragraph and sentence") in which one splits a passage into paragraphs and analyzes each sentence to explicate a classic.[12] In this approach, one can explain the meaning of a word, paraphrase a sentence, and interpret the intent of a passage. Another way of reading is called *xungu* 訓詁 ("explicating old expressions in modern language"). With this method, one deciphers the meanings of a Chinese character according to its composite parts or its sounds or simply explains its meanings in modern language. In a third way of reading, called *yishu* 義疏 ("sorting out the meanings"), one traces previous interpretations of a certain word, a sentence, or a passage and comes up with his or her own interpretation. By reading the classics meticulously, a scholar hopes to arrive at the correct understanding and, thus, to capture the true spirit of the ancient masters (Xu and Xu). Similar to the archetypical Confucian view of writing, intensive, or close, reading is a neo-Confucian scholarly means to the Way, whose ontological and epistemological underpinnings were clearly absent in Russian analytical reading. These traditional ways of reading were developed because the classics were written in an ancient Chinese almost unintelligible next to everyday Chinese. Reading such a difficult language, a scholar needs vigorous methods. By the same token, intensive reading emerged because English was a foreign language for a vast majority of Chinese learners.

However, in reality, intensive reading taught students not only analytical and synthetic reading but also comprehensive English skills. The structuralism-oriented textbooks encouraged the teaching of phonetics, grammar, reading, speaking, writing, and translation, the latter two being subservient. The reduced time in teaching English, due to political movements, made intensive reading an opportune course in which to teach these skills all together. A common way to teach a text usually started with the whole class reading aloud both the text and a vocabulary list. Then the teacher selectively analyzed some sentences and words from the text to help the students decipher their meanings, which was the original thrust of this course. To test the students' comprehension of complex sentences, the teacher would ask the students to translate them into Chinese, and then the teacher would provide the correct, standard translation. The only writing in this class occurred when students copied down passages read aloud by the teacher or when students translated Chinese sentences into grammatically sound English. Studying a text of two or three pages often took three to four hours. Juggling several language tasks in one course consumed an enormous amount of time that should have been devoted to developing students' reading skills. The teaching methods in intensive reading reflected a strong focus on grammar and translation, the emblem of the Russian analytical reading, which might explain why this course has been attributed to Russian influences.

The prevalence of this course and its negative impact in college English teaching incurred severe criticisms during the 1980s and the 1990s. A major criticism was that the course was taught in such a teacher-centered and grammar- and translation-dominant manner that it could hardly achieve the goal for which it was originally intended (Xiao Ji). Students did not reap significant benefits in any of the skills: speaking, reading, writing, or translation. Often the teacher lectured the entire time without engaging the students in any activities other than note-taking. Students were too nervous about missing language points that could be tested in quizzes or final examinations to care about developing genuine communicative competence.

The influence of intensive reading on the perception of writing and its instruction are thus apparent. The emphasis on correctly understanding texts transfigured into an emphasis on correctly expressing the writer's preconceived ideas, implying a mechanical, arhetorical view of linguistic symbols and meanings. Both the teacher and the students were extremely concerned about the grammatical correctness of whatever they wrote. They were also interested in word choice and stylistic variations. Content and organization sank to the bottom of their checklist. We may gain more insight from Yuan Shiyun's report on teaching writing in an intensive reading course. Yuan first explains students' needs in terms of writing practice: "For an adult learner, it is not the classification of English compositions that troubles his mind, but the techniques of putting his ideas into adequate English. He has not yet learned how to smooth out his language with good readable sentences and paragraphs" (345). Believing that most students translated Chinese sentences into English as they wrote, he encouraged his students to compare the two languages when reading and to pay special attention to dissimilarities in wording and syntactic structures. To enhance the students' awareness of the technique of subordination by prepositional phrases, Yuan let the students read a passage embedded with several instances of this structure. Then the students discussed the examples among themselves and translated them into Chinese using active verbs, the more common structure in Chinese. The students would be given credit if they used this English structure in their composition exercises. Yuan's effort to incorporate writing into intensive reading was shared by many teachers. Yet his perception of writing was bound by the philosophy of teaching intensive reading; that is, a mastery of vocabulary and syntactical structures was the key to accurately encoding and decoding meaning in both reading and writing.

In reformed intensive reading courses, English majors enjoyed more meaningful writing in (imagined) communicative situations in the late 1980s. The concept of teaching languages as communication became popular in the country. College English syllabi and textbooks were written according to the theoretical construct of communicative language teaching (CLT). The CLT approach was avidly experimented with in some universities. Writing was an integral component of the approach because communicative teaching focused on "a process of gradual approximation" to authentic language use when teachers were designing reading (receptive) and writing (productive) activities (Widdowson 119). These reformed intensive reading courses were sometimes termed "comprehensive English."

The CLT approach was featured in three influential college English texts.[13] *Gongneng yingyu jiaocheng* 功能英語教程 (Functional English Course Book, 1981) by the Heilongjiang University English Department combined both the structuralist and the CLT approaches.[14] *Xinbian yingyu jiaocheng* 新編英語教程 (New English Course Book, 1986) by Li Guanyi and Xue Fankang also combined the two approaches. The text claims to help students acquire authentic English, starting from text-based language and gradually moving toward life-based language. *Jiaoji yingyu jiaocheng* 交際英語教程 (Communicative English for Chinese Learners, 1987) by Xiaoju Li was born out of the Communicative English for Chinese Learners (CECL) project at Guangdong Foreign Language Institute. Since the text embodies the joint efforts of domestic and international scholars who sought to domesticate the CLT approach for the Chinese context, we will take a closer look at it.

The text emphasizes that students develop their language skills in authentic, communicative contexts. According to Li, the architect of the CECL project, CLT language activities need to meet three conditions. First, both the language situation and the language users' roles must be real. Second, real needs, purposes, and substance for communication must exist. Third, the language activity needs to allow both freedom and unpredictability when students use the language ("In Defense"). When studying a lesson, the students perform a series of tasks—listening, speaking, reading, and writing—in "authentic" contexts in the classroom, hence the course name "Comprehensive English."

Thus, the text organizes language tasks according to communicative contexts. In structuralism-oriented texts, lessons are organized according to language structures, or following a gradation of syntagmatic structures and vocabularies. In this CLT-oriented text, lessons (units) progress from one broad topical area to another. In each topical area, communicative tasks are invented; both students' roles and the context of situation in each task are defined; and linguistic competence (i.e., knowledge about grammar and vocabulary) and language skills required for performing the tasks are delineated. Take volume 2 as an example. There are eight topical areas: Getting to Places, Dealing with People, House and Home, Education, Animals and Plants, Celebrations, Health and Medicine, and Food and Drinks. In each topical area, students perform listening, speaking, reading, and writing tasks. In the listening task of Unit 4, "Education," for example, the teacher asked the students to chat among themselves about their after-school activities. The purpose was to elicit or to introduce key words and expressions that students would encounter in the forthcoming listening task. Next, students were given an outline-style note-taking sheet and were encouraged to predict the details of what they were going to hear. Then they listened and took notes on a recording of a lecture about British students' leisure activities. Finally, students checked and corrected each other's notes. Thus, they learned new words and expressions in the context of making meaning. They also acquired important skills of predicting information and making inferences in listening comprehension.[15]

Within the CLT frame, writing was taught as one of the composite skills in making meaning. However, unlike how writing was taught as a way of making meaning in U.S. college composition classes at the time, writing also served the important function of helping students acquire language structures and vocabulary. As students' proficiency level remained low upon entering college in the 1980s, communicative English pedagogy continued to place a strong emphasis on language form. In the writing task of Unit 4, the teacher would tell the students that they were going to learn how to introduce the Chinese educational system in English. First, they read about the North American educational system and listened to tapes on the British system. Next, the teacher analyzed the reading and listening materials together with the students through question-and-answer activities. Third, the students studied vocabulary and sentence structures in description, classification, comparison and contrast, explanation, and exemplification. Finally, the students prepared a speech to introduce the Chinese system in a formal situation and also revised the script, supposedly to have it published in a student magazine in an English-speaking country. Thus, in contrast to writing's marginalized status in intensive reading, it was taught as a composite skill while the students tried to enhance their holistic communicative competence. Further, students were able to connect oral composition with written composition, which restored the pedagogical affinity between the two, as Lawrence Faucett advocated in the 1920s.

The functional orientation of the CLT approach was congruent with the ideology of the Four Modernizations, in particular the *ti-yong* dualistic thinking about English language and Chinese national culture. The goal of the modernizations was to make China a strong and prosperous socialist country. In the CLT model, English was taught and used with little reference to its Western cultural origins and heritage, thus minimizing Western cultural encroachment on Chinese socialism. Robert Phillipson argues that English teaching has been increasingly deculturalized worldwide because of its alleged "political disconnection" (250) and "narrowly technical training" (262). Downplaying the teaching of grammar and Anglo-American cultures, CLT emphasizes that the purpose of learning English is to communicate. One feature of the CLT approach is that "it is learner-oriented and relies heavily on the learner's language resources, which are bound to be localized" (Tam xxii). Using materials produced in the Chinese context, such as those compiled by Xiaoju Li and his colleagues, students were partially shielded from the "evil" influences of the West. They defined their goal as mastering communicative English as they would master any advanced Western technology that would benefit Chinese modernization. However, as had been proved repeatedly in modern Chinese history, the dualistic thinking about English and Chinese culture was sinocentric and idealistic. In fact, the willing acceptance of the CLT approach marked the entry of neoliberalism—decentralized economic and political institutions—into Chinese society. For example, students studying Anglo-American educational systems and communicating with Anglo-American audiences planted seeds for reforming Chinese education, hence Chinese culture, in an interconnected world. While China joined other countries in reengineering English for its own political, economic, and cultural agendas, English continued to transform Chinese minds, as student writings will show.

Socialist Undertones in Student Writing

Writing enabled students to deal with social changes caused by the open-door policy and economic reform. After the door was opened to the outside world, Chinese youths were attracted to foreign products and Western ideas and values. Traditional Chinese and socialist values were challenged by new happenings in people's daily lives. Students struggled to come to terms with the influx of novel thoughts, values, and social issues. The following English essay, "Money Is as Beautiful as Roses," captured a student's spiritual wrestling with financial matters, which was the most important issue in the era of economic reform.

> I like reading Emerson because he told the truth about Nature, the truth about human beings. He described money exactly and correctly: "Money, which represents the prose of life, and which is hardly spoken of in parlors without an apology, is, in its effects and laws, as beautiful as roses."
>
> In China, it's true that an educated person hardly talks money without embarrassment, hardly speaks of it without an apology. I feel a little bit embarrassed now, since I want to talk of the happiness which money can bring to me.
>
> Suppose, for a few minutes, I had enough money. Because I'm so tired of having lived in dormitories where eight or more than eight people live together for eight years, the very thing I long to do is get a

home owned by myself. Its location would surely be quiet and beautiful. Within, the house would be well-equipped, beautifully decorated.

My next thing is to possess various books. I could buy any books I wanted for my private library. I dream of reading my favorite books in my beautiful reading-room. (Muehl and Muehl 74–75)

In this short passage written to her American teachers, the author voiced her desires bravely. Material constraints, such as living in a crowded dorm room and lacking variety of books, frustrated her and prompted her to dream big. The economic reform had reoriented people's sense of morality, which used to despise money talk and private property, and thus liberated their desires.

The reference to Emerson makes the piece a cultural and rhetorical hybrid. Like Chinese Daoists, Emerson keenly sought transcendental qualities of life by understanding nature and respecting its laws. If an American "Daoist" saw the value of money (capitalism) in human society, why should a modern Chinese blindly despise it? The author established her *ethos* in the contact zone by quoting Emerson and contrasting his view with that of a traditional Chinese literatus. If the student had read Virginia Woolf's essay "A Room of One's Own" (1928), which she might have done, perhaps she would have stated her desires without feeling embarrassed. In the essay, Woolf declared that a woman would need money and a quiet room of her own to produce great literary works comparable to Shakespearean plays. Writing provided an opportunity for the student to reconcile with traditional Chinese, socialist, and capitalist values. The essay embodies the ambivalent voice of an individual student implicated in a society undergoing a fast transition.

When depicting their lived experiences, however, Chinese students tended to cling to socialist themes, or to wrestle with the tensions between writing as an individual act and writing politically correct themes as a socially circumscribed practice. In a new era of the Four Modernizations, themes dealt with in both Chinese and English writing classes witnessed a depoliticizing process. Cultural determinism and class struggle were replaced by a more pragmatic agenda for social development. Composition topics gradually became apolitical and increasingly diversified. However, Marxist heuristics in selecting themes continued to shape Chinese composition. The treatment of themes remained ideological, if not explicitly political. For example, in a Chinese composition text, Lu Deqing, Shi Yaxi, and Fan Peisong postulated that themes need to be "correct," "clear-cut," and "focused." They said that for a theme to be correct, it "must abide by the Four Cardinal Principles,[16] and is in agreement with the Party's political lines, guiding principles, and policies" (20). Besides essays that were written to serve the Four Modernizations, they considered other essays equally correct, such as travel notes, essays describing the landscape of the country, and essays introducing handicraft articles as well as scientific knowledge. In their view, these other essays "offer the reader knowledge, aesthetic appeals, and positive influence" (20). By including essays that did not deal with the Four Modernizations directly, the authors encouraged students to expand the scope of cultural means to socialist and nationalist morality.

Politically correct themes permeated English composition in the 1980s, trailing a noticeable socialist undertone. In *Yingyu xiezuo shouce* (1984) by Ding Wangdao and his colleagues, discussed earlier, student essay samples are typically loaded with subtle socialist sentiments. For example, the following passage was written by a college student to describe his "good" classmates. The textbook authors quoted it to exemplify paragraph development by classification:

> According to Comrade Li, the fifteen students of his class fall into three groups. Seven of them work hard and study well. They always get good marks in examinations and are often praised by the teachers. Li calls them "good students." The monitor, the secretary of the Youth League branch, and the captain of the class volleyball team are quick in finding out what their fellow students are interested in or what they should do as a collective. They always organize proper activities at the proper time, so Li calls them "good organizers." Four other students are very kind to their classmates, always ready to lend them a helping hand. They help to clean the classroom and the corridor even when they are not on duty. Li says that they are "good comrades." "What about yourself?" someone asks him. "I'm a group by myself—a good observer." (76)

The student writer described an ordinary class in a Chinese college, but in using such terms as "Comrade," "praised," "the [Chinese Communist] Youth League," and "collective," the writer perpetuated the amicable socialist comradeship that the Communist Party encouraged. Although the passage does not address the Four Modernizations directly, it offers the reader socialist "nutrients"; therefore, it had a correct theme.

When writing for a foreign audience, students also committed themselves to correct themes. The following is a conclusion of an essay, "Use a Tractor as It Should Be Used," written by one of Carolyn Matalene's students. The author argued against the inefficient practices of Chinese agriculture:

> I am not an economic policy maker, but I have a dream of tractors singing in the fields and trucks roaring effortlessly on roads. I am not

an agricultural technical program planner, but I have a dream of seeing farmers studying science and technology and working comfortably
with machinery.

Confucius, the ancient Chinese philosopher, maintains that whatever your calling, "The first thing to do is to give everything a true
and proper name." Now, we have got a name, "tractor," it is true, "A
motor vehicle that pulls farm machinery," according to my Longman's
dictionary. What we should do now is to give every tractor a chance
to live up to its expectations. I am nothing of a philosopher, but I
have a dream that everyone of us is aware of this simple, pragmatical
idea: Call a spade a spade. Use a tractor as it should be used. (qtd. in
Matalene 804–5)

Matalene praised the student for integrating Chinese and Western rhetoric,
demonstrating "both imitative skill and extreme directness" (804). The student was indeed direct and politically correct about his position. He hoped
to see agricultural machinery being fully used and Chinese farmers being
liberated from their traditional toil. In making his argument, he repeated
the phrase "I have a dream," mimicking the voice of Martin Luther King
Jr., who wanted to liberate American blacks from racial injustice. To make
his point, the student utilized argumentative strategies commonly found in
Anglo-American tradition: definition, quotation, and idiom. However, he
used Confucius to justify the need for definition; he used an English idiom
("Call a spade a spade") rather than a Chinese one.

The passage is also reminiscent of *sanwen*, which had become a pedagogical favorite in Chinese composition. Parallelism and personification in the
first paragraph and the brief invocation of Confucius in the second paragraph
are all characteristics of "scattered writing." Quoting Confucius on the notion
of naming is a parody. Confucius emphasizes rectifying names, or assuring a
truthful representation of reality through language, because a clear prescrip-
tion and maintenance of everyone's roles and functions in society will lead to
social stability and harmony. The student wittily used the Confucian notion
of naming to argue for a nonmoral issue here. More remarkable, the student's
imaginative rendering comes close to that of the *sanwen* "Tomorrow" quoted
earlier in this chapter. Both writers envisioned a bright future for China as
a result of the Four Modernizations, two of which are the modernization of
agriculture and that of science and technology. By mentioning names such
as "economic policy maker" and "agricultural technical program planner"
in the above passage, the student insinuated the important work of these
professionals for the ongoing socialist construction.

Explicit political teaching, including morals and ethics, appeared in more than foreign language classes during the 1980s; it was part and parcel of college education. Li Peng, then a Chinese premier, for instance, reiterated its importance in 1986: "Ideological and political work among students, teachers and other faculty members of our institutes of higher education is a task determined by the nature of our socialist schools, and it guarantees success in developing specialized personnel with socialist consciousness" (qtd. in Hu and Seifman 226). In opening up the country to the West, the Communist Party had to defend its educational territory against the encroachment of Western ideology. It had to counter new challenges to the teaching of socialist values in schools. Selecting student essays that praise collectivism and socialism and packaging them into composition texts were two of the Communist Party's coping strategies. Ritualized in such an educational enterprise, the student had to negotiate between socialist teachings, the influx of Western thoughts, and the rise of an individual's liberated desires, as demonstrated in the essay "Money Is as Beautiful as Roses."

The Revival of English Writing Research

As English composition reclaimed its importance in Chinese colleges, scholarly interest in composition was rekindled. Reports on English writing research in the early 1980s were sporadic. The published literature can be divided into roughly three groups, reflecting both old and new concerns in a transitional period. The first group included some discussions on how to improve English writing, mostly based on personal anecdotes. Li Funing, for example, reflected upon his experience with learning English writing in republican China. He attributed his writing ability to his extensive reading of English translations of world literature, to his study of French, and to his retranslating of Chinese translations of English works back into English ("Tigao"). Presented as personal advice to both teachers and students, on one hand, these accounts encapsulated the rich, accumulated experiential knowledge of English composition grounded in the Chinese context; on the other hand, they revealed the historical struggle of an old generation writing in the devil's tongue.

Another part of the literature focused on introducing writing theories from overseas. The minimal English writing instruction in Maoist China made teachers rather uninformed about effective ways of teaching English composition. Looking abroad for ideas thus was a natural choice. For example, Ding Wangdao et al.'s *Yingyu xiezuo shouce* listed ten Anglo-American references in the bibliography. Tang Lixing introduced Wilga M. Rivers's theory (1968), which divides the development of writing into five stages:

copying, reproduction, recombination, guided writing, and composition. In fact, Rivers's theory was hardly new; an earlier, but similar, writing theory was articulated by Lawrence Faucett in 1927 (see chapter 2). Wang Zhigan formally introduced the process theory that was flourishing in the United States at the time. Wang elaborated on two key concepts of the theory: writing as a process of discovery and writing as a complicated, recursive process. Then he made a few suggestions on teaching English writing in China in light of the theory. The introduction of Anglo-American composition theories, whether outdated or new, indicated a strong interest among English teachers for alternative, better ways to teach writing after the Cultural Revolution.

The more significant strand of research was rooted in the Chinese context. As previously mentioned, a series of empirical investigations facilitated the redefinition and revision of English writing requirements in the national English syllabi for both majors and nonmajors. These studies uncovered the status quo of English writing instruction in Chinese colleges, the need for English writing among both students and workers, and the successes and failures of various writing classes. Experiments in teaching English writing as part of the student's communicative competence, as represented by the Communicative English for Chinese Learners (CECL) project at Guangdong Foreign Language Institute, mark yet another local effort. These locally rooted research projects sustained the century-long exploration of how English composition could better serve Chinese needs.

Despite efforts in adapting English composition to the Chinese context, scholars curiously evaded the issue of writing standards, or what constitutes good writing. A deep-seated attitude existed among scholars and teachers that English literary pieces should be used as the ideal model for writing classes. When reflecting upon his experience in learning English writing, for example, Li Funing emphasizes the importance of extensively reading literary works: "Abridged versions and English translations of world literature were written in a relatively familiar style. But the language used was still elegant, fluent, vivid, and natural, which made it easy for me to imitate and to absorb. My expressive competence in English reaped rich nutrients from those easy-to-read English writings" ("Tigao" 31). The worship of literary standards in English writing is also found in Yuan Shiyun's account of his teaching. In an intensive reading course for young teachers in 1979, Yuan taught English writing by drawing his students' attention to the dissimilarities in wording and syntactic structure between Chinese and English. Among the examples that he used to illustrate more effective and less effective English writing by Chinese students, those of effective writing emitted a strong literary flavor. He writes:

To cite an example, I should like to mention one interesting fact, that the Chinese are more apt to use verbs in many cases where the English would most probably use nouns. A Chinese who speaks English is naturally inclined to say, "I ran out when it was raining," instead of "I ran out in the rain," or "He looked around and was satisfied," instead of "He looked around with satisfaction." As the idea is conceived in a Chinese verb, the student is not aware that in English a preposition and a noun may bring out the meaning more effectively. (347–48)

It might be true that Chinese students tend to conceive ideas in verbs rather than in prepositional phrases; however, the effectiveness of the two pairs of exemplary sentences as well as that of the many more Yuan quoted in his article was judged more in the context of literary production than in any other context of communication.

The danger of applying literary standards to evaluating student writing was multifold. First, scholars and teachers perpetuated what Alastair Pennycook has called "the cultural construct of colonialism" in English teaching (161). Student writing was thought of as ineffective and full of undesirable traits of Chinese English; British and American authors were enshrined as representatives of correct, effective, and normative English writing. For example, Yuan constructed an image of Chinese students as follows: "The English taught and learned in primary and middle schools goes *à la Chinoise*. When the students get to college, they have already formed the habit of trying to say and write in English what they would in Chinese" (345). Yuan's attitude toward students' English usage was not so different from some Anglo-Americans in colonial China who condemned Chinese students for habitually placing prepositional phrases before the subject of a sentence (see chapter 2). Second, because less-polished English with clear Chinese traces was demonized, students were discouraged from transgressing Anglo-American writing conventions. Teachers foreclosed opportunities for students to experiment with English or to produce creative, hybrid texts, which are staples of contact zone writing in postcolonial, multicultural societies.

The impulse for literary-flavored writing as represented by the works of Li and Yuan stems from two discernible sources. First, many senior English teachers were trained in literature in colonial China. Anglo-American literary genres were the primary rhetorical contexts in which they could think of English writing. Within these particular contexts, the writer needed to polish the language to appeal to readers aesthetically. Second, ever since the Han dynasty, for Chinese literati, writing and rhetoric often had meant polishing words and sentences to achieve the most appealing effects. For two thousand years, with rhetorical invention confined to the spirit of Confucianism and the formulaic exam essays, literati were trained to play with words artistically to demonstrate their "good" writing. The craving for literary standards and the demonizing of student writings together reveal both the Chinese literary tradition and the deeply hidden scholarly worship of Anglo-American literary practices developed since colonial China.

However, the emergence of both the communicative language teaching and the process approach started to rally a counteractive force against the worship of literary standards in English composition. Although it came rather slowly, its impact could still be discerned. For example, in the national English syllabi for both English majors and nonmajors published in the 1980s, effectiveness of written English was defined in reference to a broad scope of communicative circumstances rather than being limited to literary production. In multidrafting and peer-reviewing activities, a student had to consider rhetorical context, audience, topical development, and organization instead of focusing exclusively on style. As English language teaching entered the 1990s, the discourse of globalization, which emphasized English as a lingua franca for international political, economic, and cultural transactions, further loosened the traditional ties between Anglo-American literature and composition in China.

To sum up, the 1980s were a time of changes and challenges in composition instruction. Marxist heuristics were reasserted in Chinese composition, which required a dialectic, objective representation of reality. In the Marxist style of writing, a writer uses accurate, clear-cut, and lively language to truthfully present materials. In broader terms, the style, though still leftist for some people, corroborated the pragmatic turn in Chinese political life. In English teaching, the notion-functional syllabus defined English learning as the acquisition of a set of communicative competences for English use, and it conceived of English writing as just such a competence. Elements of the process approach were also introduced into composition classes for English majors. Amid these conceptual and pedagogical innovations, however, the popular intensive reading course focused on vocabulary, grammar, and translation, an emphasis that perpetuated a mechanistic view of writing. While some students wrote English as though they were conscious of their communicative purposes, rhetorical situations, and audiences, most students practiced writing simply to master its technical form. Into the 1990s, students would continue to wrestle with writing instruction that was communication and meaning–oriented versus that which was form-focused.

5

WRITING AND SOCIALISM
WITH CHINESE CHARACTERISTICS

1991–2008

As further economic reforms opened up China's interior to foreign investments, transnational capitalism gained a strong footing in the country in the late 1980s. At the same time, a market economy also gradually
replaced a centrally controlled economy. A series of educational reforms
ensued, aimed at making higher education available to more students and
enhancing its versatility and accountability in the booming market economy.
English became much more valued politically, economically, and culturally
because it was seen as not only a tool for acquiring Western science and
technology but also an indispensable means of flourishing in the various
forms of transnational capitalism.

Composition instruction was adjusted to meet the requirements of the
new economic forms. While the market economy favored well-rounded, independent-minded "sovereign subjects," transnational capitalism demanded,
among other new things, "a more flexible and multifaceted subject that did
not insist on [historically obsolete notions of] 'coherence'" (Zavarzadeh and
Morton 11). Chinese composition focused on students' creativity and individuality in order to produce these kinds of subjects; the Western modes of
discourse were seriously questioned for their constraining effects on students'
creativity. However, English writing continued to be portrayed as a neutral,
objective technology governed by mechanical rules. Students were encouraged to transpose mainstream discourse into prescribed schemes rather

than to challenge or transform it. Thus, Chinese and English composition formed a new, intricate relation, continuously championing a *ti-yong* dualistic thinking while, ironically, cultural forces behind English profoundly shaped Chinese society.

Education for a Market Economy

The economic reform and open-door policy, launched as a national modernization project, successfully integrated China into global politics and economics. Through mass media, despite government censorship, the Chinese became relatively well attuned to global events. Mass media also unveiled the country's everyday happenings to the outside world, such as the Tian'anmen Square democratic movement in 1989 and the Beijing Summer Olympic Games in 2008. Modern communication technologies, such as cell phones and the Internet, broke down traditional geopolitical barriers and made China an increasingly open society. A large number of multinational corporations established their production lines in the country, turning it into "a world manufacturing center" by the late 1990s. Increased living standards and job opportunities also attracted large groups of people from other Asian countries to live in China. When China joined the World Trade Organization (WTO) in 2001, the country irreversibly plunged into economic globalization. Transnational capital brought the country into closer contact with the rest of the world.

As economic reforms progressed, the Communist Party sought a new rhetoric for the evolving socioeconomic arrangements. With the introduction of stock companies and the sale of small- and medium-sized state-owned enterprises, Jiang Zeming, the Communist Party chairman at that time, justified the market economy as the primary stage of "building socialism with Chinese characteristics" in a 1997 speech (J. Wang 63–64). However, the party was accused of no longer representing the interests of the masses but, instead, of supporting those of the bureaucrats and nouveaux riches. Indeed, the official term "socialism with Chinese characteristics" created a novel metanarrative designed to gloss over the complexity of further economic reform and to justify the party's leadership. Criticisms targeting the Communist government, regardless of their fairness, revealed precisely the continual difficulties of Chinese modernization.

In keeping with economic initiatives and new social demands, Chinese education went through a series of reforms that would deeply affect English teaching. One such major reform was the expansion of college enrollment. In the old system, the government paid for students' tuition and assigned them jobs upon their graduation. Starting in 1989, most students had to pay for part of their educational expenses. Except for job assignments in some industries that were regarded as key to the national interest, the state allowed students to seek their own jobs. As educational resources enlarged, more high school graduates could go to college. In 1990, 27.3 percent of high school graduates went to college; the number had skyrocketed to 73.2 percent by 2000 (Jiaoyubu fazhan).[1] Going to college was no longer the privilege of a few. However, the quick expansion of college enrollment also created new issues, such as larger class sizes, lower academic standards, and increased unemployment rates for college graduates.

Pressured by the fast-changing demands of global competition, higher education forged closer ties with various social forces and altered its traditional operation. To produce college graduates fit for local needs, regional governments involved themselves in the planning and management of universities. Corporate enterprises were also encouraged to work with universities, providing them with equipment, research funds, scholarships, and internship opportunities. In return, universities worked with enterprises on research projects and provided their employees with special training. By involving different social forces, higher education became more efficient, flexible, and accountable. Beginning in the 1990s, university authorities talked more about fund-raising, investment, and internationalizing higher education. Universities toiled to improve their rankings in order to attract better students and more corporate sponsorships. As Bill Readings had observed of Western universities in the late twentieth century, Chinese universities early in the twenty-first century increasingly operated as independent bureaucratic systems striving to advance their own interests.

The drive for educational excellence led to vigorous assessment in all school subjects, including English. By the late 1980s, English teaching had fully revived from its near demise during the Cultural Revolution. High school graduates studied at least six years of English before they entered college.[2] In college entrance exams, standardized English tests consisted mostly of multiple-choice questions; students were evaluated on phonetics, reading, grammar, and writing (the last by means of a direct task). Starting in 1987, college students needed to pass another standardized test, the College English Test (CET), before graduating from college. The creation of these assessment systems is evidence of the scientific approach to education that had been promoted by some Chinese educators since the early 1980s. These exams enhanced accountability of English teaching in the Chinese market economy as well as in global competition and cooperation. Both English and Chinese composition instruction were deeply influenced by these assessment systems, though in remarkably dissimilar ways.

Creativity and Individuality in Chinese Composition

The college entrance exam exerted the most impact on Chinese composition. A high school Chinese teacher could have ignored the entrance exam in the 1980s because only a few students were going to college. The teacher could no longer do so in the 1990s because a majority of the students were college bound. A plethora of composition guides and collections of student sample essays published in the 1990s testified to the high stakes associated with exam essays. Until the turn of the twenty-first century, the entrance exams were unified across the country, forming a certain common influence on Chinese composition. Thus, history repeated itself. Just as the civil service exam had done in the Qing dynasty, writing tasks in entrance exams came to shape both the students' view of writing and the teachers' pedagogical orientations.

Remaining the mainstay of Chinese socialism, the Marxist style of writing continued to characterize Chinese composition. Writing was presented as a dialectic, objective process of representing the world. Students needed to describe the observable world accurately, to state their positions in unambiguous terms, and to engage readers through lively language. The only major change was that, while the style's Marxist philosophical orientation persisted, its explicit political teaching disappeared in the 1990s. For example, in the early 1980s, writing tasks in college entrance exams all required, among other things, "correct opinions" (*guandian zhengque* 觀點正確) and "a clear-cut theme" (*zhongxin sixiang mingque* 中心思想明確). Correct opinions often meant pledging allegiance to the party's four cardinal principles (the socialist road, people's dictatorship, party leadership, and Marxist-Leninist-Maoist thought). A clear-cut theme therefore meant that a clear (and correct) ideological position guided a piece of writing. In 1983, these requirements were dropped in the entrance exam. However, the same expectations persisted among teachers and students because socialism remained their daily discourse. Students continued to pledge allegiance to the party and to celebrate the country's socialist undertakings. In the 1990s, that kind of political impulse diminished, and composition instruction shifted to other new issues.

One of the new issues involved tapping into students' creativity to meet the new demands of a market economy. This change came with the new concept of a "well-rounded education" (*suzhi jiaoyu* 素質教育), which emerged in the late 1980s. Comparisons were frequently made in the mass media between Chinese students and students in industrialized countries. The general consensus was that Chinese education had focused on imparting packaged knowledge to students instead of teaching them to become creative thinkers. Schools had produced many bookworms but few talents with well-rounded skills. The market economy needed skillful, well-rounded, and independent-minded workers. Thus, creativity became the catchphrase in the new discourse of well-rounded education.

Translated into pedagogical terms, creativity meant, among other things, encouraging reasonable imagination in students' Chinese compositions. Starting in 1990, college entrance exams sometimes required two writing tasks, one of them asking students to describe what they imagined when given a certain prompt. In the entrance exam that I took in 1991, students were asked to imagine an object in the shape of a circle and then to describe it in a particular setting. One student, writing in response to this prompt, described his imagining as follows:

> A circle gives one a sense of perfection. Every time I see it, it arouses many imaginations, particularly the imagination of our socialist New China.
>
> Our life has improved day by day since New China was born. The brothers and sisters of our fifty-six nationalities hold gather tightly. United, they hold together like a circle. The Communist Party is the people's savior. She led our people in the revolution and established a superior socialist environment. She is the center of the circle and works as our leader.
>
> The ring of a circle is inseparable from its center. Lacking one of them, the circle cannot stand. Therefore, the people cannot live without the party, nor can the party exist without the people. When the two unites, people's lives will be as sweet as honey. (qtd. in Xing Yongqing 3)

In the Maoist period, this piece might have been rated high. It connects the circle to the relationship between the people and the Communist party's leadership, which had been the most popular image painted in previous political rhetoric. However, Xing Yongqing, a veteran Chinese teacher, believes that this imaginative account fails the writing task miserably. First, it is unreasonable to imagine the "socialist New China" in the shape of a circle. Second, the author does not focus on *describing* an imagined object but rather on *exposing* it. He or she tries to compare the people to a ring and the party to the center of the circle to demonstrate the dialectic relationship between the ring and the center. Finally, the piece is rated low because pledging allegiance to the party had lost favor in the eyes of Chinese teachers in the early 1990s. In contrast, Xing thinks highly of the following description:

> Regions of water and lakes in the South have plentitude of water, thus there are many bridges. Everywhere one sees little green stone bridges

rising above the peaceful, green jade-like water. In windless days, the arch of the bridge formed a beautiful circle with its reflection in the slowly flowing water. The circle is so peaceful, and so beautiful. It looks like a rainbow standing across the water after a rain shower, or like a bright moon suddenly setting in the blue sky in autumn. Sometimes a light boat passes, leaving layers of waves to spread around the circle. After the boat passes, the water resumes its peace and forms a perfect circle again. When people walk on the bridge, their reflections seem to bypass the two sides of the "moon," climbing on it from one side and descending in the other. (qtd. in Xing Yongqing 3–4)

In this description, the author presents a reasonable and novel image of a circle: a bridge and its reflection in water. The author first compares the beauty of the circle to "a rainbow standing across the water" and then to "a bright moon suddenly setting in the blue sky." Next, the author describes the beauty of the circle in motion, as boats row in the water and pedestrians walk on the bridge. Xing comments: "The motionless circle, the moving reflections on the circle, the combination of both motion and peace creates an intriguing image. The author draws a picture of the regions of water and lakes in the South. The tone is light and elegant. The reader is thus carried away" (4). The description reflects the author's acute observation of everyday life and sensitivity to the essence of the objective world—all virtues of the Marxist style. Then, these positive attributes were united and gave rise to the author's reasonable and intriguing imagination, a kind of creativity lacking in the first passage.

Connected with creativity, individuality was also actively sought in the Chinese entrance exam. The new value attached to individuality can be seen clearly in the prompts written for the exam essays. Until the late 1980s, prompts were written either as simple titles or as complicated paragraphs that prescribed both the theme and the content of an essay. The two types of prompts are apparently traceable to those used in the eight-legged, policy, and discourse essays. In these old civil exam essays, short titles were quotes from Confucian canons and students had to explicate them along neo-Confucian exegetical lines. Policy essays often used long paragraphs as prompts to discourage students from deviating from politically correct answers. To encourage the display of individuality, in the late 1990s writing tasks no longer prescribed any modes of discourse, and students were free to choose composition titles according to their own rhetorical designs. The writing task only provided a short passage to prompt creative thinking and individual exploration. Take the prompt from 1999 as an example. It offered a scenario that reportedly some foreign scientists had succeeded in transplant-ing memory in small animals and so they were subsequently researching the possibility of memory transplant on humans. Students were asked to write a composition on "If memory can be transplanted": "Imagine boldly as long as the content is related to the topic. The specific angle and methods of writing can be diverse, for example, you can create a story, express your opinions, or envision the future. Determine the title yourself. All genres are accepted except poetry" (qtd. in Xing Yongqing 99). The prompt was highly praised in the mass media for its innovative design. By setting no limits on the theme, the content, the mode, or the genre, the 1999 prompt offered students free-dom to come up with individualized creations.

The emphasis on creativity and individuality thus partly rejected the early emphasis on scientific rhetoric. In the nineteenth century, Western scientific rhetoric materialized in the modes of discourse in Anglo-American coun-tries, which came to structure both Chinese reading and writing from the 1920s. The modes conceived of discourse on scientific terms and dissected it according to both audience and communicative intent. When reading and writing were taught following these modes, students were led to identify and analyze the constitutive and structural elements of each mode rather than the meaning of the text. Thus, the modes tended to fossilize students' thinking and hampered their creativity and individuality in writing.

In their criticisms of the modes, scholars repeatedly evoked and affirmed traditional Chinese views of writing. Such a move was significant because it first showed that Western writing styles could be complemented by or improved upon through traditional Chinese practices. The move also dem-onstrated that Western rhetorical values, such as originality, authentic voice, and *ethos*, were not absent in Chinese writing history. For example, Zhou Yulin, a Chinese teacher, compares writing to flowing water:

> Writing is used to express one's heart and mind. It is like water in an overflowing pool, which flows following ditches and tunnels of what-ever shape. Sometimes the flow is human feelings such as bitterness or happiness; sometimes it is thoughts on serving the society or living a righteous life. Whether the "water" can flow heartily or not largely depends on what is in one's heart rather than the shape of the tunnel, or the textual form. It is all about the natural way. (Zhou 22)

Zhou's analogy reconnected Chinese writing to its ancient origin—the an-cient Chinese invented writing to observe both the natural world and human society and to capture their essence. As a means to represent nature, writing should follow the most natural way to express one's thoughts and feelings, as water has taught us. The end to prescribing a particular mode in exam writing allowed students more freedom to explore their thoughts and feelings, which could flow in "ditches and tunnels of whatever shape."

While unfettering students from the modes, Chinese composition models continued to encourage dialectical thinking as featured in both traditional Chinese and Marxist styles of writing. Formal logic treats human reasoning in a formulaic, reductive, segregated, and universal manner. Dialectic reasoning is grounded in formal logic but transcends it by considering matters as evolving along the interaction of particulars. For both traditional Chinese and Marxist styles, reasoning always takes place in a certain socio-historical context. Through socially grounded, dialectical reasoning, humans reach a comprehensive knowledge of the objective world. Some essays explicitly demanded dialectical reasoning. For example, a prompt from the year 2000 started with a short story and concluded as follows: "Indeed the world is constantly evolving. Doubts rise one after another and their answers are varied and colorful. There are many cases in our lives where we can examine, come to understand, and solve an issue in more than one way, and where there is more than one answer to the issue. . . . Please write a composition related to the topic of 'The answers are varied and colorful'" (qtd. in Xing Yongqing 125). The prompt highlighted contradictory and complex relations between particulars in real life. Implicitly, the prompt encouraged liberal thinking, a style of thinking that has become increasingly crucial in an age of intercultural contact and change. To respond to the prompt, students would have to follow dialectic reasoning to examine conflicting binaries centering on any issue, thus corroborating the Marxist dialectic materialism that they studied in politics classes.

Along with these new changes, the ritualizing potential of writing continued to be valued, but the Confucian sense of ritualization, which intended to bring an individual's moral being closer to the Way of ancient sages, had become obsolete. Ritualization had come to mean both indoctrinating the writer with mainstream ideology and the writer's rendering a positive influence on the reader. In terms of ritualizing oneself, the writer was encouraged to observe everyday life closely, to think actively, and to develop his or her own sense of the "main melody" (*zhu xuanlu* 主旋律) of society, or the Way. Writing should capture the "melody" accurately and transmit it harmoniously. Such writing can positively affect the reader because it brings the reader in closer contact with others' life experiences, a process that eventually leads to the reader's refined understanding of his or her own life and of society in general. The attention to such attributes as creativity and individuality was intended to produce subjects/workers suited to the booming market economy with forms of transnational capital. Thus, Chinese composition embraced both traditional and novel elements in the era of socialism with Chinese characteristics.

The College English Test

English composition also proactively responded to changes brought in by a market economy. A syllabus for English majors issued in 1990 set more challenging requirements for juniors and seniors and laid out requirements for teaching, curricular design, and assessment. Politically correct thought, coherent structure, and error-free language were emphasized. Politically correct writing should contain "neither Western political ideas without thorough criticism nor information that misrepresents the Chinese social reality or the government policies" (Gaodeng xuexiao yingyu zhuanye yingyu 57). Development of thoughts was emphasized over either organization or style—it constituted 50 of the 100 total points in writing assessment. English majors were also expected to complete a bachelor of arts thesis before they graduated. As students steadily improved their English, naturally more attention fell on their ability to develop thoughts in writing and to function with English in their major areas. Like the English syllabi published in the 1980s, the new requirements, while continuing to shield students from baneful Western values, responded to the heightened demands for English writing in Chinese socialism.

English majors took new courses involving English writing. In the 1990s, in addition to traditional English language, literature, and culture courses, many more content courses were offered in the English department or through other departments. Students had opportunities to write in fields closely related to global circulation of capital and information, such as international trade, business, and journalism. It was hoped that curricular requirements and various course offerings would prepare students to become "professionals with multiple skills" (*fuhe xing rencai* 複合型人才) and to be more responsive to the new demands of the market economy. For many, the expanded curriculum was reminiscent of the English-based college curriculum in colonial China. However, two major differences are easily discernible: first, in republican China, the focus of English-major juniors and seniors rested on Anglo-American literature; second, with most college textbooks written in English, English was *the* language of Western science and technology. In an era of globalization, expanding the English curriculum was a proactive strategy to prepare flexible and multifaceted students for worldwide competition and opportunities. The evolving English-major curriculum also testified to the determination of the Chinese to domesticate English for their own needs.

In the late 1980s, non-English majors also found higher demands placed on their English ability reflected in the publication in 1985 of a highly regimented syllabus for science and engineering students. The syllabus divided the English course into two stages: a foundation stage (freshman and sophomore years) and a professional reading stage (junior and senior years). Teaching and learning at the foundation stage were particularized into six levels of requirements, or six bands as they have been called in China, with the first four bands signifying the basic requirements and the fifth and sixth bands signifying higher requirements. The syllabus prescribed descriptors for both basic and more advanced requirements in six different areas: vocabulary, reading, listening comprehension, writing, speaking, and translation. The two stages laid out a detailed blueprint for teaching and learning English in four-year colleges.

The six bands prescribed a gradation of writing development, revealing clear vestiges of structuralism. Bands 1 and 2 focused on constructing sentences. Bands 3 and 4 emphasized connecting sentences into paragraphs. Bands 5 and 6 were geared towards practical writing, such as correspondence and précis. To meet the basic requirements for English writing, or to reach the band-4 level, a student should "be able to employ the vocabulary, grammatical structures, and functions and notions that he/she has learned, according to the topic and prompt given, to write a short essay of approximately 100 words within half an hour, and the essay needs to convey his/her thoughts without significant grammatical mistakes" (Daxue yingyu 7). By dividing English teaching into six bands and by assigning each band specific goals, the syllabus revealed the overwhelming presence of applied linguistics in English language teaching (ELT) in China. For a long time, applied linguists had treated language as a communicative "wheel" cogged by universal, structural elements, which could be dissected and reassembled in scientific steps. This structuralist view neglected the mediating role of writing in students' thoughts and relegated writing to a technical, objective tool for communication. Once a coherent, "scientific" writing program for non-English majors was laid out, neither teachers nor students could take English writing lightly any more.

Institutionally, the 1985 syllabus marked a concerted effort by the Chinese ELT circles "to make English teaching and its evaluation a more scientific and precise enterprise" (Daxue yingyu 134). Based on nationwide surveys, the requirements of the six skill areas were carefully laid out in each of the six bands. Vocabulary size, reading speed, and writing speed were quantitatively specified for each band. All of these requirements set concrete goals for class instruction. At the same time, the syllabus also served as a yardstick for measuring college English teaching by instituting the nationwide College English Test (CET). Teaching English as a scientific and precise enterprise improved accountability within Chinese higher education. However, when English teaching and learning started to be translated into numbers, it also metamorphosed into a kind of merchandise in China's market economy, implicating teachers and students in a trading relationship.

The rise of this new economic relationship in English education could be directly attributed to the creation of the College English Test, the brainchild of Chinese testing professionals' engagement with the international educational-testing industry. Instead of relegating English proficiency certification to Anglo-American testing agencies like some post-Communist European countries (Prendergast), China built its own testing industry. According to the 1986 syllabus for non-English majors, which was a revision of the 1985 syllabus for science and engineering, students needed to take standardized tests at the end of their Band-4 and Band-6 studies (Quanguo daxue [1999]). A CET Committee was formed and the standardized tests were officially launched in 1987, one year after the Test of Written English (TWE) was added to the Test of English as a Foreign Language (TOEFL) to assess U.S. college–bound international students.[3] The Band-4 test, an imitation of TOEFL, usually consisted of five sections: listening comprehension, vocabulary, structure, reading comprehension, and writing. As the passing rate on the CET provided an index of English education at a university and as most employers required Band-4 certificates from college graduates, universities often required that students pass the Band-4 test before they could graduate from college. The pursuit of educational excellence, thus, turned the CET into an extremely contested area in modern Chinese education.

The CET writing component placed a strong emphasis on linguistic form. Students were asked to write a short composition of 100 to 120 words within 30 minutes. In the test, a prompt—such as a title, a scenario, a topic sentence, a picture, or key words—might be provided. The writing needed to be correct in expression, coherent, and without significant grammatical mistakes. And it had to cover daily life topics and general knowledge (Daxue yingyu si liu ji). Expressions such as "correct in expression," "coherent," and "without significant grammatical mistakes" in both the 1985 English syllabus and the CET syllabus suggest that correct form, rather than well-developed thoughts, was most valued in the CET writing. The focus on form, on one hand, showed the lineage of current-traditional rhetoric in writing assessment; on the other hand, it concurred with and perpetuated the notion of writing as an objective, mechanical, and neutral device for communication, a notion commonly held in applied linguistics in the 1980s and congenial to the traditional Chinese conception of English in the *ti-yong* dualism. Thus, intriguingly, just as Chinese composition started to question the technical orientation of Western modes in the late 1980s, English composition embraced this orientation wholeheartedly.

To ensure the reliability of the test, most of the writing tasks were designed as controlled compositions. The prompts were written primarily in two ways. In some cases, the initial sentence of every paragraph was given, and the students were expected to complete each paragraph, treating the first sentence as the topic sentence. More commonly, students were provided an outline in Chinese. Sometimes the outline was so detailed that, like the discourse essay in traditional Chinese civil exams, writing virtually turned into translation. For example, the topic for the CET-4 of 1995 was "Advantages of a Job Interview." A Chinese outline was provided:

1. Interviews are commonly conducted during the job-hunting process. The interviewers and the interviewees can understand each other better through personal interviews.
2. The interviewer can introduce the job, including the type of job, the working condition, the salary, and so on.
3. The interviewee will have the opportunity to make a positive impression on the interviewers. For example, the interviewee can show his or her confidence, and introduce his or her educational background and competence in work. (qtd. in Ma and Wen 37)

Using the outline provided, students were required to write within the marked boundary of meaning, which helped to secure high reliability for the test. However, the pitfall was apparent: students were deprived of opportunities to develop their own thoughts within, not to mention opportunities to transgress, this prescribed scaffold, which thus weakened the validity of the test. The fetish for controlled composition starkly contrasted the Chinese entrance exam essays, which encouraged students to seek their own voices in creative forms.

Reliability was also sought in the scoring process. First, the CET Committee announced the principles and standards for evaluating compositions. One of the principles stated: "Global scoring is used to evaluate the CET-writing section. The scorer gives points based on his or her impression (reward scores) rather than based on the number of mistakes" (Yang Huizong and Weir 134). There were five levels for scoring: 2, 5, 8, 11, or 14 points. Scorers would first decide which level a composition fell into, and then they would select the corresponding score. By comparing the composition with a sample composition of that level, scorers could add a point or subtract a point from the score. Second, scorers were recruited from different universities and went through one-day training before they started grading the compositions. In the training sessions, they would rate the five standard sample compositions and another twenty compositions that represented the scoring range from 1 to 15 points. Through statistical analysis and group discussions, the scorers were expected to develop a firm grasp of the grading scheme. Articulating scoring standards and training scorers were both crucial steps in securing reliability in writing assessment.

Despite these strenuous efforts, however, reliability was undermined by the competing interests of those involved in the CET system. After interviewing teachers who participated in scoring the CET writing, Kate Allen identified several factors that compromised the writing component's reliability. First, many teachers were unfamiliar with the holistic scoring system because they seldom used it in their own teaching. Second, during the training sessions, many teachers did not understand the statistical analysis of their own scoring. Third, every composition was read by only one scorer instead of two, owing to the limited human and financial resources. Reading an average of 150 compositions a day made it difficult for scorers to be consistent. Fourth, because participating in the scoring work was an opportunity for teachers to become insiders of the CET system, universities tried to send different teachers to do the scoring work every year, hoping that these teachers would be able to better prepare their students for the test later. Without a consistent group of scorers, the reliability of the writing section was further eroded.

The complications of achieving the desirable reliability reflected deep tension between the material condition of those involved with the CET and an idealized, scientific testing system. In a market economy that placed high values on reputation and ranking, universities wanted to excel among their peers in terms of the CET passing rate. English teachers were burdened by their heavy teaching load and were unmotivated to learn anything beyond their immediate concerns. The CET Committee was primarily interested in securing high reliability and validity that would satisfy certain psychometric standards. The colliding interests of the three parties made high reliability and validity of the writing component hard to come by, which spoke to the complexity of scientific, objective testing in Chinese society.

After the CET was launched, non-English majors' writing ability improved significantly. For example, out of a total score of 15 points for the writing section, the national average rose from 4.37 points in 1990 to 7.13 points in 1997 (Quanguo daxue [1996]; Yang Huizhong and Weir). However, the improvement was far from satisfactory from the standpoint of effective written communication. For example, even the 8-point level of composition proficiency was still low in terms of communicative effectiveness, as its own definition stated: "The basic topic is evident, but there are places where the expressions are not very clear. The sentences are linked with great effort; there are relatively numerous language errors, among them quite serious ones" (Yang Huizhong and Weir 134). Therefore, the CET Committee set 6 points as the minimum score for the writing section in the late 1990s. Without achieving this score or higher, a student's total CET score would be automatically lowered. That meant that a student who achieved a passing score, say 60 points on the entire test, but did not get 6 points or above for the writing section would still fail the test (Quanguo daxue [1996]). Setting the minimum score for the writing section further spurred students to improve their writing.

Thus, the CET generated enormous pressure for students, teachers, and school administrators. When facing one of the hurdles for graduation, some students found ways to cheat on the test, such as paying someone to take the test for them, stealing test papers, and receiving answers from someone through electronic devices. Occasionally, students boycotted the test or committed suicide after failing the test.[4] Their mentality resembled that of students taking the old civil service exam—without passing the test, they would not be able to receive their diploma; without a diploma or a Band-4 certificate, they would have difficulty finding an esteemed job and, therefore, would disgrace themselves and their families. As the CET passing rate would influence a university's reputation, administrators pressured foreign language departments to focus their resources on the test, and the best English teachers were arranged to teach sophomore classes. At Northwestern Polytechnic University, a well-ranked institution where I once taught, English teachers were encouraged to guess the essay topics in the forthcoming CET. The one who made a correct guess would receive a large cash reward from the university. Students were also asked to memorize dozens of sample essays on topics that might occur in the test. In short, the pressure of the test wracked everybody's nerves, turning the CET into a tool of oppression by Chinese educators themselves.

The "Five-Legged Essay" Paradigm

Both the English syllabi and the CET directly affected writing instruction for non-English majors. As prescribed in the 1985 syllabus, writing was taught in a progression from sentence construction to paragraph writing. Several widely used textbooks adopted this gradation approach in the late 1980s and the 1990s. *Daxue hexing yingyu* (College Core English) by Yang Huizhong, Zheng Shutang, and Zhang Yanbin, a text first published in 1987 and used in many universities, was such an example. Students used both the reading and writing manual and the listening manual every semester during their freshman and sophomore years. In the reading and writing manual, each unit contained three reading passages followed by grammar, vocabulary, transla- tion, and writing exercises, all of it mimicking the types of questions that appeared in the CET test. For the writing component, instruction focused on word choice and sentence-combining in the students' freshman year and cohesion and paragraph-writing in their sophomore year. Graded, controlled composition instruction placed a strong emphasis on correct grammar and vocabulary usage, consistent with the spirit of the CET syllabus.

Non-English majors practiced writing mostly in the intensive reading class. Students took three English classes in their first two years—intensive reading, extensive reading, and listening—and writing was most conveniently taught and practiced in the intensive reading class. Many teachers related their experiences of teaching English reading and writing in professional journals. For example, Hu Meihua asked her students to write outlines and summaries for passages read in the intensive reading class. Tian Dexin used read-to-write exercises of three difficulty levels in his teaching. He asked low-level students to practice constructing sentences, connecting sentences together to build paragraphs, and connecting paragraphs to form a text. He asked intermediate-level students to write passages that modeled reading pas- sages from the textbook and to write outlines and summaries for each reading passage. He asked high-level students to research the different aspects of a reading passage—such as the author's biography, the style and the purpose of the passage, and the major historical events mentioned in the text—and to write reports about their investigations. Mao Zhongming encouraged oral discussions on both reading passages and students' responses to these passages. In each case, when writing was taught in intensive reading classes, it was taught as controlled composition with much of the attention paid to vocabulary and grammatical structures, which had been the traditional focus of intensive reading.

Students practiced writing intensively in the fourth semester when the CET-4 was approaching. Special attention was devoted to helping students construct complete passages. As the focus shifted to preparing students for the CET, the reading-writing connection was suddenly severed. Teachers might continue to lecture on readings from the textbook in the intensive reading class, but the students paid scant attention to the readings. They focused on practicing CET-styled writing tasks as well as grammar, vocabu- lary, and the sorts of questions that would appear in the CET. Often they practiced simulated writing tasks based on the CET-4. The simulations were expository in nature and most of the time provided prescribed outlines or structures. During the fourth semester, student-centered teaching meant preparing students for the menacing CET.

In Chinese market economy, English composition was increasingly commercialized, a development which led to new values and practices in its teaching. Students purchased books from publishers and bookstores on CET writing; they paid teachers for after-class tutorials and CET simulations. A certificate from the CET Committee potentially meant a well-paying job. Some English teachers systematically studied CET writing, and their theories on preparing for it also became products for trade. The full circle of production, circulation, and consumption of the CET writing thus gave rise to what I call a "five-legged essay" paradigm in writing instruction.

The rise of the new paradigm could directly be attributed to the wide circulation of reference books on the CET. Into the 1990s, experienced English teachers and former CET scorers were often invited by publishing houses to write books coaching students for the test. A series written by Cai Jigang on CET writing was extremely influential because it successfully integrated both Anglo-American and traditional Chinese conventions and values in academic writing. Cai made suggestions on textual organization, theme, invention, and preparation for exam-oriented writing. Stretching over more than a decade, his books represented the trajectory of thoughts in teaching exam-oriented writing among English teachers, thus warranting scrutiny here.

Cai emphasized practicality in his exam-oriented books. To be "practical" meant preparing students for the kinds of writing tasks that would appear in domestic and international English tests, including the CET, the Chinese graduate school entrance exam, the English Proficiency Test (EPT) for Chinese civil servants, and the TOEFL. "Get your money's worth from this book," he explains in *Yingyu kaoshi gaofen zuowen* 英語考試高分作文 (High-Score Compositions for English Tests, 1994):

> Regarding the types of writing, this book only addresses expository argumentation (*lunshuowen* 論說文), analyzing in detail several of its variations in the tests, rather than narration, description and practical writing which must be dealt with in general composition books but will never appear in the tests. In terms of the writing samples used in this book, whether presented as positive or negative, they all come from student writings, particularly from the previous tests, rather than from famous British and American literary works. They are familiar to the students and therefore learnable. As to the writing tasks designed for your practice, they are ones that will appear most probably in the tests rather than those that will never, such as "My Classmate," "A Memorable Trip," and "A Walk on the Campus." (2)

Cai was candid about what money could buy in his book. College students who bought the book were guaranteed satisfaction whether they wanted to graduate from college, to enter graduate school, to become a civil servant, or to study abroad. Orienting the students towards various tests, Cai narrowed the scope of reading and writing to exposition, in the process eliminating other modes or types of writing that normally were not assessed. In unambiguous terms, Cai highlighted exposition as the only valuable item in the market of English tests.

Studying writing prompts from previous tests, Cai identified four primary patterns in expository argumentation. He first laid out the four patterns in his *Yingyu kaoshi gaofen zuowen* (1994) and *Yingyu xiezuo gaofen zhidao* 英語寫作高分指導 (A Guide to High-Score English Compositions, 1998) and finally elaborated on them in *Yingyu wuduan zuowen fa* 英語五段作文法 (A Five-Paragraph Approach to English Composition, 2002). Of the four patterns, the first one was explanation: the writer would be asked to explain the causes of a social phenomenon or an issue or the reasons for doing or not doing something. The second pattern was analysis: the writer would be asked to analyze the influences or consequences of an event or a phenomenon. The third pattern was comparison: the writer would be asked to compare objects, events, or opinions; to identify their features, strengths, or weaknesses; and finally to take a position. The fourth pattern was commentary: the writer would be asked to comment on an object, a social phenomenon, or a controversy. He or she would first take a position and then prove it by analyzing the different aspects of the subject matter. According to Cai, the four patterns all fit into a five-paragraph scheme. Thus, writing was simplified as consisting of five pre-calculated rhetorical moves, clearly reminiscent of the five to eight rhetorical moves prescribed in the eight-legged essay.

For the five-paragraph structure, Cai prescribed a deductive reasoning pattern no different from the five-paragraph themes practiced in the United States. In the introductory paragraphs, the writer introduces the topic and states his or her opinion on the topic. Cai emphasized raising the readers' interest in the introduction by quoting someone's words, offering an event, providing statistics, asking a thought-provoking question, or using a contrast. In the middle paragraphs, the writer explains why he or she holds the particular opinion or attitude. The writer must ensure that the middle paragraphs are united under the main argument of the essay and show lines of reasoning, such as exemplification, comparison, analogy, statistics, and appeals to authority. For the last paragraph, the writer needs to "touch upon the dragon's eye" (*hua long dian jing* 畫龍點睛), or hit the thesis once again before ending the essay (Cai Jigang, *Yingyu wuduan*). The suggested reasoning pattern and ways to open and close the exposition also resemble the moves within the eight-legged essay.

In terms of the themes used in CET writing, Cai suggested four guidelines (*Yingyu kaoshi*). First, as the writing tasks were all expository, the topics needed to elicit discussions of opinions. Second, the topics should fit the student's "knowledge structure" (*zhishi jiegou* 知識結構), that is, they should be familiar to the student so that he or she would have enough to say about the topics. Topics related to the current concerns of Chinese society were therefore offered as good ones. Third, the topics also had to fit the student's cultural background and generational features; therefore, topics related to college students' lives, studies, and life goals were suitable. Fourth, the student's linguistic competence, including lexical and syntactic repertoires, should be factored in choosing the topics. Under these guidelines, according to Cai, CET writing tasks naturally fell into four general themes: the impact of science and technology on society and human life, social issues, campus life, and youth issues. It is worth noting that Cai did not emphasize the importance of politically "correct" themes, or themes that abided by the Four Cardinal Principles. Thus, as in the case of Chinese school writing in the 1990s, explicit political rendering had also fallen out of popularity in English composition. Technical attention to reliability and validity of the writing tasks partially kept political concerns at bay.

Within the given scope, invention was meant to promote the collective wisdom of contemporary Chinese society. Because a composition had been neatly mapped out by the prompt, there was little discussion, and indeed no need for discussion, on invention in Cai's books. Based on sample student writings in his books, he clearly encouraged students to conform to rather than to challenge or transform mainstream perceptions and opinions on any topic. In *Yingyu wuduan zuowen fa*, for example, on the popular topic of "Studying Abroad," the sample student writing echoed what many people in China thought about international education—studying abroad provided opportunities to use a foreign language; it provided opportunities for understanding other nations and their values as well as one's own people and their values; and it begot frustrations and pains, which could be turned into precious assets for an individual. Some writing samples offered students much-needed consoling in a fast-changing Chinese society. For example, a sample essay, "Job Problems for College Graduates," enumerated reasons why college graduates find it increasingly difficult to secure a job and concluded by suggesting that students need to develop a positive attitude toward this issue. Responding to an increasing number of suicides in Chinese colleges, another sample essay suggested three ways to reduce students' stress. Some sample writings reinforced moral and legal judgments. For example, an essay discussed the intellectual and moral dangers of cheating on exams and suggested preventive measures for stopping this phenomenon. These sample writings exposed readers to a wide scope of national and transnational issues. However, by and large they perpetuated and promoted the mainstream ideology on these issues, or the mainstream perceptions of the Way of Chinese society and the world. Therefore, invention (within the conventions of the CET writing) meant submitting to the collective thought on a topic, and any deviation from the mainstream was discouraged.

Cai suggested that students use the sample essays as they were traditionally used in Chinese writing practice. Chinese exam takers habitually studied and memorized old exam essays, which made publishing student essay collections a lucrative business ever since the Tang and the Song dynasties (618–1279 C.E.). Cai urged students to write essays on every topic and to compare theirs with the sample essays. Students were advised to study each sample carefully, and preferably memorize and imitate it. Cai explains:

> Most of the sample essays deal with China and its current social issues. There is a great chance that you will encounter writing tasks on similar topics . . . Even if you do not happen to come across any topics that you have recited, you may still integrate some relevant chunks from the samples into your own writing to argue or to prove your points. Most importantly, some beautiful sentence structures in the sample essays are panacea; they can be used to express your thoughts all the time. It is these beautiful and native-sounding sentences that will make your writing stand out (*Yingyu kaoshi* 3–4).

For Cai, therefore, the method of learning how to write for exams involved studying, imitating, and reciting the sample essays; copying a sample directly onto the answer sheet as the student's own; or integrating chunks of the samples into the student's own writing. The Anglo-American notion of plagiarism was not an issue. Again, the method confirmed that topical exploration and personal voices were not valued as much as elegant expression of received knowledge. Thanks to traditional Chinese writing practice and its pedagogical convenience, Cai's method was well received by many college English teachers as the default approach to preparing students for CET writing.

Thus, this homegrown English composition pedagogy shows a great resemblance to the *bagu-ce-lun* paradigm in Chinese composition from a century ago, suggesting yet another major pedagogical adaptation. First, both pedagogical approaches emerged from nationwide testing situations in which writing bore high stakes for both teachers and students. Second, the reasoning pattern in CET essays was limited to five paragraphs, similar to the five or eight rhetorical moves found in an eight-legged essay. Third, the themes in CET essays conformed to mainstream ideology and did not allow any deviant voices, just as the themes in the eight-legged essays were confined to the Confucian canons endorsed by the ruling class. Fourth, with the rhetorical moves prescribed and the meaning very much predetermined by the prompts, neither the CET essay nor the eight-legged essay allowed students much space for rhetorical invention. Students were deprived of opportunities to critically engage with any topics. As a result, like students in the Qing dynasty, contemporary students were encouraged to focus on arrangement and style (such as word choice and grammar) in English compositions. A century ago, current-traditional rhetoric took the place of the *bagu-ce-lun* paradigm by integrating narrative and descriptive writing in Chinese composition. At present, the five-paragraph pedagogy narrowed the scope of English composition by excluding narration, description, and practical writing. The pedagogy was a most recent attempt to adapt English composition to the national education agenda.

However, recent exam-centered writing instruction has not gone without criticism. In professional journals, for example, both Fen Yuzhu and Wang Peigen have criticized universities for devoting too much attention to the CET and for ignoring regular-hour classroom instruction and the college English syllabus. Yang Xiaorong has enumerated problems in invention, arrangement, and style that he observed in English majors' writing, problems he attributes to the influences of CET-style writing instruction. According to Yang, students have become narrow-minded and unmotivated to explore a topic: "Lacking the habit of close observation and active thinking, the students suddenly blank their minds in the exam and have nothing to write about" (71). Moreover, without active thinking, the five-paragraph scheme immediately became a handy formula for students to fill in ideas without careful calculation. Finally, many students develop a fabricated, exaggerated, and empty style. Without active and creative thinking, students may have to swiftly fabricate ideas that they do not truly hold. Without concrete details to support a point, students tend to reiterate worn-out and meaningless slogans. Without something of substance to write about, they use many clichés to fill in space. These are exactly the vices Liang Qichao censured in the 1920s, vices that have been repeatedly corrected in Chinese composition instruction ever since. In a market economy, evidently these vices disserved the effort to cultivate broad-minded, multifaceted workers.

While it is justifiable to criticize test-driven composition for harming students, it is equally necessary to situate the criticisms within the material conditions of average English teachers. The "five-legged essay" pedagogy was the best solution to many issues that they faced. An English teacher commonly taught three to four classes each semester, with the total number of students ranging from 60 to 200. With a relatively low salary and lots of opportunities to make more by teaching extra hours on or off campus, teachers hardly found enough time to grade student essays, not to mention time to encourage students' individual voices. With most English departments running on a tight budget, most teachers were not funded for attending professional conferences and, therefore, could hardly keep track of new practices in teaching English writing. Furthermore, like American women working in the labor-intensive, low-division writing courses (Enos), females staffed most of the English courses for non-English majors. Besides their teaching, they needed to perform many traditional roles at home. Overwhelmed by their daily duties, such teachers found the "five-legged essay" pedagogy efficient and effective in meeting their own needs.

The Free Spirit of Student Writing

Exam essays constricted students' thoughts; however, their minds were active and open when tests were less of an immediate concern. Students, particularly English majors, were often encouraged by their teachers to keep journals and to write essays, short stories, and poetry. Some students submitted essays to China-based ESL magazines and newspapers that had flourished since the early 1990s, periodicals such as *English Salon* and *The Twenty-first Century*. Some composed speeches for nationwide English-speaking contests. The Internet provided another venue for using English in domestic and international communications. Like Chinese writing instruction in high schools, there was virtually no limit put on students' creativity in English writing. They observed and reflected on the ever-changing Chinese society, sustaining English composition as a unique medium in Chinese cultural reformation.

Students tended to take a pro-Communist Party stand on political issues, not because they were afraid of government censorship or legal retribution, but often because they had been steeped in mainstream discourse and became fluent in and sympathetic to the party's positions on various political issues. Sometimes they defended government policies as a way to show their patriotism. Their intricate feelings toward the Communist Party, the state, and the ongoing economic reform were exemplified in student journal entries. One student commented on the military training required of all freshmen after the 1989 Tian'anmen event. In her commentary, she placed the interests of the state as her top concern:

It's sunny, the first year students are doing their military training. They walked again and again. Although the sweat is dropping down from their head, they can't stop without the permission of their leader.

Of course, in this way, they know how hard the army life is. Their spirits can be discouraged.

Everyone should have a strong sense of patriotism, especially the college students. Our state costs a lot of money to educate them. They should be faithful to their motherland. Army force is a symbol of the power of a country, so it is necessary to have some knowledge about military. In 1989, there was a student movement in Beijing. For the youth, their thoughts don't ripe and they don't have their own ideas, so the surroundings can influence them easily. Also they can't tell the truth from the fault. Where there is exciting thing, they turn up. After the movement, our state decides to have military training in college, to make them understand that it is not easy to obtain our present life. (qtd. in Hessler 15–16)

To a Western audience, the author's patriotic commentary sounds almost like a naive cliché. She blames college students for their immature and misdirected thoughts during the 1989 democratic movement. Writing as a mouthpiece for the state and chanting political slogans like Red Guards during the Cultural Revolution, she simply repeats the government's version of the events. What reads to outsiders like irony, sarcasm, and mimicry in the last paragraph could have resulted from the student's misinformation about the event. In a private textual space, the student might have expressed her sincere feelings. Implicated in a more private and imaginary relation to her material conditions, she conveyed her own take on the official discourse of the event.

Less obvious to a Western reader is that the journal entry deployed a traditional Chinese rhetorical strategy called *jie ti fahui* 借題發揮, or literarily "seizing on an incident to exaggerate matters or to extrapolate associated meanings." The author started with a concrete, impersonal subject, namely military training, and then shifted to express her own thoughts and feelings on the relationship between individuals and the state. This key strategy to traditional scattered writing (*sanwen*) allowed a writer to transcend his or her particular experiences to reach an abstract, heightened understanding of the world, or the Way. A writer sometimes seizes the opportunity to criticize or satirize ruthless acts of the government.[5] However, the student chose not to challenge or to mock the official discourse. The impulse to get hold of the Way was so strong that she quickly moved on to her rendering of patriotism after a brief description of students' military training.

Amid the urge to deliberate on moral and ethical matters, many students grew more attentive to their personal lives or their individuality. Immersed in a culture of fashion, information, and a market economy, they embraced capitalist logic and expressed their feelings and desires more boldly than students in the 1980s. On a well-publicized website that featured student essays, for example, students related significant events in their lives and expressed their evolving feelings. The website was born out of an ongoing research project conducted at Guangdong University of Foreign Studies in which students were encouraged to write long essays to improve their English. In a narrative called "My Cell Phone," one author contrasted her early resistance to cell phones (developed from not wanting her parents to keep track of her) with her later indulgence in them. In the following passage, the author describes her ecstasy after purchasing her first cell phone:

> I could wait no longer! The styles of the cellphones were so wonderful that I was deeply attracted by them. What is more, the prices of them kept going down. At last I got one. I still remember the first night I got it. How excited I was! I found out all my friends' cellphone numbers and sent short messages to each of them, telling them that I had bought a mobile phone! Then, of course, I received a lot of short messages back from them. At that time, I seemed to forget all about the money I spent on messages and sent them crazily. For a week, I was always busy sending messages and my friends around me all thought that I was mad. (Fan Jie)

This essay is significant both thematically and stylistically. In the passage, the author is attracted to cell phones' stylish designs and falling prices, which suggests the subjugating power of a market economy on average Chinese youths. Writing mediates the student's experience of both social and psychical forces, embodied in what Thomas Rickert has termed "*jouissance* (enjoyment/sensual pleasure), desire, and fantasy." The juxtaposition of short and long sentences vividly captures her anxiety, excitement, and joy. This personal narrative would have been discouraged by teachers who wanted to teach the CET-styled essay, which favored a sober, objective, and impersonal voice. Once the author published the narrative on the Internet, it opened a "window" through which the student honestly shared her private world with a large audience.

Exposure to a wide variety of genres also inspired students' creativity with the English language. English majors often found the opportunity to write essays, short stories, dramas, and poems in various English classes. When I was an undergraduate senior, I took an American poetry class. After we read Henry Wadsworth Longfellow's poems, my American teacher asked us to write an English poem ourselves. So I composed mine, titled "Mount Pavilion Yugu":

> Feeling on the mossy wall,
> I see rows of mountains tall.
> When Xin Qiji mused amid the smog,
> Some battle fires burned distant logs.
>
> Red houses were demolished.
> He felt badly, astonished.
> Travelers hurried to and fro with fears,
> He composed his poem with tears.
>
> The sands of time keep flowing,
> The east wind now starts blowing.
> Toward the east, never halting to stay,
> The Gan River threads its way.
>
> Has he reality found?
> Modern buildings rise around,
> Bridges lie on river pretty,
> Rail leads to royal city.

In the poem, I recalled a recent visit to an ancient pavilion in my city called the Pavilion of Sorrow and Loneliness (*yugu tai* 鬱孤台). The building is connected with the renowned poet Xin Qiji, who mounted the pavilion and wrote a famous poem eight hundred years ago. In his piece, Xin described the feelings of a traveler tossed by continuous wars in the North. Mounting the same pavilion, I reconstructed the scene of Xin, a sorrowful and lonely man, musing at the Gan River and composing his heartrending poem. I concluded my piece by juxtaposing the sad past with the bright present. Modern buildings, new bridges, and the Beijing-Kowloon (Hong Kong) Railway symbolize a peaceful and prosperous country unimaginable to Xin.

The poem demonstrates an average Chinese student's ability to cross literary traditions and cultures. When composing the piece, I counted beats and sought rhymed words, all key features in both traditional Anglo-American and Chinese poetry. I unknowingly plagiarized by borrowing "the sands of time" directly from Longfellow's poem "Psalm of Life," one of whose stanzas reads,

> Lives of great men all remind us
> We can make our lives sublime
> And, departing, leave behind us
> Footprints on the sands of time.

I adopted the metaphor because it was vivid and conveyed a deep sense of history commonly found in ancient Chinese poetry. The parallel metaphor "the east wind" was uniquely Chinese, signifying a favorable weather condition or an uplifting social development. In this creative piece, I not only juxtaposed the past with the present but also infused Chinese literary sensibilities into an Anglo-American genre. The interplay of two literary traditions offered me inspiration for creative expression.

The binary division between private and public, the psyche and the social, and national and international collapses when students compose for television audiences, creating what Homi Bhabha has described as "an 'in-between' temporality that takes the measure of dwelling at home, while producing an image of the world of history" (19). Starting in 1996, the *21st Century Cup*, an English-speaking contest, swept across Chinese college campuses, attracting thousands of participants every year. In 2002, CCTV, which had become an international broadcast medium that reached all continents, launched an equally influential English-speaking contest. These contests involved both prepared and impromptu speeches.[6] The following prepared speech, "A Strategy for Saving the World," delivered in the 2006 CCTV contest final, centered on the relationships between the individual, the nation, and the world, a theme that had captivated Chinese literati for thousands of years:

> Ladies and gentlemen, the globe is warming, the sea level is rising, and the world is in danger. I am not crying a false alarm. We are suffering more and more severe natural disasters every year and have just experienced the warmest October in fifty years. The danger is real and present.
>
> Who was the culprit? The human being ourselves! Or rather, the wrong idea of development that drives us mad. Under the name of development, we want to live in bigger and bigger houses, to have fancier and more comfortable cars, and to consume more and more material gadgets. Our small globe can hardly bear the burden of this kind of development. Scientists predict, if we do not take action immediately, then a hundred years from now, we would use up nearly all energy resources and destroy the environment.
>
> Alas, all these costs do not increase our sense of happiness. According to some statistics, people in some [of the] most developed countries have much lower index of happiness. If so, why we have to develop at the cost of our mother earth? Ladies and gentlemen, if we want to save the world, the only strategy we can employ is to change our view of development. We do want development, the development

of spiritual fulfillment based on moderate material consumption. It should be measured not by GDP or per capita income or other material things, but by index of happiness, literacy rate, equity level and other factors of social harmony.

Thank you very much, ladies and gentleman! (Wang Rong 262)

Although dwelling in China, the speaker produces an image, or a discourse, of human history. As CCTV audiences were both domestic and international, she wisely chooses a topic that mattered to everyone on earth: social development and our natural environment. She argues that, in the face of a major cause of natural disasters, we need to alter our ill-conceived notions of development and extravagant life styles.

Situated in a historical, transnational contact zone, the speaker adopted classical and modern rhetorical strategies with both local and international flavors. First, she structured her speech using a problem-solution pattern, familiar to both Anglo-American and Chinese audiences. Second, she used parallelism and an example ("the warmest October in fifty years") to raise a sense of urgency among the audiences. Her example could easily evoke images spread by the media of natural disasters, such as sand storms and droughts in north China, Hurricane Katrina in the Gulf Coast of the United States, and the disappearing ice cover at the North Pole. Third, the speaker used hard science ("scientists predict" and "according to some statistics") to bolster her points about energy resources and the index of happiness. After the Cultural Revolution, Chinese leaders praised science and technology as the most important productive force. Resorting to scientific evidence, the speaker secured the audience's trust in what she said. Fourth, she aligned her solution to the government's policy statements. After three decades of rapid industrialization, Chinese society acutely realized the danger of blindly pursuing economic development at the cost of clean air, public health, and social equality. Thus, at its national convention in 2005, the Communist Party shifted its emphasis from pursuing high GDPs to constructing a "harmonious socialist society." While appealing to the official discourse of science to support new policies, the speech also lightly mocked the Communists' dysfunctional leadership in China's industrialization. Addressing both local and international listeners, the speaker adopted rhetorical strategies that were no longer purely Chinese.

Rooted in a particular social-historical context, Chinese students' free spirit did not mean free expression. Their expression was constrained in the mainstream discourse of constructing socialism with Chinese characteristics. Students experienced the discourse firsthand, being surrounded by a chattering mass media, glamorous merchandise, competing lifestyles, and the depressing contrast between the "haves" and the "have-nots." While learning Western thoughts and expressions, they were also entangled in Chinese literary and rhetorical traditions. Chinese ways of reasoning and expression often crept into their English writing. Therefore, students' expression was a complex hybrid, infusing their interpretations of mainstream discourse with Western and Chinese literary traditions and their own spontaneous creativity. Within this hybridized schema, the students' free spirit prevailed.

Writing Research with Chinese Characteristics

English composition scholarship underwent a strong drive for both localization and internationalization during the 1990s. Influenced by international scholarship in applied linguistics and composition, published research moved quickly from sheer classroom observations to more systematic investigations using quantitative and qualitative methods. Issues related to teaching writing to non-English majors received much more attention, as such students constituted the majority of college student bodies. The heavily researched areas included the types of difficulties faced by students in English writing, their composing processes, writing pedagogies, computers and writing, and the interaction of Chinese and Anglo-American rhetorical traditions in student writing. Apparently, Chinese scholars borrowed these topics from American composition studies and ESL writing and used them as parameters to examine English composition in the Chinese context. However, influenced by scientific positivism in applied linguistics, most of the studies adopted a reductionist, micro view of writing. They conceived writing as taking place in a sociocultural vacuum and dissected it into variables for closer examination. The positivist epistemology in composition research, although limiting, accorded perfectly with the scientific fetish of English syllabus design and assessment.

The area of research in Chinese students' composing processes has been particularly enlightening to bilingual writing practice. Modeling studies by Linda Flower, John Hayes, Sondra Perl, and Vivian Zamel, Chinese scholars used think-aloud protocols to trace students' mental activities. Different from American researchers, who had only focused on composing in English, Chinese scholars sought the differences between students' composing processes in both Chinese and English. An early study was conducted by Zhang Zuocheng involving sixteen non-English majors. Zhang asked the students to think aloud when composing two writing tasks, one in Chinese and the other in English. He found that the composing processes in both languages were recursive and that all students went through the prewriting, writing, and revision phases. However, students revised more frequently on both the syntactic-lexical and semantic levels than on any other levels when they were writing in English. When composing in Chinese, they often used clauses or sentences when thinking aloud to approach a complete discourse, whereas they tended to use words or phrases to think aloud when composing in English and often used Chinese to guide their thoughts and to deliberate on word choices. Substitution and avoidance were two common strategies that students used when unsure of how to express an idea in English. Focusing on the use of Chinese in the composing process, Wang Wenyi and Wen Qiufang conducted another think-aloud study involving English majors who represented different English proficiency levels. They found that students tended to depend on Chinese when managing their writing processes and generating and organizing ideas but were more likely to use English when undertaking task-examining and text-generating activities. The use of Chinese declined as a student's English proficiency level increased. Both studies confirmed findings about ESL composition in other countries, such as the recursive nature of composing processes and the similarities and differences in writers when composing in their first and second languages. More importantly, both studies showed that Chinese plays a positive, enabling role in students' English writing processes. Empirically, they confirmed teachers' traditional, experiential knowledge that translation could be an effective strategy in second or foreign language writing. American scholarship informed Chinese researchers and encouraged them to tease out the complexities of Chinese students' composing processes.

International scholarship also stimulated pedagogical innovations. In the late 1970s, with the help of Canadian language experts, the Communicative English for Chinese Learners (CECL) project was conducted at Guangdong Foreign Language Institute, now Guangdong University of Foreign Studies. Continuously fascinated by students' communicative use of English, scholars in the same institute, for example, conducted a series of empirical studies in the late 1990s, which gave rise to the so-called "length approach" (*xie chang fa* 寫長法) in teaching English. The earliest study was reported by Wang Chuming, Niu Ruiying, and Zheng Xiaoxiang. The researchers first rationalized their study based on Chinese students' material conditions and on second language acquisition (SLA) theory: students lack the natural environment for using English for communication; they fear losing face in speaking English; and writing offers them a safe zone to practice the language and internalize vocabulary and structures through a comprehensible output. Scholars sought composition and applied linguistic theories to combat a very thorny issue: a majority of Chinese students still lacked a natural environment for using English even after the country had been open to the outside world for two decades.

The researchers then conducted a case study to investigate the role that extensive writing plays in developing students' communicative use of English. The study involved 200 English-major freshmen in a reading-centered class over one semester. Every week, the students each wrote an essay at home on a topic of their choice. They were encouraged to write the essay as long as possible since length was a criterion on the grading rubric. One or two well-written student essays would be read in the class each week. The entire class commented on these essays' development, organization, and use of language. The teacher tried to make minimal corrections but offered brief, positive comments. Results revealed that writing long essays enhanced the students' confidence in English writing, that exploring topics of their own choice stimulated students' interest in learning English, and that the length approach improved their English ability holistically. Later, this approach was replicated in other universities and with non-English majors; similar results were found.[7]

After its pedagogical success, scholars did not waste any time to give the homegrown approach some theoretical embellishment. Their theoretical efforts were deployed in two disciplinary camps, applied linguistics and composition. For example, Ouyang Huhua identified the approach as a hybrid pedagogy that embraced theoretical elements in SLA, the process approach, and current-traditional rhetoric. Similarly, Zheng Chao evoked Peter Elbow's categorization of "high-stakes writing" and "low-stakes writing" in his theoretical deliberation of the length approach. He suggested that students do not encounter much pressure when performing low-stakes writing and therefore are able to express themselves freely. They can truly experience the writing process and improve their ability to deal with high-stakes writing (Zheng, "Yi xie cu xue"). In their efforts to theorize the length approach and to justify the significance of their pedagogical innovation, scholars furnished the approach an eclectic theoretical framework.

While applied linguistics offered Chinese scholars theoretical guidance, it hindered critical studies of English writing instruction. Applied linguists promoted a positivist epistemology about language and language teaching in China. The positivist epistemology holds that we can best understand language or language teaching by breaking it up into discrete parts. Applied linguists accordingly searched for the elements whose removal from a causal chain would alter the outcome of language learning and language performance. In composition research, for instance, it was believed that if the construct of students' English writing based on skill levels could be established, then we could predict and control the outcomes of their English writing performance (Grabe). Due to its positivist orientation, composition research focused on those aspects that could be studied objectively, such as the students' composing processes and products.[8] Other "nondiscursive" aspects—such as broad sociocultural contexts, language-in-education policies, institutional establishments, and teachers' and students' socioeconomic conditions—were hardly researched at all.

An example of the negative influence of positivist epistemology emerged in a series of studies on Chinese students' rhetorical preferences during the 1990s. Taking a structuralist view of writing, these studies reduced rhetorical practices to textual organization. Furthermore, these studies embodied a strong assumption among Chinese scholars that Anglo-American English speakers were the only legitimate users of English and were, thus, *the* audience and *the* arbitrator of Chinese students' English writing. For instance, when Zhao Yongqing asked his students and a native speaker to respond to an English essay written by a Chinese student, he found that Chinese- and English-speaking audiences preferred different reasoning patterns in expository writing. Then Zhao drew a pedagogical implication: "The unique reasoning patterns commonly found in Chinese written discourse, such as the thesis statement appearing in the end, appearing in the middle, or hidden in the text, leads to a negative transfer in Chinese students' English writing. The teacher should never underestimate the greater harm caused by these patterns" (26). Zhao failed to recognize the fluidity of language, audience, and the rhetorical situation. Although students were writing hypothetically for a native-speaker audience, in reality students tried to communicate with their Chinese audiences (i.e., teachers and peers) who truly mattered in the rhetorical situation (i.e., class assignments or tests). Positivist epistemology constricted scholars to a static, essentialized view of English language, Anglo-American people, and their culture.

At the same time, fortunately, a few scholars reconsidered the place of Chinese rhetorical traits in English writing more positively (e.g., Ge Chuangui; Li Wenzhong; Wei Yun and Fei Jia).[9] Within the framework of World Englishes, Chinese linguistic and rhetorical traces were regarded as a natural part of an emerging variety of English in China. As this book has demonstrated so far, Chinese students have always brought Chinese rhetorical practices into their English writing since the earliest days that English was taught in the country. They have been able to draw on rhetorical and linguistic resources from multiple traditions in their Chinese and English composition. Some historical knowledge of Chinese students' writing practices becomes critical to appreciating Chinese rhetorical traces in English writing.

The open-door policy introduced Chinese scholars to the international arena of composition research and offered them opportunities for appropriating overseas theories. Starting in the 1980s, an increasing number of China-based studies were published in international ELT journals, such as *College English, College Composition and Communication, ELT Journal, TESOL Quarterly, The Journal of Second Language Writing, System,* and *World Englishes.* The International Conference on ELT in China, launched in 1985, has been held regularly in recent years. In the 2004 conference, of the nearly 500 presentations, 49 dealt with teaching English writing in Chinese colleges (You, "New Directions"). As Chinese teachers and scholars joined the international community of composition research, they saw the advantages of putting overseas theories to the test locally. As the studies on the length approach have showed, they appropriated the imported theories to tinker, gild, or justify their own practice of teaching English writing. In the end, the homegrown pedagogical practices and theories were hybridized by the foreign import, a positive move toward producing competent multilingual writers for both local and international communications.

In China's continual educational reforms since the late 1980s, Chinese and English composition instruction followed different paths. Through the leverage of college entrance exams, Chinese school writing encouraged creativity and individuality, while retaining the Marxist style of writing and the traditional notion of writing as a means to the Way. Western modes of discourse were seriously questioned; students were encouraged to let their thoughts and feelings reign over form. Like Chinese composition, English writing was emphasized in various national exams. However, it was conceived of as a neutral, objective technology governed by static, mechanical rules. Therefore, English composition was laid out in college English syllabi as a set of scientifically structured mini-tasks and was assessed in a highly controlled schematic form. In the CET, students were encouraged to translate Chinese mainstream discourse into the prescribed format of three or five paragraphs. Pedagogically, they were encouraged to study, memorize, imitate, or even borrow expressions from sample essays. Despite the different paths that Chinese and English composition instruction took, together they aimed to cultivate well-rounded multilingual professionals with a competitive edge in the market economy.

6

WRITING IN OUR TONGUE

In recent discussions of English education in China, the perception of English as a devil's tongue has started to shift. The old framing that associated English with English-dominant nations is being replaced by a neutral, technological framing. The new framing, I suggest, continues the old sinocentric *ti-yong* dualism that reduces English to a practical tool alien to Chinese cultural essence. In fact, each nationality exposed to English finds a way to repurpose it to their own needs, to exercise control and a degree of sovereignty over the language. English becomes a technocultural means owned by its users, regardless of their national, racial, linguistic, class, or gender background. Rhetorical and sociolinguistic factors associated with people's use of English, rather than the old monolithic notion of the language, are central to understanding the ownership of English. From this perspective, the history of English composition in China is no different from that of Chinese composition—they both involve Chinese people writing to engender a modern Chinese culture in our tongues, "our" in the sense of all users of English and their mother tongues in the world. I conclude the book with some consideration of how American composition studies may respond to the worldwide teaching of English in light of the Chinese history of English composition.

Redesigning English Literacy

Ever since China joined the World Trade Organization (WTO), influences of globalization have been strongly felt in English education. English was described by the mass media as an international language for global political, economic, and cultural transactions. Responding to the rising demands for English, the Ministry of Education required that primary schools teach the language from the third grade on, starting in 2002. For college English, the ministry issued a new educational decree, College English Curriculum Requirements, in 2007 laying out new goals and requirements for teaching English to non-English majors (Jiaoyubu, Daxue yingyu [29 Sept. 2007]). Before the document was officially published, the stipulations were implemented in 180 universities as a yearlong experiment in 2004 (Jiaoyubu, Daxue yingyu [2004]).[1] Adopting the discourse of international educational norms, the decree reinforced the demands of globalization by transposing them into institutional and pedagogical discourses. Thus, the decree offers an excellent entry point for examining how English literacy education is redesigned in a non-English dominant country amid the discourse of globalization.

Compared to previous syllabi for non-English majors, the decree required not only the teaching of language knowledge and skills but also that of cross-cultural communication skills. Why were cross-cultural communication skills emphasized? The answer was suggested in an article published prior to the release of the decree by Zhang Yaoxue, the chair of the Department of Higher Education under the Ministry of Education. In a section titled "Primary Conditions," Zhang defined English as a means for international communication: "The world economy is increasingly globalized; our country has joined the WTO; scientific exchanges become internationalized; international communication is getting more and more frequent; all of which have turned English into a daily tool just like a driver's license" (par. 6). Phrases like "a daily tool" and "a driver's license" replaced any old ideological connotations of English that used to connect it with foreign dominance and oppression in modern Chinese history. English was no longer fixedly associated with a particular people, a nation-state, or a culture but simply became a communicative means. With a driver's license, someone is entitled to operate a vehicle to travel from one locale to another. With a good command of English, someone is capable of communicating across both Anglo-American and non-Anglo-American cultures. The projected image of English as a device for international transactions thus warranted the inclusion of cross-cultural communication skills in the new English literacy. The bold statement defining English as "a daily tool" culminated from the instrumental, pragmatic emphasis in English teaching after the Cultural Revolution.

English literacy was further defined with a clear emphasis on English for academic purposes (EAP), indicating China's desire to participate in a globalized knowledge market. The "Teaching Requirements" section of the decree set three well-articulated levels for language skills: the basic, intermediate, and advanced levels. At the intermediate level, students should "be able to understand, by and large, courses in their areas of specialty taught in English" (par. 9), "be able to understand the main ideas, major facts and relevant details when reading summative literature in their areas of specialty" (par. 11), and "be able to compose English abstracts for theses in their own specialization, and write short English papers on topics in their field" (par. 12). The new demand for teaching EAP goes hand in hand with an ambitious bilingual education project currently underway in Chinese higher education. As part of this project, some high-ranking universities were asked by the Ministry of Education to increase the number of courses taught in English in different majors (Zhang).

The new English literacy, setting EAP as the terminal goal of college English teaching, was reminiscent of English teaching decades before. College English was largely taught for academic purposes in republican China. However, these two similar historical trends were rooted in different ideologies. In republican China, the urgency to salvage the nation from foreign exploitation and oppression prompted the study of Western subjects. With most foreign textbooks not yet translated into Chinese, academic English opened a gate to Western knowledge. In contrast, entwined in the discourse of globalization, college students nowadays are persuaded to believe that mastery of both Chinese and English will earn them a competitive edge in scientific research, industry, business, and culture. EAP is no longer framed as a means to surviving the death threats of the foreign devils but rather as an instrument for winning global competitions.

The decree included the call for technology in designing the new English literacy. Addressing pedagogical models, the decree states that "the new model should be built on modern information technology, particularly network technology, so that English language teaching and learning will be, to a certain extent, free from the constraints of time or place and geared towards students' individualized and autonomous learning" ("Pedagogical Models" section, par. 1). Students can choose the learning materials, and they can record and assess their progress. Studying English in an information technology–facilitated environment, students will have the opportunity to develop individualized learning strategies vital to their academic success; more important, they will practice with technologies that will constitute their future workplace. Like cross-cultural communication skills, conceptualized in broader terms, computer/network literacy makes up part of English literacy.

The redefinition of English literacy echoed discussions of English teaching in other countries and perpetuated a literacy myth, celebrating literacy as a means of achieving wealth and citizenship. For example, in a report submitted to former Japanese prime minister Keizo Obuchi in 2000, the

Commission on Japan's Goals in the Twenty-first Century claimed that the possession of global literacy skills would determine whether or not a citizen could expect to enjoy a better life in the new century. The global literacy defined by the commission includes the mastery of modern information technologies, such as computers and the Internet, and a strong working knowledge of English that helps a person with "learning about and accessing the world" (Matsuura, Fujieda, and Mahoney 471). In the Chinese context, global literacy is particularized as a good command of English language skills for both academic and cross-cultural communication as well as familiarity with modern information technologies. It needs to be noted that both the Chinese and the Japanese definitions of global literacy rest on the assumption that students all at the same time develop strong competence in their mother tongue. English literacy is a "value-added" discourse that intends to help them live and work in the global economy successfully.

To achieve the new English literacy, the curriculum requirements emphasize a functional view of computer-mediated teaching and English as a medium for acquiring subject knowledge. The decree instructs schools to promote computer network–based courses. English courses are no longer conceptualized simply as helping students acquire English, but rather as the media that "allow the students to learn about science and technology and Western society and culture" ("Curricular Arrangements" section, par. 4). The shift towards computer network–based courses with a clear emphasis on content-rich subject matter presents a concrete curricular infrastructure for achieving the new literacy. However, these new curricular requirements encourage a pedagogy with narrower social and cultural goals than those of the pedagogy of multiliteracies advocated by the New London group, which has deeply influenced computer-mediated teaching in the West. The group argues that traditional literacy pedagogy is inadequate in the post-Fordism era in which communication channels and media have multiplied and cultural and linguistic diversity have increased.[2] A pedagogy of multiliteracies assumes that "language and other modes of meaning are dynamic representational resources, constantly being remade by their users as they work to achieve their various cultural purposes" (Cope and Kalantzis 5). While the computer network–based courses have actively responded to the multiplied modes of communication in our lifework, they often fail to engage students in using multiliteracies to achieve, in addition to academic purposes, other cultural and social goals. Ignoring the rhetorical and critical uses of multiliteracies (Selber), these computer network–based courses have disseminated a technological, pragmatic view of English and other literacies.

Working toward the new literacy, the decree promulgates student-centered assessment. Besides the traditional summative evaluation, like midterms and finals, the decree introduces methods of process-based, student-centered evaluation. Universities should observe, evaluate, and monitor students' progress through in-class and extracurricular records, students' self-learning online records, portfolios, interviews, and teacher-student conferences. For each exit level, the decree provides benchmarks for self- and peer-evaluation of the five language skills. At the relatively high level, for example, students can gauge their writing ability by answering "yes" or "no" to statements like the following: "I can write for daily purposes, conforming to the standard structure and expression of a particular genre." "Based on reference materials, I can write disciplinary reports, expositions, and speech scripts with clear structures and rich content." "Within half an hour, I can write a 160-word narrative, descriptive, expository or argumentative piece with complete content, clear structure and fluent language" (Appendix 2, chart 2).

The introduction of process-based, student-centered evaluation has the potential to lead to student-centered teaching and learning, an outcome that has been valued in the discourse of international educational norms. The process-based evaluation closely connects learning and assessment, stimulating students in their entire learning process rather than having them focus on midterms and finals. The reform of both curriculum and assessment was a timely response to the heightened issue of educational accountability in globalization.

By conceptualizing English as "a daily tool" and by implementing the new decree, English education in China took a historical turn at the advent of the twenty-first century. English was no longer conceived of as a foreign devil's tongue but rather as an additional language for educated Chinese. It had become the second or third language of at least 300 million Chinese by 2005.[3] Since English is now being taught in elementary schools, the number of Chinese users of English is sharply increasing. After the Cultural Revolution, college English focused on producing students who would be able to read and translate in their disciplines; its current goal is to produce students who will be able to function competently in both their academic fields and future workplaces with English. English has transcended its historical function of assimilating Chinese into Western learning and has become a medium of international exchange, cooperation, and competition.

A History of Writing in "Our" Tongue

The seemingly drastic change in the societal view of English did not happen overnight. The change culminated from relentless political, economic, and cultural struggles that had taken place in Chinese society since its disheartening encounter with the West. English teaching has been deeply rooted in the throes of a nation transitioning from a feudal to a socialist/capitalist society. It has a history of educated Chinese striving to acquire an additional language to inscribe their experiences, feelings, and desires for multicultural audiences. Their experiences of acquiring a devil's tongue were far from being rosy or uneventful. Mediating in local cultural politics, English was virtually no different from local Chinese languages and dialects. In fact, Chinese composers turned English into "our" tongue in pedagogical, rhetorical, linguistic, and discursive terms, factors that ensured its vitality in the Chinese context.

English composition in China has been marked by a continuous, critical search for effective pedagogies over the years. When English writing was first taught in the mid-nineteenth century, Chinese students were practicing the civil service exam essays, the gateway to feudal officialdom. In the early twentieth century, Chinese language teachers adopted Western modes to replace exam essays, indicating a pedagogical rejection of feudalism. They drew students' attention away from political, moral, and historical topics and led them toward making sense of their everyday lives. Similarly, the modes liberated students in their English composition. Into the 1950s, attention to grammar and textual analysis in English reading reinforced the current-traditional approach to English composition. This approach survived the ups and downs of English teaching in the People's Republic, and the four modes continue to structure English composition instruction for English majors even today. The success of the modes can be attributed to their early resistance to feudalism and alignment with bourgeois capitalism and to their later affinity with Chinese proletarian rhetoric. When English composition for non-English majors surged in the late 1980s, test-centered teaching promoted expository argumentation while marginalizing narration and description. The promotion of the former resulted from a compromise between exposition's great practicality in a business-oriented culture and the traditional Chinese interest in expository argumentation. Teachers' and scholars' critical search for composition pedagogies sensitive to the evolving Chinese context has never stopped.

English composition took on both Anglo-American and Chinese rhetorical traditions at the same time. Confucian rhetoric dominated Chinese school writing for two thousand years. In the Confucian epistemology, truth is the Way, or the essence of the evolving universe, which manifests itself in human society through virtuous human behaviors. A good rhetor is also a virtuous person who advocates and exemplifies the Way. In the early twentieth century, Western scientific rhetoric made its way into both Chinese and English composition and was strengthened in Chinese proletarian rhetoric in the 1950s. This new rhetoric located truth in the external, sensible world; the rhetor needed to convey truth to the audience objectively. Both rhetorical traditions not only negotiated with each other in pedagogical terms but also found creative expressions in English composition. In students' speech scripts, political essays, or journal entries, Chinese rhetorical traces never stopped creeping in: the ritualizing function of writing, the scattered style of *sanwen*, the parallelism in rhymed prose, and the dialectic reasoning in Confucian canons all made their way into students' English writing. Students were not poor learners of the devil's tongue, but rather they used English to describe their thoughts and feelings for both Chinese and international audiences and to experiment with, in Patricia Bizzell's words, "the textual arts of the contact zone" (168). Schooled with a scientific attitude and subjected to the local cultural signification, students had to adulterate the devil's tongue to signify their intended meanings.

Students' appropriation of English to their own purposes and ideas was also reflected linguistically. For example, in one of the student essays written at Tong Wen Guan quoted in chapter 1, the writer used "the God" to refer to Jesus Christ. Since he was in the process of secretly learning about Christianity, it can be conjectured that he placed Jesus Christ side by side with the Chinese God of Heaven (*huangtian* 皇天), whose earthly son was the emperor. In an essay written at Ginling College in the 1920s, a female student related her struggles in pursuing higher education. Her father warned her that it was very difficult to "jump the stairs of study," a Chinese expression that vividly captured household discourse on education. During the Cultural Revolution, students translated Mao's works into English and compiled them into their English textbooks. They consciously used literal translations to retain the original signification of Chinese expressions. Thus, it was common to see that students praised the People's Liberation Army for adhering to the military disciplines in their fight against "the paper tigers" and that they vowed to "do revolution" following Mao's teaching. In these instances of "bastardized" English, students used writing to describe their actual, imagined, and possible lives within a Chinese cultural context.

English composition also enabled students to participate in the discourse of Chinese modernity. After the Opium Wars, English learning revived from the nation's deeply felt humiliations. Through English, students of foreign affairs schools could sample Western science and culture and relativize the Chinese feudal structure. In the early twentieth century, students at mission colleges edited English newspapers and magazines to deliberate on the relationship between the individual and the state in a national crisis. They discussed how China could learn from industrialized countries while resisting the vices of capitalism and imperialism. During the Second World War, students vented their hatred for Japanese invaders in their English writing, signifying a discursive combat with foreign imperialists. During the Maoist period, students wrote about their experiences working in factories or on farms. They chanted Maoist phrases and tried to connect Mao's teaching to their daily activities. Since the late 1980s, students have been asked to discuss current social issues in the CET writing. Reading and writing on various topics, students continuously reflected on and responded to novel issues that emerged in Chinese society. Thus, like Chinese composition, over the last 150 years English composition has become a discursive ritual through which students are acculturated into mainstream discourse. It has furnished them with much-needed cultural and symbolic capital to function in the society.

From the very moment English entered Chinese schools, it has engaged the Chinese, a few in the beginning to a large number nowadays, in search of new meanings for Chinese modernization. The Chinese government constantly adjusted its English-in-education policies to socially engineer students, turning them into serviceable scientists, technicians, bureaucrats, and cultural workers for the state. Teachers sought composition theories and pedagogies that would work in the evolving educational context. Students interwove Chinese rhetorical and linguistic features with English writing to capture their new sensibilities. They wrote about their daily events and deliberated on urgent social issues, which in turn shaped their lives. Through the constructive, multidomain use of English in the endless search for Chinese modernity, rather than a devil's tongue, English has become "our" tongue for its numerous Chinese users.

Viewed from such a historical perspective, the current emphasis on English as "a daily tool" in Chinese mainstream discourse is partial and flawed. Naming English as an instrument continues the old cultural logic manifest in the *ti-yong* dualism, or Chinese learning as the essence versus Western learning for practical use. A clear line has always been drawn between Chinese and English since the Qing dynasty. English was viewed as a foreign tongue, external to the Chinese cultural essence which was historically anchored to classical Chinese. However, the Chinese history of English composition has showed that both modern Chinese and English are deeply involved in the reformation of Chinese culture. English has also taken on the anchoring position, just as modern Chinese and Western science and technology have done. As English saturates Chinese society more deeply, its anchoring role will become more prominent. Thus, an alternative view of the language calls for a critical assessment of the notions of English as a devil's tongue and as "a daily tool" and calls for a celebration of English as "our" tongue, an additional language of the Chinese.

The Chinese history of writing in "our" tongue can shed new lights on the contact zone theory. First, in an increasingly connected world, contact zones emerge when cultures meet with each other regardless of whether they form symmetrical or asymmetrical relations of power. If Anglo-American and Chinese cultures interacted with each other in an asymmetrical power relation in colonial China, their relation became more symmetrical in the People's Republic. Under either power relation—as revealed in student writings, composition theories and pedagogies, and scholarly research—these two equally learned cultures met, clashed, and grappled with each other. Through these contact zones, the teaching of composition in China developed transpacific relations with that in Japan and the United States. Second, when two major cultures meet, the way they intersect and grapple with each other varies as time elapses. For example, in colonial China, Western scientific culture and democratic ideals contended with Confucian philosophy and ethics. In Maoist China, Chinese revolutionary culture interacted with international Communist and Western capitalist cultures. After the Cultural Revolution, Chinese socialist culture vied for power with Western neoliberal and transnational capitalist cultures. The various ways that Western and Chinese cultures engaged with each other, as Chinese students' writings have demonstrated, made the global contact zone fluid, multifaceted, and generative. Third, global politico-economic dynamics constantly interact with the contact zone, and the interconnectivity between them further mobilizes the global contact zone. For example, Western colonial powers invaded Qing China and forced Chinese literati to acquire Western learning, hence the rise of the global contact zone. The contact zone provided the Chinese with opportunities to cultivate political and cultural leaders with modern consciousness, who then, through the arts of the global contact zone, led the Chinese people to the fight against colonialism, fascism, and imperialism in the world. The rich history of English composition in China, a history of Anglo-American and Chinese cultures engaging with each other through the teaching of English, offers scholars a rare opportunity to expand their understanding of the contact zone theory.

Globalization and Composition Studies

The mediating role played by English in Chinese modernization is not entirely unique in world history. In the expansion of British and American imperial powers over previous centuries, English was the language of dominance and control. At the same time, it also presented a particular cultural practice that contributed to the discourse of modernity in different locales. For example, at the turn of the twentieth century, English was taught in the Philippines by American soldier-teachers, who significantly improved the local literacy level (Alberca; Gonzalez and Fortunato; Isidro). English teaching was implicated in the Filipino experience of breaking away from Spanish control, falling into American colonization, and finally achieving national independence. In India, although English teaching served British governance for centuries, it was also adopted as a lingua franca to unite different ethnic communities in their fight for national integrity and independence. Over the last century, Indian writers produced large numbers of literary works in English that have captured their nation's experience and have helped to create a national identity. By the end of the twentieth century, English writing had been taught at the university level in all major Pacific Rim countries (Kaplan, *Teaching*), a phenomenon inseparable from the United States' politico-economic presence in the region. The historical process of a community adopting English for its own needs should not be taken lightly. It often happened because social elites considered that the native tongue was inadequate for modern needs and that English was a language of higher cultural capital. In ways similar to the Chinese case, English composition was deeply rooted in those communities' pursuit of their modern dreams and visions.

In the world history of English composition, Anglo-American teachers have made their contributions in different continents. However, as an academic field, American composition studies has remained largely indifferent to the worldwide teaching of English writing and to the global contact zones created by the worldwide spread of Anglo-American political and cultural forces. Canagarajah's description of English teaching in Sri Lanka (*Resisting Linguistic Imperialism*), Muchiri et al.'s report of English composition in Africa, Prendergast's ethnographic study on English in post-Communist Slovak, and my own historical account of composition in China have revealed the penetrating influence of Anglo-American theories and pedagogies in the rest of the world. If we agree with Muchiri et al.'s postcolonial positioning, what is the entry point that will allow American composition to engage in conversation with the rest of the world?

The most urgent task might be, in light of the international windows that we have opened, reassessing American composition studies' assumptions in relation to the dynamics of globalization. Horner and Trimbur suggest that a tacit policy of unidirectional English monolingualism has haunted first-year composition for more than a century and has confined composition to U.S.

national interests. Overshadowed by English monolingualism, English has been conceived as a discrete, value-free tool for serving a homogenous U.S. population. English teaching has been, in Min-Zhan Lu's words, "promoting a fluency that requires a willingness to presume (and therefore, prescribe) a set (fixed and specific) context and purpose for all users of English, on serving the interests of those with the most say in the designing of English, the realities of the Othered, and the world order" (43). Comments like those by Horner and Trimbur and by Lu have encouraged us to examine American composition studies' assumptions and practices. However, their comments remain largely U.S.-centric and might be at risk of excluding some of the histories that we can now draw on to support a global understanding of English.

Examined against the increasingly connected relations among linguistic, economic, social, political, and cultural fronts resulting from the global diffusion of market modes of operation, English composition can no longer stand as a purely American "business." The incessant information flow has turned the composition classroom into an international economic and cultural space. A student no longer composes as an independent, authentic self—as the old modernist ideology once made us believe—but rather as one of billions of intelligent "processors" in the network of information flow. These students are future business leaders, farmers, tourists, politicians, scholars, CEOs, and employees of multinational corporations, whose work requires regular border crossing and shuttling between speech communities. In a world of catastrophe and injustice, Min-Zhan Lu argues, composition has undeniable responsibility because of its unfathomable impact on students of American English or other Englishes. Composition teachers in both China and the United States need to reexamine and reform pedagogical approaches, rhetorical preferences, and writing practices to make sure that they live up to new responsibilities.

Working in a globalized space, we should produce responsive and responsible users of multiple Englishes who will transcend the narrow interests of a particular group and will embrace justice and equality for all peoples. My historical narrative has provided a detailed view on how American composition theories and practices were profoundly connected to social changes in China over the last century. We clearly see that some composition pedagogies produced responsible users of both English and Chinese, who liberated the people from the oppression of feudalism, imperialism, and capitalism. For example, when the four modes gradually replaced the *bagu-ce-lun* pedagogical system in the early twentieth century, they revitalized description and narration and nurtured an empiricist generation no longer content with pure metaphysical discourse. These educated young men freed the Chinese minds by instilling the spirit of science and democracy. However, any liberating pedagogical approach could be stifling as time passed. Into the 1980s, the four modes were judged too formulaic; they hampered students' creativity and individuality, traits that are vital to success in the modern workplace. The rise and fall of the modes in the United States reflects a similar political-cultural logic (Connors). In a tensely interconnected "global village," American pedagogies and writing practices will continue to spread and influence other parts of the world. Owing to the high stakes of our everyday work, we should always question ourselves as to whether our approaches will be liberating, not only for users of American English but also for users of other Englishes and other languages in the world.

Attention to the international ramifications of our work also means that we need to be sensitive to rhetorical traditions and practices in different linguistic and ethnic communities. We need not only to celebrate the multiplicity of cultures that students represent but also to critically interrogate the way these cultures are constructed and circulated in classroom contact zones. Every user of English or of other languages comes from several communities—family, school, district, nation-state, and so on. Every community teaches the language user a set of rules of socialization and communication. When students write, they will necessarily rejoin the cultures of communities in which they identify themselves. The history of English composition in China illustrates that Chinese students brought in their preferred rhetorical strategies to construct and circulate their cultural experiences. Sensitivity to and respect for various rhetorical traditions will help us to appreciate our students' creative use of English to construct their lived cultures in contact zones.

Students' use of rhetorical strategies reflects their sense of self, that is, an understanding rising from past and present lived experiences and from their dreams and desires for their futures. These rhetorical strategies embody students' perceived relations with the various communities and cultures in which they participate or relate to. Too often we discuss concepts such as rhetorical situation, audience, *ethos*, *pathos*, *logos*, arrangement, and style in our classes without urging students to explore how these concepts are actuated in their particular communities, cultures, and languages. We sometimes give our students a false impression that there is only one correct, standard parameter in which these concepts should operate in their discourse. In different communities, these rhetorical concepts play out in remarkably divergent ways. Our students always bring with them their cultures' preferred ways of thinking, speaking, and writing, which are resources that we must capitalize on in our teaching.

While composition remains a teaching profession in both China and the United States, we should not lose sight of the larger picture of students' writing practices. Too often we focus on technical aspects of a text, discussing invention, organization, style, and grammar in our class. Alan France argues that in the postmodern era, composition, together with literary studies, should continue to be the central province of liberal education, or "the cultivation of the intellect for its own sake" (146). He suggests that composition instruction should encourage students to look beyond the text and ask themselves how much of their experience is the free expression of agency and how much is the product of cultural determination. School writings are never produced in a political and cultural vacuum. They will always traverse the realm of the intellect and impact the present and future lives of others. Over the last 150 years, English writing mediated between Chinese students' deliberation of their everyday lives and the relationship between the self and the state. For example, the first generation of Chinese female students at Ginling College wrote about the hardships of pursuing higher education and expressed their conviction in defending human dignity. Students wrote about their commune work during the Cultural Revolution to show the worth of combining education and physical labor. These student writings might seem trivial when viewed on an individual, technical basis against a static time reference. Placed in a historical spectrum, none of them was insignificant. These pieces represented the critical consciousness of intelligent human beings who eventually made a difference in modern China. Writing practices, whether taking place in high school or college, in American English, other Englishes, or other languages, are all grounded in the dreams and possibilities of our students who shape human history.

American composition scholars and teachers are not alone when facing new challenges of globalization. Segregated by geopolitical boundaries, teachers in many parts of the world have to figure out ways to teach English writing by themselves, and they continue to be influenced by Anglo-American monolingual and monocultural modes of writing. Until now, there has been rather limited worldwide communication among English teachers, particularly between teachers in English-dominant and non-English-dominant countries. A cursory survey of English-language teaching journals published in English reveals that discussions and reports about English composition in non-English-dominant contexts remain scarce. American composition studies need to pay more attention to those locales where their work has repercussions. Professionals in those locales need to be invited to discuss English composition issues. Frequent two-way communication will establish a sustainable network through which composition professionals all over the world can share visions and take joint actions for positive social change.

To foster an international alliance, teachers and researchers in the United States need to be humble and inclusive. American composition studies need to entertain new, fundamental values about the English language. It needs to forsake completely its anachronistic assumption that English mainly serves its native speakers, and in turn, that native speakers set the standards for English use. For centuries, English has not been statically connected to a particular community, nation-state, or culture; rather, it has been utilized by both monolingual and multilingual users for various situated needs and desires. The field needs to accept that all users of English are legitimate owners of the language and that they can use the language in ways that will best serve their particular needs. English literacy is no longer a national issue that matters to Caucasians, African Americans, Hispanics, or "visa" students in English-dominant countries, but it has become an international issue concerning users of multiple Englishes and other languages. Composition scholars in North America should work closely with scholars and users of these Englishes in other locales to negotiate standards of English use, to formulate appropriate language policies, and to discuss how to effectively teach the language in light of local conditions. Min-Zhan Lu has spelled out an international obligation for the field of composition: "It is our responsibility to call attention to the potential desires, capabilities, and needs of all users of English to actively participate in the redesigning of standardized Englishes with the highest Market values and to do so in intra- and international *jiaos* 交 [networks] on all levels of life" (44). This revolutionary vision is a proactive lifeline for composition, which will eventually turn a devil's tongue of many into an "our" tongue for all.

APPENDIXES

NOTES

WORKS CITED

INDEX

APPENDIX A: A SKETCH OF RHETORIC AND ENGLISH COMPOSITION COURSES AT MISSION COLLEGES, 1900–1950

This sketch is compiled largely based on course announcements and catalogs of mission colleges in China. It is intended to show the curricular dynamics, not the comprehensiveness, of rhetoric and English composition instruction at the mission colleges. Only courses directly related to rhetoric and composition are listed in the sketch; other English courses are omitted. Where there are large gaps between years it is because there were no significant changes in the rhetoric and composition courses offered until the next given year. Textbooks mentioned were required reading.

Fukien Christian University 協和大學, Fuzhou (est. 1910)

1916   Fukien Union College
- English Language and Literature (freshman; weekly themes in narration and description)
- English Language and Literature (sophomore; weekly themes in exposition and argumentation)

1919–26   Fukien Christian University
- Freshman Composition (weekly themes in narration, description, and exposition); Scott, *Bulletins in English Composition* (starting in 1924)
- Sophomore Composition (practice in exposition and writing magazine articles; weekly themes); Greever and Jones, *The Century Collegiate Handbook* (starting in 1925); Bough, Kitchen, and Black, *Writing by Types* (starting in 1925)
- Advanced Composition (extension of Sophomore English)

1929
- Freshman Composition (required)
- Sophomore Composition (elective)
- Advanced Composition (elective)
- Public Speaking (sophomore, elective)

Ginling College 金陵女子文理學院, Nanjing (est. 1913)

1913
- Rhetoric and Theme Course (topical writing, short themes)
- Short Story Course (discussion of readings, writing of short stories, story-telling)

1920
- Literature (freshman; including oral composition)
- Rhetoric and Composition (sophomore; paragraph structure)
- Rhetoric and Composition (junior; exposition and description)
- Rhetoric and Composition (senior; narration and development of short story, argumentation, and public speaking)

1931
- Language and Literature (freshman, required; including parliamentary practice)
- Composition and Literature (sophomore, required; development and structure of the novel)

1933–35
- Language and Literature (freshman)
- Composition and Literature (sophomore)
- Composition (for students showing insufficient mastery of English at the end of sophomore year)
- Thesis (for English majors)

1938
- English Composition and Literature

1941
- Freshman English (required)
- Sophomore English (required for non-English majors; essay, outline, and prose writing)
- Composition and Literature (including reading reports)
- Advanced Composition (junior and senior; emphasizing creative writing)
- English Essays
- Translation
- Debate
- Thesis (individual research report)

1947
- Freshman Writing
- Sophomore Writing
- Exposition
- Argumentation
- Junior Composition (criticism)
- Senior Composition (original writing)
- Translation
- Journalistic Writing
- Thesis

Hangchow University 之江大學, Hangzhou (est. 1897)

1904   Hangchow Presbyterian College
- Art of Letter-Writing (1st year)
- Exposition on Current Affairs (2nd year)
- Translation from English to Chinese; Rhetoric (3rd year)
- Translation from Chinese to English; Rhetoric (4th year)
- Debate (5th year)

1910
- Composition
- Literature
- Grammar (freshman, sophomore, junior, and senior)

1913   Academy (four years): no requirements for English composition
College (four years):
- Translation; Logic (junior)
- Translation; Letter-Writing (senior)

1921   Hangchow Christian College
Junior College:
- Composition and Rhetoric (1st year; weekly composition); Clippinger, *Written and Spoken English*, vol. 1; Davis, *Practical Exercises*

- Composition and Rhetoric (2nd year; weekly drill in written essays); Clippinger, *Written and Spoken English*, vol. 2

Senior College:

- Advanced Composition and Rhetoric (1st year; weekly essays); Herrick and Damon, *New Composition and Rhetoric*
- Public Speaking (2nd year); Winans, *Public Speaking*

1925
- Composition and Rhetoric (I); Ball, *Construction English*
- Composition and Rhetoric (II); Herrick and Damon, *New Composition and Rhetoric*

Hua Chung College 華中大學, Wuchang (est. 1929)

1908 Yali Middle School
- 1st year English: Oral and Written Drill; *Hyde's Course*, vol. 1
- 2nd year English: Reed and Kellong, *Graded Lessons in English*
- 3rd year English: Grammar and Composition; *Mother Tongue*, vol. 2
- 4th year English: Literature and Composition; *Mother Tongue*

1916 The College of Yale-in-China
- English (freshman): Rhetoric, Composition, and Literature
- English (sophomore): Composition and Survey of English Literature
- English: Nineteenth-Century Prose Writers

1932–36
- Freshman Composition; Smart, *Handbook of Effective Writing*
- Sophomore Composition
- Advanced Composition (junior; starting in 1936)
- Senior Composition (starting in 1936)

Lingnan University 嶺南大學, Guangzhou (est. 1888)

1900 Christian College in China, Macao
- Freshman English (focused on composition)
- Sophomore English (focused on composition)

1909 Canton Christian College
Preparatory:
- Composition (1st year; themes thrice weekly); *Mother Tongue*, vol. 1; *Seaside and Wayside*, vol. 2; *Jones' Third Reader*; *Baldwin's Third Reader*
- Grammar and Composition (2nd year; composition work in the classroom and themes thrice weekly)
- Grammar and Composition (3rd year; themes twice weekly)
- Composition and Rhetoric (4th year; theme practice in application of first principles of rhetoric and a short study of the various kinds of simpler composition)

College:
- Advanced Rhetoric and Composition (freshman)

1913 Middle School:
- Composition (4th year)
- Composition (5th year)

College:
- Composition (freshman and sophomore; both emphasizing writing on themes of other courses)

1923
- English Composition (freshman, required; rhetoric, reading, themes and conferences); Genung and Hanson, *Outlines of Composition and Rhetoric*; Burke, *Speech on Conciliation with America*; Tennyson, *Idylls of the King*; Webster, *First Bunker Hill Oration*; Campbell and Rice, *A Book of Narratives*
- English Composition for College of Agriculture Students (freshman, required; themes on subjects taken from the practical work and the texts of the courses in agriculture)
- Rhetoric (for sophomores with good standing; forms and methods of writing)

1925
- Composition and Reading (freshman, required); Thomas, Manchester, and Scott, *Composition for College Students*; Campbell and Rice, *A Book of Narratives*; Denney and Raymund, *Good Reading*, vol. 1; Tennyson, *Idylls of the King*
- Rhetoric (forms and methods of writing)

1929
- Composition and Reading (freshman, required; organization of sentence, paragraph, and theme); Greever and Jones, *Century of Collegiate Handbook*; Hart and Perry, *Representative Short Stories*
- Advanced Composition (practice in the writing of essays, dialogues, short stories, letters, and book reviews); Fulton, *Writing Craftsmanship*; Grose, *College Composition*
- Special Problems in Writing (not offered in 1929–30; the writing of original essays, sketches, and other forms)

1934
- Freshman English (including sentence and paragraph construction and theme writing)
- Advanced English (practice in the more common forms of present-day writing based on the study of contemporary models)
- Debate and Oratory (development and presentation of formal speeches)
- Thesis

1946
- Freshman English
- Sophomore English

Soochow University 東吳大學, Suzhou (est. 1900)

1919 Middle School:
- 1st Year English
- 2nd Year English; *Graded Lessons*
- 3rd Year English; *Mother Tongue*, vol. 2
- 4th Year English: Advanced Grammar and Composition

Junior College:
- 1st Year English: Composition and Literature; Lewis and Hosic, *Practical English for High Schools*
- 2nd Year English: Composition and Literature; Genung and Hanson, *Composition and Rhetoric*, vols. 1 and 2

Senior College:
- Composition and Literature (1st year); Genung and Hanson, *Composition and Rhetoric*, vol. 3

- The English Essayists (1st year); Bryan and Crane, *The English Familiar Essay*

1934
- Freshman English; Dakin, *The Mastery of the Sentence*; Kies, *Handbook of Composition*
- Sophomore English; Jones, *Practical English Composition*; Beaty, Lamar, and Leisy, *Facts and Ideas*
- Composition Correction (for students who plan to teach English in middle schools)

1935   Law School:
- English (freshman, required; grammar and sentence structure in the 1st semester; structure of paragraphs and the whole text in the 2nd semester); Arnold, *Manual of Composition*; Dickens, *David Copperfield*

1938
- Language and Composition (freshman)
- Essays (sophomore)

St. John's University 聖約翰大學, Shanghai (est. 1879)

1907   St. John's College
- Freshman: Rhetoric and Composition; Genung, *The Practical Elements of Rhetoric*; English and Chinese
- Sophomore: Rhetoric and Composition; Genung, *The Practical Elements of Rhetoric*
- Junior: Composition and Poetics
- Senior: Composition and Oratory

1932
- Composition 1, 2: the clear, concise, and direct treatment of facts; frequent individual conferences for criticism of themes
- Composition 3, 4: intensive work in the various types of composition with frequent individual conferences, special attention being paid to letter writing; Lomer and Ashmun, *The Study and Practice of Writing English*
- Composition 5, 6: lectures on style and structure; weekly expository essays based on the work done in other departments with individual conferences; Curl, *Expository Writing*

1938
- Freshman English
- Freshman Composition
- Sophomore Composition
- Advanced Composition

University of Nanking 金陵大學, Nanjing (est. 1889)

1909   Primary:
- English and Chinese Writing (3rd year)
  Intermediate:
- Copy-Book Writing (1st year)
- Elementary Composition Lessons; Copy-Book Writing (2nd year)
- Copy-Book Writing (3rd year)
  High School:
- 1st year: Carpenter; *Mother Tongue*, vol. 2; *Commercial Writing*

- 2nd year: *Mother Tongue,* vol. 2; *Elocution and Essay Writing*
- 4th year: English Language and Literature

College:

- English (elective).

Writing-related courses include:

- Rhetoric and Essay Writing
- Prose Masterpieces
- Synonyms Discriminated

1914   High School (four years):

4 semesters of English

- Elementary Idiomatic Composition (2nd semester)
- English Composition; Letter Writing and Elementary Elocution (3rd semester)
- Essay Writing and Elocution (4th semester)

College:

- Composition and Rhetoric (required of all freshmen); Merkley, *Modern Rhetoric;* writings of Macaulay and Stevenson
- Readings in English Prose (sophomore, required; principles of rhetoric and composition but emphasis on the development of literary appreciation)
- Advanced Composition (emphasizing translating English into Chinese, and vice versa, given in connection with the courses in Chinese literature)

1919   Primary Higher:

- Language: oral and written composition (7th year); Emerson and Bender, *English Spoken and Written,* vol. 2

Middle School:

- Language (1st year): narration, description, exposition, argumenta-tion, letter-writing, advertising, and telegram-writing; Emerson and Bender, *English Spoken and Written,* vol. 3 (pts. 1 and 2)
- Language (2nd year): narration, description, exposition, and argu-mentation; Emerson and Bender, *English Spoken and Written,* vol. 3 (pt. 3)
- Language (3rd year); Maxwell and Smith, *Writing in English*
- Readings in Science (4th year); Caldwell and Eikenberry, *General Science*

Junior College:

- Language (1st year): Principles of Composition and Rhetoric; Holmes and Gallagher, *Composition and Rhetoric;* Warren, *Stories from English History*
- Language and Literature (2nd year; not for agriculture and forestry students): Clippinger, *Written and Spoken English;* Speare and Norris, *World War Issues and Ideals;* Bryan (ed.), *The World's Famous Orations*
- Language and Literature (2nd year; for agriculture and forestry students): Herrick and Damon, *New Composition and Rhetoric;* J. C. Bowman (ed.), *The Promise of Country Life*

College of Arts:
- 1st year: Essay: the history and nature of English essays in comparison to the Chinese (1st year); Bryan and Crane, *The English Familiar Essay;* Tanner, *Essays and Essay Writing*

1924   Middle School:

The curriculum resembles that of 1919.

College:

Pre-freshman:
- Composition and Language

Freshman required:
- Language and Literature for Arts Students (including theme writing and oral composition); Lomer and Ashmun, *Study and Practice of Writing English*
- English for Agriculture and Science Students (including theme writing and oral composition); Brede, *English in Modern Thought;* Lomer and Ashmun, *Study and Practice of Writing English*

Junior, Senior electives:
- The English Essay; Smith (ed.), *Essays and Studies*
- Advanced Composition (principles of good prose, theme writing in all forms except argumentation); Baldwin, *College Composition; Century Collegiate Handbook*
- Argumentation; Foster, *Argumentation and Debating*

1931   College:
- Fundamentals of English; White, *English Study and English Writing*
- Freshman English for Arts Students (required; literary structure and values, plot and character development, oral and written theme); Dickens, *Tale of Two Cities;* Lomer and Ashmun, *Study and Practice of Writing English*
- Freshman English for Agriculture and Science Students (required); Eliot, *Silas Marner;* Lomer and Ashmun, *Study and Practice of Writing English*
- Reading and Composition (freshman, required; composition related to readings); Hanson and Gross, *Short Stories of Today*
- Scientific Essays and Composition (2nd semester, for science students; compositions dealing with scientific problems); Cummingham, *Adventures in Science*
- The English Essay (English majors, required)
- Advanced Composition (study of principles underlying good prose, practice of theme writing in all forms except argumentation); Pence, *College Composition*
- Public Speaking

1936   • Pre-freshman Grammar and Composition
- Freshman Composition (1st semester, required)
- Readings and Composition (2nd semester, required)
- Sophomore Composition (3rd semester, required; nature of essays, discourse structure, theme writing on all forms with special attention to narration)
- Individual Composition Training (elective)

1946   Writing-related courses offered include: Sub-freshman English; Freshman English; Sophomore Composition; Exposition; Directed Writing; Junior Composition; Senior Composition; Translation; Thesis

University of Shanghai 滬江大學, Shanghai (est. 1906)

1920   Shanghai College
- Rhetoric (freshman; detailed study of the principles of rhetorical composition as illustrated in texts used in other departments); Clippinger, *Written and Spoken English*
- Composition (sophomore; further study of the principles of rhetoric for effective interpretation and expression)
- English Essay (sophomore; the mastery of the thought as well as the principles of rhetoric contained in the English essays studied)
- Public Speaking (principles and practice of public speaking); Winans, *Public Speaking*

1924–29
- Rhetoric and Grammar (sub-freshman)
- Written English (sub-freshman, starting from 1929)
- Rhetoric (freshman; oral and written composition based upon the textbook: Ward, *Theme Building*)
- Non-detailed Reading and Composition (sophomore; written compositions and outlines based on the novels and English magazines read)
- Essays (preparation of summaries and outlines for the essays read); Bowman, *Essays for College English*
- Public Speaking (starting in 1929)
- Short Story Writing (starting in 1929)

1938   University of Shanghai
- Composition and Rhetoric
- Essays
- Creative Writing

West China Union University 華西協合大學, Chengdu (est. 1910)

1915–22   Junior Division
Reading and Rhetoric, different focus at different year levels:
- 1st year: Paragraph study, theme, writing from dictation
- 2nd year: Description and narration
- 3rd year: Exposition and argumentation, with debates

Senior Division
English Language and Literature, different focus at different year levels:
- 4th year: Dictation, abstract writing, and translation from Chinese periodicals
- 5th year: Theme writing, dictation, class orations, translations
- 6th year: Book reviews, translation, dictation, and thesis

1926
- The Art of Writing English (pre-collegiate, 4 semesters); *Writing English; Arabian Nights*
- Rhetoric and Composition (freshman or sophomore, required; theme writing, conversation)

1931
- Short Stories (freshman, required; including composition writing assignments)
- Freshman Composition (required)
- Rhetoric and Composition (sophomore, required; theory and practice of narrative, descriptive, expository, and argumentative speaking and writing)
- Advanced English Composition (elective)
- Expository English (elective)

1937
Required for all students:
- 1st Year English Prose
- 1st Year Composition
- 2nd Year English Composition

Required for students in Division of English Literature:
- Rhetoric and Composition

Electives:
- Advanced Composition
- Modern Essays and Other Prose
- Expository English
- English Essayists

Yenching University 燕京大學, Beijing (est. 1870)

1920
Peking University
Junior College:
- Composition (1st year): oral and written work; weekly themes; Clippinger, *Written and Spoken English*, vol. 1
- Composition (2nd year): oral and written work; weekly themes

Senior College:
- Composition and Rhetoric (1st year): exposition; study of the paragraph and its development
- Composition (2nd year): exposition, narration and description; oral reports on subjects of personal investigation
- Composition (3rd year): argumentation
- Composition (4th year): both original work and the accurate translation of Chinese articles into good English
- Public Speaking

1923–26
- Pre-freshman English; Clippinger, *Written and Spoken English*, vol. 1
- Freshman English (required); Clippinger, *Written and Spoken English*, vol. 2
- Sophomore English (required; development of paragraph, weekly short themes with one long theme each semester)
- Parliamentary Law (elective; written and oral practice)
- Argumentation and Debate (elective)
- Advanced Composition (elective, added in 1925)

1936
Yenching University
- Freshman English (required; sentence, paragraph, letter writing, note-taking, exposition, description, narration, and argumentation)

- Sophomore English (required; essay writing)
- Advanced Composition I and II (electives; creative writing)

1946

- Freshman English (required)
- Sophomore English (required)
- Advanced Composition and Study of the Development of Modern English Prose Style (elective)

APPENDIX B: SAMPLE CORRECTED STUDENT ESSAYS AT GINLING COLLEGE, 1923

The following are student essays from Dorothy Lindquist's classes at Ginling College in the spring of 1923. The first one seems to be a sample that Dorothy, or Ms. Stendel, as her students called her, created to exemplify the symbol system she used to mark errors in her student essays. The second and third essays were written by two of her students.

Sample No. 1

Name   Date

(Autobiografy) Title   _____

se   I was born in 19_0 we then lived

s   in Utah the City of Ogden

s   When I was (6) years old ther

s   was a big flood there everybody

se   was going around in boats an boats

?   It was coused by a big river

  clooted by a big river clooted by

s   about a year afterward we got a

s   big camp wagen and started up throu

se   rakes then on up into Montana

se   we saw many bages beaes mountain

gr   lioms once we ran over a snake (3) in

se   round and about (6 ft) long I killed

gr   many snakes up there one day

s   we was going down around a big lift

s   and the road was just big enough

s   for the wagen to go aerost we darnnear

gr   fell in the lake down below

gr   It took us about (8) more months to

s   get back then about two years we

s   got a car and started on a nother trip

cp se gr   we was going down to califorina we did

s   not wont to go through the navada

"Autobiography"

Sample No. 2

Ginling College,
Nanking, Kiangsu
March 26, 1923

Dear unknown friends:—

You may wonder who(m) I am and why I am writing to you. So I shall explain. I am a (member) *student* of Ginling College. Since we are Christians and the children of our heavenly Father. Although we don't know each other very well (but) *yet*, we are related in His name. Therefore I think it would be good for us to have correspondence (between one another,) and to know some thing more (among) *between* us, and to make the friendship seeming real to us.

(I am a Chinese who has not new thing to tell you) Would you like to hear some thing about our native land? If so, I (am) *do* not hesitate to (do it) *tell you*. But I want to ask you several questions before I open my story. Do you wear silk? How *Where* does it come from? It is not a vegetable fibre but simply comes from a caterpillar. I am very glad to tell you the story of silkworm.

China is the native home of *the* silk- worm. We wore silk robes before Great Britain was in existence. But the silkworm is not raised all over China. Most of the worms are raised in the central part along the

"A Letter" (Li Dzeh-Djen)

Sample No. 3

My First Year at Ginling College.

Time passes quickly. Unconsciously I have studied one year in Ginling college. As I recall the time when I entered the Ginling gate, I found everything disagreeable to me. Everything was different from high school, but as I stayed longer and longer I liked Ginling more and more. Things gradually became accustomed to me. Day by day, I began to seek the things I liked and enjoyed. There are several points which I regard (them) as the privileges in college.

Firstly I can have the pleasure to associate with different kinds of people from all parts of the world. In contact with them I can learn their interests, their ideas, their habits and their personalities. They brought new thoughts and new ideas to me, which may influence my thoughts and personality.

Secondly, I have the opportunity to hear the lectures of our professors and of great men. They made me (to) realize the important duty and the great opportunity of a college girl of China. My mind became broader than before. My whole life may be changed and influenced by them.

"My First Year at Ginling College" (Li Hwei-Siu)

NOTES

Preface

1. "Composition Studies Saves the World!" was the title of a talk given by Patricia Bizzell at Pennsylvania State University, University Park, in 2008. She spoke in response to claims about freshman composition made by Stanley Fish in his book *Save the World on Your Own Time* (2008). The rest of the statements are panel titles at the 2008 and 2009 Conferences on College Composition and Communication.

Introduction

1. See Meisner for a critical analysis of the 1989 democracy movement, including its sociopolitical background, the evolution of the movement, and its politico-economic consequences in the early 1990s.

2. According to *Shuowen*《說文》, a Chinese dictionary compiled in the first century A.D., *gui* 鬼 refers to "what humans will metamorphose into after they return" (*Hanyu* 4427). Thus, it actually refers to "ghosts" or "spirits" that the Chinese imagined living in a different world. In the *Analects*, Confucius famously admonishes that a gentleman "who by respect for the Spirits keeps them at a distance may be termed wise" (120), meaning that humans should not probe the other world. Therefore, dubbing Westerners "foreign devils" indicated the prevailing Occidentalism among the Chinese. They believed that foreigners came from a mysteriously unknown, dangerous world to which only the deceased would return and from which the sane would stay away. By inventing a series of terms such as *yangguizi* 洋鬼子, *guiqian* 鬼錢 (devil's money), and *guitong* 鬼統 (devil's weapons), the Chinese portrayed the Western world as part of the other world that ancient Chinese sages warned them to avoid. These terms also confirmed the deep-seated Chinese contempt of almost anything foreign. They considered things from outside of the Middle Kingdom as worthless, thus unworthy of knowing. For a brief cultural history of the term *yangguizi*, see Meng.

3. The Conference on College Composition and Communication (CCCC) issued a statement on second language writing and writers in 2001, urging writing teachers and writing program administrators "to recognize the regular presence of second-language writers in writing classes, to understand their characteristics, and to develop instructional and administrative practices that are sensitive to their linguistic and cultural needs" (CCCC Committee 230). However, the isolationist mentality and the assimilationist stance taken toward both international and generation 1.5 students (those who immigrate to a new country before or during their early teens) persisted in American composition. For discussions of the mentality and corresponding administrative and pedagogical practices and of the issues thereby created for both students and their teachers, see Harklau, Losey, and Siegal; and Matsuda, Ortmeier-Hooper, and You.

4. Mainstream scholarship and graduate training have reciprocally sustained the hegemony of Western rhetoric in American composition studies. Influential U.S. composition histories by James Berlin, Robert Connors, Sharon Crowley, and Thomas Miller all traced the teaching of English composition back to Greek and Roman traditions, without considering non-Western traditions. Only recently, scholars such as Keith Gilyard, David Gold, Jacqueline Jones Royster, Jean C. Williams, Ronald L. Jackson, Elaine Richardson, and Stephen Schneider have started to rewrite U.S. composition history by considering the influence of African American rhetorical tradition. A collection of essays recently edited by Ernest Stromberg also reveal American Indians' rhetorical practices in American composition history. Thus, it is not surprising that almost all graduate programs in rhetoric and composition offer courses in classical Western rhetoric but few offer courses dealing with non-Western traditions. See a 2004 survey of programs in rhetoric and composition studies conducted by Brown, Torres, Enos, and Juergensmeyer.

5. According to Paul Kei Matsuda, ESL writing was part of American composition studies and then was marginalized when teaching English to speakers of other languages (TESOL) became an independent field of research in the 1960s. Ever since, ESL writing has existed in the fissure between composition studies and second language studies, using ESL students in North American universities as its primary subject of research ("Situating ESL Writing"; "Composition Studies").

6. Bill Readings argues that in the context of globalization, universities, particularly Western universities, are operating for their internal interest as bureaucratic systems instead of with any ideological imperatives bound to modern nation-states and, therefore, that Althusser's conception of a university as an ideological state apparatus is no longer applicable. Presumably, Readings's conceptualization of Western universities is correct. I will argue, however, that the function of Chinese universities can still be understood within Althusser's framework, at least before China joined the World Trade Organization (WTO) in 2001, a development that has been widely perceived as marking the country's full entry into economic globalization. Admittedly, with the increase of international trade and the penetration of mass media in China, the country joined the globalization process as early as the late 1970s. But for the entire economic reform and "open-door" period, Chinese universities were consciously engaged in nation building under the slogan of "Four Modernizations," i.e., the modernization of agriculture, industry, national defense, and science and technology for building a powerful, modern socialist country.

7. The discursive inequality is clear in several observations that I made during my archival research. First, English composition was mostly taught by Anglo-American teachers before the 1920s; therefore, they dominated the pedagogical discourse until a significant number of local teachers joined the English teaching profession. Second, a large number of materials related to English teaching were destroyed or lost in wars and political movements in both republican China and the People's Republic. Third, numerous materials are stored at overseas universities and research institutes because of their resourcefulness and historical connection with American missions in China. For example, rich materials related to American mission colleges are stored at some American liberal arts colleges, such as Carleton, Claremont, DePauw, Dickinson, Grinnell, Haverford, Mt. Holyoke, Oberlin, Smith, Wesleyan, Wellesley, and Yale Divinity School (see the American Context of China's Christian Colleges Project).

8. An alternative interpretation of the sentence, provided by Hui Wu, in a review of this book manuscript, is that "writing is the result of the understanding of the Way through reading and is a means to share a writer's insight of the Way to enlighten people."

9. Unless specified otherwise, the term *rhetoric* is used in a broad sense in this book, referring to artful communication through symbols. Therefore, by "rhetorical education" I mean training for effective communication both inside and outside schools.

1. Encountering the Devil's Writing, 1862–1918

1. After China was defeated in the great Sino-Japanese War over Korea in 1894–95, the Chinese intelligentsia became rather dubious about the single-minded promotion of Western learning. Some went to study in Japan and translated Western scientific developments through Japanese texts. See a discussion of the attitudinal change toward Western learning among Chinese literati in Elman's *A Cultural History of Modern Science in China*.

2. Hart played such a crucial role in Tong Wen Guan's operation that William A. P. Martin's *Gewu rumen* 格物入門 (Elements of Natural Philosophy and Chemistry, 1868), the academy's earliest science textbook, was dedicated to Hart "in recognition of his influence in the organization of an institution, so full of hope for the future of China."

3. See Brunero for a historical review of the Chinese Maritime Customs Service, 1854–1949.

4. There were also military degrees in the civil service exam. Examinees were tested in military skills (archery, horse riding, and weight lifting), military policy, and essay writing. See Yu Jingxiang for a brief historical review of the military examination.

5. Western science was first tested in the provincial exam for the BA degree (*xiucai* 秀才) in 1887 (see Du Bose) and in the triennial metropolitan exam for the MA degree (*jüren/kü jǎn* 舉人) in 1889. In the first triennial exam for science students, 32 students passed the preliminary exam and 13 of them came from *Tong Wen Guan* ("Triennial Examination"), indicating the important role that the academy played in Western scientific training in the late Qing.

6. Chain reasoning works in interconnected propositions, such as "If A then B; if B then C." The following is an example of such reasoning: "Therefore as an emperor, he rectifies his heart in order to rectify the court; he rectifies the court in order to rectify hundreds of officials; he rectifies hundreds of officials in order to rectify millions of people; he rectifies millions of people in order to rectify the world." Another example is the quote about the relationship between the self, the state, and the universe from the *Great Learning* in the beginning of this section.

7. The title of this eight-legged essay was quoted from a verse in Confucius's *Analects*—"The Master said, I for my part have never yet seen one who really cared for Goodness, nor one who really abhorred wickedness. One who really cared for Goodness would never let any other consideration come first. One who abhorred wickedness would be so consistently doing Good that wickedness would never have a chance to get at him. Has anyone ever managed to do Good with his whole might even as long as the space of a single day? I think not. Yet I for my part have never

seen anyone give up such an attempt because he had not the strength to go on. It may well have happened, but I for my part have never seen it" (103). Comparing the verse to Tang Xianzu's essay, one can clearly see the way Tang "translated" the Confucian verse—a mediation of Confucius's original thought, Tang's own interpretation, and the appropriate codes that govern the exam discourse.

8. Such a question, given for the 1685 metropolitan exam, and the answer of a successful student, Lu Kentang, who later passed the palace exam with the highest honor, are quoted in full in Chang Weijen, "Qingdai". Also see Man-Cheong for a detailed analysis of three policy essays written in the 1761 palace exam.

9. See a sample discourse essay written by a successful candidate, Shang Yanying, in the 1903 metropolitan exam, in Shang 269–70.

10. The writing pedagogy at elementary level was called *zhui zi fa* 綴字法, literally meaning "connecting characters." William A. P. Martin gave a brief account of this pedagogy in his *Report on the System of Public Instruction in China*. He illustrated the pedagogy with some typical exercises that Chinese students performed in the late Qing. Students first practiced connecting a simple subject with a predicate. For example, the teacher writes "wind blows," and the pupil adds "rain falls;" the teacher writes "rivers are long," and the pupil adds "seas are deep." Then students practiced more complex structures. For example, the teacher writes, "The Emperor's grace is vast as heaven and earth," and the pupil matches it with "The Sovereign's favor is profound as lake and sea" (18).

11. An alternative to the civil exam-oriented education also existed in the late Qing. Some Confucian literati, such as Woren, argued that instead of producing future officials, education should set its primary goal on *xiushen* 修身, or self-cultivation, to cultivate in students the desired virtues. Traditional virtues such as benevolence and filial piety could be developed through reading classics, reflecting upon one's daily behaviors, and recording one's thoughts everyday. Some academies in the low Yangtze region adopted this neoclassicist model (Keenan). Students studied classical works beyond the neo-Confucian canon, such as philology from the Han dynasty, belle lettres and composition from the Tongcheng literary school, and history, mathematics, and astronomy. Instead of emphasizing recitation, the teacher often analyzed the readings at the vocabulary level through lectures, believing that philology would help to clarify the meanings of the classics. In those academies, students wrote monthly eight-legged essays and kept a diary reflecting upon their daily readings and behaviors. Reading and writing in those academies thus exposed the students to more diversified Chinese rhetorical styles and encouraged them to develop their own thoughts.

12. See a survey of Mohist rhetorical theory and practice in Xing Lu (*Rhetoric in Ancient China*).

13. See a comprehensive survey of the late Qing educational reform that modeled the Western school system in Cai Yuanpei et al.

14. However, students of the Capital Teachers Learning Institute practiced English writing on topics similarly found in the civil exam, dealing with Confucian moral philosophy and state making. For example, the English essay topic for the graduating class of the translation college was a quote from the *Analects*, "Pondering over it [public business] untiringly at home; carrying it out loyally when the time comes" (Beijing daxue 276; Confucius 167).

15. During the Sino-Japanese War (1931–45), enrollment at mission colleges reached an unprecedented high (20 percent in 1941) because the Japanese were generally careful in respecting American properties and kept their interference with the academic work at the mission colleges to a minimum (Caldwell).

16. Two points are worthy of notice here about missionary education and the civil service exam. First, although Chinese classics were taught in mission schools, mission educators were rather reserved about their students taking the exam. They discouraged Chinese Christians from taking it on several grounds: the heathen rituals of Confucius-worshipping performed after the exam, the difficulty of observing Sabbath properly during the exam months, the expenditure of time and money, and the temptations to pride and worldliness that the exam would bring to students (Hartwell). Second, missionaries took advantage of the civil service exam by disseminating Christian ideology among Chinese literati, whom they considered the hardest to convert. Missionaries handed out Christian tracts and handbills during and after triennial metropolitan exams. They encouraged students to submit Chinese essays on several topics after they had carefully studied the Christian literature. They rewarded those who displayed some understanding of Christianity with cash prizes. See Hill for reports of such proselytizing activities in Taiyuan of Shanxi Province and for a discussion of student essays on Christianity ("The Triennial Examinations for the Ku Jan Degree"; "The Kü Jǎn Examination").

17. In a survey of 35 mission and 20 government schools conducted in 1919, Elam J. Anderson attributed Chinese students' low English proficiency to several reasons: the limited length of time devoted to English instruction, low-level middle school English curricula, English teachers with low credentials, and outdated textbooks and pedagogies imported from overseas.

18. See the diverse composition textbooks used at mission colleges in Appendix A.

19. See Ye Junjian's account of both his struggles and his liberation when shifting from reading the Confucian canon to reading about foreign matters in his English classes in the 1920s (Ye, "Xuexi").

20. See composition courses offered at mission colleges in Appendix A.

21. See Appendix B for samples of corrected student essays from Ginling College in 1923.

22. See courses that combined literature and composition in Appendix A.

23. Writing across the curriculum also took place at some state universities. See Li Funing (Li, "Reminiscences") and Zhao Zhaoxiong (Zhao) for their experiences of writing English in content courses at National Hsinghua University in the 1920s and the 1930s.

24. See Crofts for his experience of studying in a British-controlled secondary school in Chefoo (Qüfu) of Shandong Province.

2. Writing and Decolonization, 1919–49

1. See Tomasi for a history of Western rhetoric in Japan and its interactions with sociopolitical forces that eventually gave rise to modern Japanese literature and culture.

2. Students at the teachers' college studied memorials, biographies, rhymed prose, and poetry in their third year and historical evolution of traditional Chinese genres in their fourth year. See Beijing daxue 92.

3. The stylistic innovations in vernacular Chinese include parenthetical clauses and interjections, elaborate embedding of attributives and transposition of clauses, fragmentation and disjunction, and even pseudo-parallelism. See Gunn.

4. The new school curriculum standards were implemented nationwide in 1928. According to the new standards, one of the goals for Chinese language education in both junior and senior middle schools was "to develop the ability of using the vernacular Chinese to articulate matters and express feelings freely" (cited in Li and Gu 127) rather than the ability of using classical Chinese and rhymed styles (*yunwen* 韻文). Hu Shi prepared the reading list for both junior and senior middle schools. The list included both classical and modern works that consisted of such genres as prose, novels, short stories, dramas, songs, and poems. See the outline standards of the new school curriculum in Curriculum Committee.

5. The Educational Association of China was founded in 1890 by foreign mission educators to coordinate mission schools and textbook publishing in China. Because of its foreign and evangelic nature, the organization changed its name to the Christian Educational Association of China in 1915.

6. The disciplinary nature of the ritual of honesty was most clearly seen at St. John's College. For years, the college prescribed rules for student behaviors in its annual catalogs. For example, it stated in the "discipline" section of the 1907 catalog, "Dishonesty in examinations, card-playing, cigarette smoking, wine drinking, gambling, and reading improper literature are considered serious offences, and will be punished with great severity" (34).

7. Religious and philosophical disputation was studied and practiced in Chinese Buddhist monasteries during the early and medieval periods (until the twelfth century). Indian Buddhist texts on logic and disputation, particularly those of the Nyaya School, were translated and widely studied (Garrett, "Chinese Buddhist"). See a discussion of such a text, *Nyaya Sutra*, in Lloyd.

8. Public speaking was practiced in Chinese as well. As early as 1891, students of Tengchow College wrote policy essays and delivered them orally in their literary society. According to its school catalog, "performers are appointed and subjects assigned two weeks previous. Every student, from the time of his admission until the senior year, is required to perform in order. The teachers attend as critics and judges. The students are not only trained to write and speak but also to conduct business according to parliamentary rules" (Tengchow College 6).

9. See Appendix A for the significant decrease in both the number and the kinds of composition courses offered in mission colleges during the war with Japan. As different parts of the country were taken over by the Japanese at different times, the direct impact of the war on different colleges came at varying moments.

10. The book was a published version of Faucett's Ph.D. dissertation at the University of Chicago with a more theoretical title, "The Revision of Scientific Language Principles for Oriental Application in the Teaching of English" (1926).

11. See "Introduction to Volume IV" in Smith for a brief discussion of the impact of the Oxford English Course series in different parts of the world.

3. Writing and the Proletarian Revolution, 1950–76

1. In Taiwan, the Nationalist-controlled province, colleges continued to offer English composition as a discrete course. According to Li Hongli (personal interview), who studied English in the 1950s and the 1960s and taught English in Taiwanese

middle schools and colleges until 2000, composition continued to be offered to English-major freshmen after 1950. After they had studied English reading, writing, and conversation intensively in their first year, students moved on to study American and British literature and culture.

2. To support the civil rights movement in the United States, Mao Zedong delivered the speech "Supporting the Blacks' Struggles against Racial Discriminations in the United States" in 1963 (*Mao Zedong waijiao*). After Martin Luther King Jr. was assassinated in 1968, the Chinese Communist Party issued an announcement to "support the blacks' struggle against violence" and organized a mass rally involving more than a million people in Tian'anmen Square.

3. See debates on the issue of authentic language use in the Soviet English textbooks at Zhongshan University in Wang Zongyan ("Liuge").

4. For a teacher's perspective in teaching college English composition in the 1950s, see Ge Chuangui ("Yingyu").

5. Works by Chinese authors, notably Mao Zedong's writings, were originally written in Chinese and then translated jointly by domestic and foreign scholars.

6. The eight-volume textbook was a collective endeavor, involving more than twenty writers. Xu Guozhang, Yu Dayin, and Xu Yanmou served as the head writers. Xu Guozhang was responsible for the first four volumes (1962), Yu Dayin for volumes 5 and 6 (1964), and Xu Yanmou for volumes 7 and 8 (1964).

7. Chen Lin et al.'s *Daxue yingyu keben* (1957) shares a similar pedagogical approach with Xu Guozhang et al.'s eight-volume *Yingyu* (1962–64) under the influence of structural linguistics. One of its objectives was to permit "students [to] gain a well-round development (listening comprehension, speaking, writing, and reading) through exercises in phonetics, grammar, and vocabulary."

8. The earliest adoption of structuralism in English textbook writing in China was probably by Lin Yutang (1895–1976), who graduated from the University of Leipzig with a Ph.D. in linguistics. In *Kaiming yingwen duben* (1929) and its later revision *Kaiming di'er yingwen duben* (1933) for secondary schools, Ling emphasizes oral work, grammar, phonetics, and reading. He also highlights the primacy of oral English and encourages teachers to use the question-and-answer method to develop students' oral ability. Regarding grammar, he takes a descriptive stand, stating that "grammar is *the correct and accurate observation of the forms and usage of words*" (*Kaiming di'er* 10, emphasis original). In terms of pronunciation, students conduct phonetic analysis by transcribing given words according to the International Phonetic Alphabet "to give the students a vivid and accurate idea of the normal sound-values of the vowels, diphthongs and consonants" (11). Exercises such as the translation and dictation of sentences play a subservient role, employed "to test accuracy of hearing and spelling" (13).

9. A new section called "word study" was added in volumes 2 and 3 to help students master some commonly used verbs.

10. There are other exercises, such as "revision exercises" and "oral and written work." However, they appear rather irregularly across the first four volumes of *Yingyu*. For example, "oral and written work" only appears in volume 3. In other volumes, it becomes part of the "exercises to the text."

11. The Red Army refers to military forces led by the Chinese Communist Party before 1937. It was founded on August 1, 1927, during the Nanchang Uprising when troops of the Nationalists rebelled under the leadership of Zhu De and Zhou Enlai.

In 1937, the Communist military forces were nominally integrated into the National Revolutionary Army of the Republic of China to combat the Japanese invaders. They formed the Eighth Route Army and the New Fourth Army units. After the Anti-Japanese War, the Communists merged the two groups and renamed its forces the People's Liberation Army, intending to liberate Chinese people from the oppression of feudalism, imperialism, and bureaucratic capitalism.

12. The concept of "socialist realism" originated from a speech given by Andrei Zhdanov at the first All-Union Congress of Soviet Writers, held in Moscow in August 1934. According to the subsequent formulation of a specific statute in the Writers' Union constitution, an artist needs to provide "a truthful, historically concrete representation of reality in its revolutionary development," and "[a]t the same time, truthfulness and historical concreteness of artistic representation of reality must (or should) be combined with the task of ideologically remaking and training the laboring people in the spirit of socialism" (qtd. in Chung x). When the concept was introduced into and practiced in other countries, it went through reformulation processes to adapt to local cultural traditions and political realities. See Chung for comparative studies of the concept's theoretical reformulations and the concept-inspired literary practices in China, East Germany, and the former Soviet Union.

13. See Fanon for the efficacy of the proletarian rhetoric in the decolonization of African countries.

14. Surely, proletarian rhetoric as formulated by Mao Zedong and Liu Shaoqi before 1949 was leftist in the eyes of many people now and then, particularly Western observers. However, it was not as leftist as it later evolved into in the late 1950s. The extremely leftist rhetoric prompted the Great Leap Forward movement and reached its zenith during the Cultural Revolution.

15. The assertion that "imperialism and all reactionaries are paper tigers" was first brought up by Mao Zedong in August of 1946 in an interview with American journalist Anna Louise Strong. By dubbing reactionaries, or enemies of the masses, as "paper tigers," Mao's assertion greatly inspired the Communist military forces and the people who stood with the Communists in the ongoing civil war between the Communists and the Nationalists (1946–49). See the complete interview with Strong in Mao Zedong, "Talk".

16. The three time-honored texts (*lao san pian* 老三篇) were written during the Anti-Japanese War period (1931–45). "Serve the People" (1944) was a speech delivered to commemorate a Communist soldier's death. The soldier was praised for his wholehearted devotion to the cause of the masses. "In Memory of Norman Bethune" (1939) is Mao's remembrance of Bethune as another unselfish Communist soldier and a representative of internationalism. Bethune, a Canadian physician, was sent by the Canadian Communist Party to assist the Chinese in combating Japanese invaders in 1938. He died in 1939 of blood poisoning from a cut received while performing surgery. "The Foolish Old Man Who Removed the Mountains" (1945) was a speech delivered at the seventh CCP National Congress. In the speech, Mao used a Chinese fairy tale about a foolish old man who was determined to remove two mountains from in front of his house. In the tale, the old man's determination deeply touched God, so God helped him to remove the mountains. Mao compared the two mountains to imperialism and feudalism that the Chinese people had to remove at the moment.

He encouraged the party to be determined and to overcome difficulties along the way of removing the two "mountains."

17. See Renmin jiaoyu for criticisms of a series of arguments that were raised in the early 1960s against the heavy use of politically charged texts and translated works in foreign language classrooms.

4. Writing and the Four Modernizations, 1977–90

1. See Liu Yunhua; Yan Binggang; and Martin, *Hanlin Papers*, for missionaries' negotiations with Confucian thought since the seventeenth century.

2. The text retained elements of current-traditional rhetoric. This is clear from the section headings, where written modes and style hold preeminent positions: "Introduction," "Materials," "Theme," "Structure," "Language," "Narration and Expression of Emotion," "Description and Conversation," "Commentary and Exposition," "Revision," and "Style of Writing."

3. The term "new long march" alludes to the historical Long March (*changzheng* 长征), a massive military retreat undertaken by the Red Armies of the Communist Party to evade the pursuit of the Nationalist Army between 1934 and 1936. The Red Armies escaped in a circling retreat to the west and north, which reportedly traversed some 12,500 kilometers (8,000 miles) over 370 days. As the route passed through some of the most difficult terrain of western China, "long march" has become a general term referring to daunting tasks in the national modernization project.

4. See Heilker for a discussion of the Western essay tradition.

5. A notional-functional syllabus is a way of organizing a language-learning curriculum. In such a syllabus, instruction is organized in terms of *notions* and *functions* rather than in terms of grammatical structures. In this model, a *notion* is a particular context in which people communicate. A *function* is a specific purpose for a speaker in a given context. For example, the "notion" of shopping requires numerous language "functions," such as asking about prices or features of a product and bargaining.

6. Most of the English writing books published between 1976 and 1987 were about writing for specific or practical purposes, including letters, correspondence in international trade and business, scientific abstracts, papers, and documents. These topics reflect the urgent demands for practical writing ability in Chinese society in the early years of the "open door" era.

7. The book was so popular that it had its fifth printing by 1991, its second edition in 1994, its Chinese edition in 1997, and its twenty-third printing in 2000. By 2005, over 1.1 million copies had been sold.

8. These seven U.S. composition texts are *American English Rhetoric* (Robert Bander, 1971), *The Random House Handbook* (Frederick Crews, 1974), *Heath's College Handbook of Composition* (Langdon Elsbree, Frederick Bracher, and Nell Altizer, 1977), *The Little Brown Handbook* (H. Ramsey Fowler, 1980), *Harbrace College Handbook* (John Hodges and Mary Whitten, 1977), *Subject and Structure* (John Wasson, 1970), and *Practical English Handbook* (Floyd Watkins, William Dillingham, and Edwin Martin, 1974). The British sources include *From Paragraph to Essay* (Maurice Imhoof and Herman Hudson, 1976), *Designs in Prose* (Walter Nash, 1980), and *A Short Guide to English Style* (Alan Warner, 1961).

9. See a discussion of the origin of the intensive reading course in Gui Shichun, "Yingyong."

10. In *The Principles of Language-Study* (1921/1964), Palmer defines intensive reading as a pedagogical approach in which students "take a text, study it line by line, referring at every moment to our dictionary and our grammar, comparing, analyzing, translating, and retaining every expression that it contains" (111).

11. See Cooper and Liu for Grace Liu's criticisms of the English reading pedagogy in Chinese colleges in the 1950s. She considered it a continuation of the reading pedagogy used in republican China, which centered on grammar and translation.

12. Classical Chinese writing uses minimal punctuation symbols to mark sentences and no markers for paragraphing.

13. The CLT approach was also featured in some imported texts. The most widely used foreign text in Chinese colleges was Longman's *New Concept English* (1967) by Louis George Alexander. See Liu Tianyou and Lin Jingyi for a report on how the text was used at Shanghai Teachers' College in the 1980s.

14. See Chen Chuanguo and Jia Yuxin for the rationale of *Gongneng yingyu jiaocheng* and suggested classroom activities.

15. The pedagogical procedures in teaching the listening task and the writing task (in the next paragraph) were described by Xiao Huiyun, who participated in the CECL project.

16. The Four Cardinal Principles were completely inherited from the Maoist period; the principles refer to the socialist road, the people's democratic dictatorship, the leadership of the Communist Party, and the thought of Marxism-Leninism and Mao Zedong.

5. Writing and Socialism with Chinese Characteristics, 1991–2008

1. China's Compulsory Education Law (1986) guaranteed school-age children the right to receive at least nine years of education (a six-year primary education and a three-year secondary education). A large number of middle school students would not go to high school at the end of their three-year secondary education. Thus, the percentage of college-age youths (age 18–21) going to college was actually 3.4 percent in 1990 and 11.5 percent in 2000 (Jiaoyubu fazhan).

2. English teaching started in the third grade in some elementary schools in 2002. Thus, students entering college in 2011 will have studied English for nine years.

3. See Spolsky for the history of TOEFL and TWE.

4. Two news reports related to the CET are worthy of notice here. These reports were widely circulated in Chinese colleges. According to Daozou, he boycotted the test by writing a Chinese essay in the answer sheet for the CET writing task in 2005. According to another report by Xu Li, Wang Qi, and Yao Shuo'ang, on 28 February 2006, due to his failure to pass the CET-4, a senior student of Chengdu University of Electronic Science and Technology committed suicide by jumping off a five-story building.

5. See Martin (*The Chinese*) for an elaborated discussion of this rhetorical strategy in traditional Chinese prose writing.

6. See an introduction to these two major national English-speaking contests in Su, Wang, and Fan.

7. After experimenting with the length approach at Guangdong University of Foreign Studies and other institutions for nine years, Zheng Chao and his colleagues published *Yingyu xiezuo tongyong jiaocheng* in 2008. Rather than teaching writing in a structuralist orientation, such as the traditional gradation from sentences to paragraphs and discourses, the course book focused on meaning making by teaching students multiple genres, such as essay, fiction, and news story. The authors believed that extensive practice in multiple genres would lead to improved writing even in short exam essays.

8. The dominance of positivism in English composition research can be clearly seen in three proceedings that came out of the Chinese EFL Writing Teaching and Research Conferences from 2003 to 2006 (Hu Xiaohua; Wang Lifei and Zhang Zoucheng; Zheng Chao, *Yi xie cu xue*). Gao Yihong, Li Lichun, and Lü Jun also note the positivist trend in applied linguistics research in China, evidenced by the predominant use of the quantitative rather than the qualitative approach.

9. Allegedly, Ge Chuangui was the first person to argue for the Chinese variety of English. He stated in an article in 1980: "Every country is unique to some extent. Whether in old or in new China, for example, we have China-specific things to express when we speak or write in English, such as *Four Books* (*si shu*), eight-legged essay (*baguwen*), May Fourth Movement (*wusi yundong*), xiucai (*xiucai*), Mr. Science (*sai xiansheng*), baihua (*baihua*), ideological remoulding (*sixiang gaizao*), and four modernizations (*sige xiandai hua*). All these translated terms are words of China English rather than Chinese English or Chinglish" ("Mantan" 2).

6. Writing in Our Tongue

1. See a further discussion of the nationwide experiment in a book chapter that I authored, "Globalization and the Politics of Teaching EFL Writing" (2006).

2. *Post-Fordism* refers to the dominant system of economic production, consumption, and associated socioeconomic phenomena in most industrialized countries since the late twentieth century. Post-Fordism departs from Fordism, a system formulated in Henry Ford's automotive factories, where workers on a production line perform specialized tasks repetitively.

3. According to the National Bureau of Statistics of China, the number of people who received secondary or tertiary education rose from 371.9 million in 1990 to 685.8 million in 2005 (Zhonghua renmin). As English was a compulsory course for secondary and tertiary education, the statistics indicate that by 2005 more than 300 million Chinese had studied English as a school subject for at least three years.

WORKS CITED

Alberca, Wilfredo L. "English Language Teaching in the Philippines during the Early American Period: Lessons from the Thomasites." *Philippine Journal of Linguistics* 25.1–2 (1994): 53–74.

Alexander, Louis George. *New Concept English*. London: Longman, 1967.

Allen, Kate. "The College English Test Band Four Writing Section: The Constraints on Reliability in a Large-Scale Writing Test." *Asian Pacific Journal of Education* 17.1 (1997): 86–95.

Althusser, Louis. "Selected Texts." *Ideology*. Ed. Terry Eagleton. New York: Longman, 1994. 87–111.

The American Context of China's Christian Colleges Project. "The American Context of Chinese Christian Colleges and Schools." 5 Nov. 2004 <http://www.library.yale.edu/div/colleges>.

Anderson, Elam J. *English Teaching Efficiency in China*. Shanghai: Commercial, 1925.

Aristotle. *On Rhetoric: A Theory of Civic Discourse*. Trans. George A. Kennedy. New York: Oxford UP, 1991.

Arnold, Sarah Louise, and George Lyman Kittredge. *The Mother Tongue*. Vol. 1, *Lessons in Speaking, Reading and Writing English*. Rev. ed. Boston: Ginn, 1908.

Arnot, R. Page. "The Great Leap Forward." *Daxue san nianji yingyu keben.* 大學三年級英語課本 [English Textbook for the Juniors]. Nanjing daxue waiyuxi san nianji yingyu jiaocai bianzhuan weiyuanhui 南京大學外語系三年級英語教材編撰委員會 [English Textbook Compiling Committee, Juniors of the Nanjing University Foreign Languages Department]. Beijing: Shidai Chubanshe, 1960. 3–10.

"Autobiography." 1923. Lindquist Papers.

Beijing daxue 北京大學 [Beijing University]. *Beijing daxue shiliao diyi juan (1898–1911)* 北京大學史料第一卷 (1898–1911) [Beijing University Archives, vol. 1 (1898–1911)]. Beijing: Beijing daxue chubanshe, 1993.

Beijing shifan daxue zhongwenxi 北京師範大學中文系 [Beijing Normal University Chinese Department]. *Xiezuo jichu zhishi* 寫作基礎知識 [Essentials in Writing]. Beijing: Beijing chubanshe, 1979.

Beijing waiguoyu xueyuan 北京外國語學院 [Beijing Foreign Language Institute]. *Yingyu jiaokeshu (xiaolei shiyong)* 英語教科書 (校內使用) [English Textbook (for Use within the Institute)]. Beijing: Beijing waiguoyu xueyuan, 1962.

Benda, Jonathan P. "Rhetorical Education in Martial-Law Taiwan: A Case Study of Tunghai University." The 10th Biennial Conference of the Rhetoric Society of America. Las Vegas, Nev., 23 May 2002.

Berlin, James. *Rhetoric and Reality: Writing Instruction in American Colleges, 1900–1985*. Carbondale: Southern Illinois UP, 1987.

———. *Writing Instruction in Nineteenth-Century American Colleges*. Carbondale: Southern Illinois UP, 1984.

Bernstein, Basil. *The Structuring of Pedagogic Discourse.* New York: Routledge, 1990.

Bhabha, Homi. *The Location of Culture.* New York: Routledge, 2004.

Bizzell, Patricia. "'Contact Zone' and English Studies." *College English* 65.2 (1994): 163–69.

Bourdieu, Pierre. *Language and Symbolic Power.* Cambridge: Harvard UP, 1991.

Brereton, John C. *The Origins of Composition Studies in the American College, 1875–1925: A Documentary History.* Pittsburgh: U of Pittsburgh P, 1995.

Brockman, F. S. "How to Retain to the Church the Service of English-Speaking Chinese Christians." *Chinese Recorder* 34.7 (1903): 319–29.

Brooke, Robert. "Underlife and Writing Instruction." *College Composition and Communication* 38.2 (1987): 141–53.

Brown, Stuart C., Monica F. Torres, Theresa Enos, and Erik Juergensmeyer. "Mapping a Landscape: The 2004 Survey of MA Programs in Rhetoric and Composition Studies." *Rhetoric Review* 24.1 (2005): 5–12.

———. "2004 Survey of Master's Programs in Rhetoric and Composition Studies." *Rhetoric Review* 24.1 (2005): 13–127.

Brown, Wenzell. "An Analysis of Failures in the English Entrance Examinations of Lingnan University." *Chinese Recorder* 72 (February 1941): 75–77.

Brunero, Donna. *Britain's Imperial Cornerstone in China: The Chinese Maritime Customs Service, 1854–1949.* New York: Routledge, 2006.

Burke, Kenneth. *On Symbols and Society.* Ed. Joseph Gusfield. Chicago: U of Chicago P, 1989.

Cai Jigang 蔡基剛. *Yingyu kaoshi gaofen zuowen* 英語考試高分作文 [High-Score Compositions for English Tests]. Shanghai: Shanghai jiaotong daxue chubanshe, 1994.

———. *Yingyu shiju zuowen fa* 英語十句作文法 [A Ten-Sentence Approach to English Composition]. Shanghai: Fudan daxue chubanshe, 1999.

———. *Yingyu wuduan zuowen fa* 英語五段作文法 [A Five-Paragraph Approach to English Composition]. Shanghai: Fudan daxue chubanshe, 2002.

———. *Yingyu xiezuo gaofen zhidao* 英語寫作高分指導 [A Guide to High-Score English Compositions]. Shanghai: Shanghai jiaotong daxue chubanshe, 1998.

Cai Yuanpei et al., eds. *Wanqing sanshiwu nian yi lai zhi zhongguo jiaoyu (1897–1931)* [Chinese Education since the Late Qing (1897–1931)]. Hong Kong: Longmen shudian, 1969.

Caldwell, Oliver J. "Chinese Universities and the War." *School and Society* 55 (1942): 230–33.

Campbell, George. "The Philosophy of Rhetoric." *The Rhetoric of Blair, Campbell, and Whately.* Ed. James L. Golden and Edward P. J. Corbett. Carbondale: Southern Illinois UP, 1990. 143–271.

Canagarajah, Suresh. *A Geopolitics of Academic Writing.* Pittsburgh: U of Pittsburgh P, 2002.

———. "'Nondiscursive' Requirements in Academic Publishing, Material Resources of Periphery Scholars, and the Politics of Knowledge Production." *Written Communication* 13.4 (1996): 435–72.

———. "The Place of World Englishes in Composition: Pluralization Continued." *College Composition and Communication* 57.4 (2006): 586–619.

———. *Resisting Linguistic Imperialism in English Teaching*. New York: Oxford UP, 1999.

———. "Toward a Writing Pedagogy of Shuttling between Languages: Learning from Multilingual Writers." *College English* 58.6 (2006): 589–604.

Canton Christian College. *Catalogue, 1909–1910*. Canton, 1909.

———. *Catalogue, 1923–1924*. Canton, 1923.

———. *Catalogue of the College Department*. Canton, 1915.

Cao Weifeng曹未風. *Xinbian dayi yingwen* 新編大一英文 [New Freshman English]. Shanghai: Shanwu yingshuguan, 1950.

CCCC Committee on Second Language Writing. "CCCC Statement on Second Language Writing and Writers." *Journal of Second Language Writing* 10.4 (2001): 229–33.

Chang, Iris. *The Rape of Nanking: The Forgotten Holocaust of World War II*. New York: Penguin, 1998.

Chang Weijen. "Qingdai de faxue jiaoyue (shang)" 清代的法學教育(上) [Legal Education in Qing China (Part 1)]. *Guoli Taiwan daxue faxue luncong* 國立臺灣大學法學論叢 [National Taiwan University Journal of Legal Studies] 18.1 (1988): 7–24.

Chang, Wejen. "Legal Education in Ch'ing China." *Education and Society in Late Imperial China, 1600–1900*. Ed. Benjamin Elman and Alexander Woodside. Berkeley: U California P, 1994. 292–339.

Chen Chuanguo 陳傳國 and Jia Yuxin 賈玉新. "Gongneng jiaoxue fa de ketang jiaoji huodong" 功能教學法的課堂交際活動 [Communicative Activities in Classes That Use the Functional Approach]. *Jichu yingyu jiaoxue lunwenji* 基礎英語教學論文集 [Collected Papers on Teaching English to Chinese Students: Approaches and Methods at the Foundation Stage]. Ed. Hu Wenzhong 胡文仲. Beijing: Waiyu jaoxue yu yanjiu chubanshe, 1985. 68–78.

Chen Guh-Hsiang. "My First Year at Ginling College." 1923. Lindquist Papers.

Chen Jiebai 陳介白. *Xin zhu xiucixue* 新著修辭學 [New Rhetoric]. Shanghai: Shijie shuju, 1936.

Chen Lin 陳琳 et al. *Daxue yingyu keben* 大學英語課本 [College English Textbook]. Beijing: Shidai chubanshe, 1957.

Chen Qingchang 陳慶昌, Yang Huizhong 楊惠中, and Huang Renjie 黃人傑. "Keji waiyu shehui xuyao diaocha" 科技外語社會需要調查 [An Investigation of the Social Need for Foreign Languages for Scientific Purposes]. *Waiyu jiaoxue yu yanjiu* 外語教學與研究 [Foreign Language Teaching and Research] 2 (1984): 64–68.

Chen Wangdao 陳望道. *Zuowen fa jiangyi* 作文法講義 [Lectures on Written Composition]. Shanghai: Minzhi shuju, 1922.

Chen Yilun 陳羽綸, ed. *Shi tu pian: Zhuanjia xuezhe jiaoshou tan yingyu xuexi* 識途篇：專家、學者、教授談英語學習 [Knowing Your Way: Experts, Scholars, and Professors Talk about English Learning]. Beijing: Shanwu yingshuguan, 2000.

Chen Zhongsheng 陳中繩. "Ba yikao benzhuyu yuanze tigao yibu, geng youxiao de yingyong zijue bijiaofa" 把"依靠本族語原則"提高一步，更有效地應用"自覺比較法" [To Further Promote the Mother Tongue–Based Principle and to More Effectively Use the Contrastive Method]. *Waiyu jiaoxue yu fanyi* 外語教學與翻譯 [Foreign Language Teaching and Translation] 7 (1959): 1–5.

China English Language Education Association. *ELT in China: Papers Presented at the International Symposium on Teaching English in the Chinese Context*

(ISTEC), Guangzhou, China, 1985. Beijing: Foreign Language Teaching and Research, 1990.

Chou Kang-mei, Shen Chiung-sheng, and Lu Shih-shih. "The Labor Program" (ms.). Archives of the United Board for Christian Higher Education in Asia—Addendum. RG 11A, Series IV, Box 98A, Folder 1375: "Students, Labor, 1957–1965." Yale Divinity School Lib., New Haven, Conn.

Christian College in China. *Catalogue, 1900–1911.* Macao: "China Mail" Office, 1900.

Chung, Hilary, ed. *In the Party Spirit: Socialist Realism and Literary Practice in the Soviet Union, East Germany and China.* Amsterdam: Rodopi, 1996.

Cicero. *On Oratory and Orators.* Trans. and ed. J. S. Watson. Carbondale: Southern Illinois UP, 1970.

Clippinger, Erle E. *Written and Spoken English: A Course in Composition and Rhetoric.* Boston: Silver, Burdett, 1917.

"Communiqué of the Third Plenary Session of the Eleventh Central Committee of the Communist Party of China." *Beijing Review,* 29 December 1978.

Confucius. *The Analects of Confucius.* Trans. Arthur Waley. Vintage, 1989.

———. "The Great Learning." *Confucian Analects, The Great Learning and The Doctrine of the Mean.* Trans. James Legge. New York: Dover Publications, 1971. 355–81.

Connors, Robert. *Composition-Rhetoric: Backgrounds, Theory, and Pedagogy.* Pittsburgh: U. of Pittsburgh P, 1997.

———. "The Rise and Fall of the Modes of Discourse." *College Communication and Composition* 32 (1981): 444–55.

———. *Selected Essays of Robert Connors.* Ed. Lisa Ede and Andrea A. Lunsford. New York: Bedford/St. Martin's, 2003.

Cooper, Eleanor McCallie, and William Liu. *Grace in China: An American Woman beyond the Great Wall, 1934–1974.* Montgomery, Ala.: Black Belt, 1999.

Cope, Bill, and Mary Kalantzis, eds. *Multiliteracies: Literacy Learning and the Design of Social Futures.* New York: Routledge, 1999.

Courses Offered by Ginling College, Hangchow Christian College, University of Nanking, University of Shanghai, Souchow University and St. John's University. Shanghai, 1938.

Crofts, Alfred. "Vernacular of an English School in the Orient." *American Speech* 10.1 (1935): 24–29.

Crook, David. "School Examinations in China." *Eastern Horizon* 14.4 (1975): 22–26.

Crowley, Sharon. "Linguistics and Composition Instruction, 1950–1980." *Written Communication* 6.4 (1989): 480–505.

———. *The Methodical Memory: Invention in Current-Traditional Rhetoric.* Carbondale: Southern Illinois UP, 1990.

Curriculum Committee of the Conference of Federated Provincial Associations of China. *The Outline Standards of the New System Curriculum.* Shanghai: Commercial, 1925.

Dai Liuling 戴鎦齡. "Lue tan tigao xuesheng waiyu xiezuo nengli wenti" 略談提高學生外語寫作能力問題 [A Brief Discussion of Issues in Enhancing Students' Foreign Language Writing Ability]. *Waiyu jiaoxue yu yanjiu* 外語教學與研究 [Foreign Language Teaching and Research] 1 (1962): 11–12.

Daozou de congming ya 倒走的聰明鴨 [Clever Duck That Walks Backward]. "Zuihou yici kao siji wo yong zhongwen dati chedi zaofan" 最後一次考四級我用中文答題徹

底造反 [I Rebelled by Giving Chinese Answers in My Last College English Test]. *Xinlang jiaoyu* 新浪教育 [Sina Education]. 2005. 25 Oct. 2006 <http://edu.sina.com.cn/exam/2005–10–27/11439653.html>.

Davin, Delia. "Imperialism and the Diffusion of Liberal Thought: British Influences on Chinese Education." *Chinese Education and the Industrialized World*. Ed. Ruth Hayhoe and Marianne Bastid. New York: M. E. Sharpe, 1987. 33–56.

Daxue yingyu jiaoxue dagang xiuding gongzuozu《大學英語教學大綱》修訂工作組 [College English Syllabus Revision Team]. *Daxue yingyu jiaoxue dagang (gaodeng xuexiao ligongke benke yong)* 大學英語教學大綱（高等學校理工科本科用）[College English Syllabus (for Science and Engineering Students)]. Beijing: Gaodeng jiaoyu chubanshe, 1985.

———. *Daxue yingyu jiaoxue dagan (xiuding ben) (gaodeng xuexiao benke yong)*. 大學英語教學大綱［修訂本］（高等學校本科用）[English Syllabus for Four-Year Colleges]. Rev. ed. Beijing: Gaodeng jaoyu chubanshe, 1999.

Daxue yingyu si liu ji biaozhun kaoshi sheji zu 大學英語四、六級標準考試設計組 [College English Test Design Team]. *Daxue yingyu siji kaoshi dagang ji yangti* 大學英語四級考試大綱及樣題 [College English Band-4 Test Syllabus and Sample Tests]. Shanghai: Shanghai waiyu jiaoyu chubanshe, 1994.

Ding Wangdao丁往道. "Guanyu jichu jieduan de xiezuo lianxi he xiezuo ke" 關於基礎階段的寫作練習和寫作課 [On Writing Exercises and the Writing Class at the Foundational Stage]. *Jichu yingyu jiaoxue lunwenji* 基礎英語教學論文集 [Collected Papers on Teaching English to Chinese Students: Approaches and Methods at the Foundation Stage]. Ed. Hu Wenzhong 胡文仲. Beijing: Waiyu jiaoxue yu yanjiu chubanshe, 1985. 248–54.

———. "Lue tan biyu he biyu ke" 略談筆語和筆語課 [A Brief Discussion of English Writing and the Writing Class]. *Waiyu jiaoxue yu yanjiu* 外語教學與研究 [Foreign Language Teaching and Research] 3.4 (1959): 213–14.

——— et al. *Yingyu xiezuo shouce* 英語寫作手冊 [A College Handbook of Composition]. Beijing: Waiyu jiaoxue yu yanjiu chubanshe, 1984.

Dong Chuncai 董純才. "Gaige women de zhongxue yuwen jiaoxue" 改革我們的中學語文教學 [To Reform Our Middle-School Chinese Language Teaching]. *Zhongxue yuwen jiaoxue de gaijing* 中學語文教學的改進 [The Improvement of Chinese Language Education in Middle Schools]. Ed. Jiaoyu ziliao congkan she 教育資料叢刊社. Beijing: Renmin jiaoyu chubanshe, 1951. 1–17.

Du Bose, Hampden C. "The Soochow Examination." *Chinese Recorder* 18 (1887): 481.

Dzung, T. C. "The First Step of China's Independence." *St. John's Echo* 15 (1904): 19–21.

Elman, Benjamin A. "Changes in Confucian Civil Service Examinations from the Ming to the Ch'ing Dynasty." *Education and Society in Late Imperial China, 1600–1900*. Ed. Benjamin Elman and Alexander Woodside. Berkeley: U of California P, 1994. 111–49.

———. *A Cultural History of Civil Examinations in Late Imperial China*. Berkeley: U of California P, 2000.

———. *A Cultural History of Modern Science in China*. Cambridge: Harvard UP, 2006.

Emig, Janet. *The Composing Process of Twelfth Graders*. Research Report No. 13. Urbana: NCTE, 1971.

Enos, Theresa. *Gender Roles and Faculty Lives in Rhetoric and Composition.* Carbondale: Southern Illinois UP, 1996.

Fan Jie. "My Cellphone." *Yi xie cu xue yingyu xiezuo zhuanti wangzhan* 以寫促學英語寫作專題網站 [Write to Learn: English Composition Website]. 19 May 2005. Guangdong University of Foreign Studies. 1 Jan. 2006 <http://www.writetolearn.com/Article_Show.asp?ArticleID=401>.

Fanon, Frantz. *The Wretched of the Earth.* New York: Grove, 2004.

Faucett, Lawrence W. "The Revision of Scientific Language Principles for Oriental Application in the Teaching of English." Diss. U of Chicago, 1926.

———. *The Teaching of English in the Far East.* New York: World Book, 1927.

Fen Yuzhu 馮玉柱. "Quanmian lijie he shenru guanche daxue yingyu jiaoxue dagang (gaodeng xuexiao ligong ke benke yong)" 全面理解和深入貫徹大學英語教學大綱 (高等學校理工科本科用) [To Understand Comprehensively and Implement Thoroughly the College English Syllabus for Science and Engineering Students]. *Waiyujie* 外語界 [Foreign Language World] 1 (1990): 18–21.

Ferguson, John C. "The Work of Our Association." *Records of the Triennial Meeting of the Educational Association of China Held at Shanghai, May 2–4, 1893.* Shanghai: American Presbyterian Mission, 1893. 17–26.

Fish, Stanley. *Is There a Text in This Class? The Authority of Interpretive Communities.* Cambridge: Harvard UP, 1980.

———. *Save the World on Your Own Time.* New York: Oxford UP, 2008.

Flower, Linda S., and John R. Hayes. "A Cognitive Process Theory of Writing." *College Composition and Communication* 32 (1981): 365–87.

France, Alan W. "Dialectics of Self: Structure and Agency as the Subject of English." *College English* 63.2 (2000): 145–65.

France, Peter. "The Rhetoric of Translation." *Modern Language Review* 100 (supp.) (2005): 255–68.

Freemantle, Anne, ed. *Mao Tse-Tung: An Anthology of His Writings.* New York: New American Lib., 1962.

Fukien Christian University. *Catalogue and Announcements.* Fuzhou: C. M. S. Mission, 1924–29.

———. *College of Arts and Sciences* [catalog]. Fuzhou, 1921–23.

Fukien Union College. *Catalogue of Fukien Union College, 1916.* Fuzhou: Hua Mei, 1916.

Gaodeng xuexiao yingyu zhuanye jichu jieduan yingyu jiaoxue dagang zhiding zu 高等學校英語專業基礎階段英語教學大綱制定組 [Task Force for Developing the College English Syllabus for English Majors at the Foundation Stage]. *Gaodeng xuexiao yingyu zhuanye jichu jieduan yingyu jiaoxue dagang* 高等學校英語專業基礎階段英語教學大綱 [College English Syllabus for English Majors at the Foundation Stage]. Shanghai: Shanghai waiyu jiaoyu chubanshe, 1989.

Gaodeng xuexiao yingyu zhuanye yingyu jiaoxue dagang gongzuo xiaozu 高等學校英語專業英語教學大綱工作小組 [Task Force for Developing the College English Syllabus for English Majors at the Advanced Stage]. *Gaodeng xuexiao yingyu zhuanye gaonianji yingyu jiaoxue dagang (shixing ben)* 高等學校英語專業高年級英語教學大綱 (試行本) [College English Syllabus for English Majors at the Advanced Stage (trial ed.)]. Beijing: Waiyu jiaxue yu yanjiu chubanshe, 1990.

Gao Junhua 高駿驊. "Tamen shi zenyang pigai gaonianji yingwen zuowen de?" 他們是怎樣批改高年級英文作文的? [How Do They Grade Advanced Students' English Compositions?]. *Waiguoyu* 外國語 [Foreign Languages] 5 (1982): 63–64.

Gao Yihong, Li Lichun, and Lü Jun. "Trends in Research Methods in Applied Linguistics: China and the West." *English for Specific Purposes* 20 (2001): 1–14.

Garrett, Mary M. "Chinese Buddhist Religious Disputation." *Argumentation* 11.2 (1997): 195–209.

———. "Classical Chinese Conceptions of Argumentation and Persuasion." *Argumentation and Advocacy* 29 (1993): 105–15.

Ge Chuangui 葛傳槼. "Mantan you han yi ying wenti" 漫談由漢譯英問題 [Random Thoughts on Some Problems in Chinese–English Translation]. *Fanyi tongxun* 翻譯通訊 [Chinese Translator's Journal] 2 (1980): 1–8.

———. "Yingyu jiaoxue wangshi tan" 英語教學往事談 [My Past Experiences in Teaching English]. Li and Liu 62–77.

———. *Yingwen zuowen jiaoben* 英文作文教本 [A Textbook of English Composition]. Shanghai: Jingwen shuju, 1941.

———. *Yingyu xiezuo* 英語寫作 [The Writing of English]. Shanghai: Shanghai yiwen chubanshe, 1985.

Genung, John F., and Charles L. Hanson. *Outlines of Composition and Rhetoric.* New York: Ginn, 1915.

Gilyard, Keith. "African American Contributions to Composition Studies." *College Composition and Communication* 50.4 (1999): 626–44.

Ginling College. *Bulletin of Ginling College: Announcement.* Nanjing, 1915–33.

———. "Course List for Fall 1947." Nanjing, 1947.

———. *Ginling Catalog.* Nanjing, 1941.

———. *Ginling College Handbook.* Nanjing, 1918.

———, Class of 1919. *The Pioneer.* Shanghai: Presbyterian Mission, 1919.

Gold, David. *Rhetoric at the Margins: Revising the History of Writing Instruction in American Colleges, 1873–1947.* Carbondale: Southern Illinois UP, 2008.

Gonzalez, Andrew, and Teresita Fortunato. "The Teaching of Writing in English and in Filipino in the Philippines." Ed. Robert B. Kaplan. Spec. issue of *Journal of Asian Pacific Communication* 6.1 (1995): 85–101.

Grabe, William. "Notes toward a Theory of Second Language Writing." *On Second Language Writing.* Ed. Tony Silva and Paul Kei Matsuda. Mahwah, N.J.: Lawrence Erlbaum, 2001. 39–57.

"Greeting." *St. John's Echo* 1.1 (1890): 1.

Gui Shichun 桂詩春. "Kaizhan jiaoyu ceshixue yanjiu, shixian woguo kaoshi xiandaihua" 開展教育測試學研究, 實現我國考試現代化 [Conducting Research in Educational Assessment to Modernize Examinations in Our Country]. *Xiandai waiyu* 現代外語 [Modern Foreign Languages] 1 (1982): 1–6.

———. "Yingyong yuyanxue yu wo" 應用語言學與我 [My Relationship with Applied Linguistics]. Li and Liu 343–65.

Gunn, Edward. *Rewriting Chinese: Style and Innovation in Twentieth-Century Chinese Prose.* Stanford: Stanford UP, 1991.

Guoli Beijing daxue 國立北京大學 [National Peking University]. *Guoli Beijing daxue ruxue shiyan shiti* 國立北京大學入學試驗試題 [National Peking University Entrance Examination Papers]. 1935. Beijing University Archives, Beijing.

———. *Guoli Beijing daxue yuke ruxue shiyan shiti (minguo liu nian qi shiyi nian zhi)* 國立北京大學預科入學試驗試題民國六年起十一年止 [National Peking University Precollege Entrance Examination Papers, 1917–22]. 1922. Beijing University Archives, Beijing.

————. "Guoli xinan lianhe daxue sanshiyi niandu xinsheng ruxue kaoshi guowen shiti" 國立西南聯合大學三十一年度新生入學考試國文試題 [National Southwest Associated University Entrance Examination of 1942, Chinese Language Paper]. 1942. Tsinghua University Archives, Beijing.

Guoli Wuhan daxue 國立武漢大學 [National Wuhan University]. *Guoli Wuhan daxue yilan* 國立武漢大學一覽 [National Wuhan University Information and Curriculum]. Wuhan, 1930–38.

Guy, R. Kent. "Fang Pao and the Ch'in-ting Ssu-shu-wen." *Education and Society in Late Imperial China, 1600–1900.* Ed. Benjamin Elman and Alexander Woodside. Berkeley: U of California P, 1994. 150–82.

Hangchow Christian College. *Announcements.* Shanghai: Methodist Publishing House, 1921–25.

Hangchow Presbyterian College. *Catalogue, 1913–1914.* Shanghai: Presbyterian Mission, 1913.

————. *Hangzhou yuying shuyuan zhangcheng* 杭州育英書院章程 [Hangzhou Presbyterian College Bulletin]. Shanghai: Presbyterian Mission, 1904.

Hanyu da cidian 漢語大辭典 [A Grand Chinese Dictionary]. Chengdu: Sichuan cishu chubanshe and Hubei cishu chubanshe, 1995.

Harklau, Linda, Kay M. Losey, and Meryl Siegal, eds. *Generation 1.5 Meets College Composition: Issues in the Teaching of Writing to U.S.-Educated Learners of ESL.* Mahwah, N.J.: Erlbaum, 1999.

Hartwell, C. "The Relation of Christians to the Examinations." *Chinese Recorder* 1.11 (1869): 217–20.

Harvey, David. *The Condition of Postmodernity.* Cambridge, Mass.: Blackwell, 1990.

Heilker, Paul. *The Essay: Theory and Pedagogy for an Active Form.* Urbana, Ill.: NCTE, 1996.

Heilongjiang daxue yingyu xi 黑龍江大學英語系 [Heilongjiang University English Department]. *Gongneng yingyu jiaocheng* 功能英語教程 [Functional English Course Book]. Beijing: Waiyu jiaoxue yu yanjiu chubanshe, 1981.

Herrick, Robert, and Lindsay T. Damon. *New Composition and Rhetoric for Schools.* New York: Scott, Foresman, 1911.

Hessler, Peter. *River Town: Two Years on the Yangtze.* New York: HarperCollins, 2001.

Hill, David. "The Kü Jän Examination." *Chinese Recorder* 11 (1880): 143–46.

————. "The Kü Jän Examinations." *Chinese Recorder* 10 (1879): 303.

————. "The Triennial Examinations." *Chinese Recorder* 19 (1888): 282–83.

————. "The Triennial Examinations for the Ku Jan Degree." *Chinese Recorder* 10 (1879): 463–64.

Holborow, Marnie. *The Politics of English: A Marxist View of Language.* Thousand Oaks, Calif.: Sage, 1999.

Holden, R. *Yale in China: The Mainland 1901–1951.* New Haven, Conn.: Yale-in-China Assoc., 1964.

Horner, Bruce, and John Trimbur. "English Only and U.S. College Composition." *College Composition and Communication* 53.4 (2002): 594–630.

Hu, Shiming, and Eli Seifman, eds. *Education and Socialist Modernization: A Documentary History of Education in the People's Republic of China, 1977–1986.* New York: AMS, 1987.

Hua Chung College. *Catalog of the School of Arts, the Yale-in-China School of Science, [and] the School of Education for the Academic Year 1932–1933.* Hankou: Religious Tract Society, 1933.

———. *Catalogue, 1936–1937.* Wuchang, China, 1937.

Hu Meihua 胡美華. "Daxue yingyu xiezuo jiaoxue zhi buzu yu kexing duice" 大學英語寫作教學之不足與可行對策 [The Weaknesses in College English Writing Instruction and Possible Solutions]. *Waiyujie* 外語界 [Foreign Language World] 1 (1994): 24–28.

Hu Shi 胡適. *Hu Shi wencun* 胡適文存 [A Collection of Hu Shi's Works]. Vol. 1. Taipei: Yuandong tushu gongsi, 1953.

———. "Jianshe de wenxue geming lun" 建設的文學革命論 [On a Constructive Literary Revolution]. *Hu Shi wencun* 55–73.

———. "Shiyan zhuyi" 試驗主義 [Experimentalism]. *Hu Shi wencun* 291–341.

———. "Wenxue gailiang chuyi" 文學改良芻議 [An Initial Discussion on Literary Innovation]. *Hu Shi wencun* 5–16.

Hu Wenzhong 胡文仲. "Kexue yanjiu yu jiaoxue dagang" 科學研究與教學大綱 [Scientific Research and Syllabus]. *Waiyu jiaoxue yu yanjiu* 外語教學與研究 [Foreign Language Teaching and Research] 2 (1983): 32–37.

———, ed. *Jichu yingyu jiaoxue lunwenji* 基礎英語教學論文集 [Collected Papers on Teaching English to Chinese Students: Approaches and Methods at the Foundation Stage]. Beijing: Waiyu jiaoxue yu yanjiu chubanshe, 1985.

Hu Xiaohua 胡小花, ed. *Yingyu xiezuo jiaoxue yu yanjiu* 英語寫作教學與研究 [English Writing Teaching and Research: Proceedings of the 2nd ESL Teaching and Research International Seminar]. Xi'an: Xibei gongye daxue chubanshe, 2006.

Hymes, Dell. *On Communicative Competence.* Philadelphia: U of Pennsylvania P, 1971.

Isidro, A. S. "The Development of Written English Expression of Filipino Children." Diss. U of Chicago, 1934.

Jackson, Ronald L., and Elaine B. Richardson, eds. *African American Rhetoric(s): Interdisciplinary Perspectives.* Carbondale: Southern Illinois UP, 2004.

———, eds. *Understanding African-American Rhetoric: Classical Origins to Contemporary Innovations.* New York: Routledge, 2003.

Jensen, J. Vernon. "Values and Practices in Asian Argumentation." *Argumentation and Advocacy* 28 (1992): 153–66.

Jiang Jinzhi 蔣津芝. *Daxue yingyu xiezuo* 大學英語寫作 [Writing in English for College Students]. Wuhan: Hubei jiaoyu chubanshe, 1986.

Jiaoyubu 教育部 [Ministry of Education]. "Daxue yingyu kecheng jiaoxue yaoqiu" 大學英語課程教學要求 [College English Curriculum Requirements]. 29 Sept. 2007 <http://www.jiaodong.net/examin/system/2007/09/27/010095479.shtml>.

———. "Daxue yingyu kecheng jiaoxue yaoqiu (shixing)" 大學英語課程教學要求（試行）[College English Curriculum Requirements (for Trial Implementation)]. 2004. 17 June 2004 <http://www.edu.cn/20040120/3097997.shtml>.

Jiaoyubu fazhan guihua si tongji xinxi chu 教育部發展規劃司統計資訊處 [Statistic Information Office of the Development and Planning Department, Ministry of Education]. "2000 nian quanguo jiaoyu shiye tongji zhuyao zhibiao ji jianxi" 2000 年全國教育事業統計主要指標及簡析 [Some Major Statistical Figures for Chinese Education of the Year 2000 and a Brief Analysis]. 2001. 21 Jan. 2002 <http://www.edu.cn/20010910/3000909.shtml>.

Johns, Ann M. "Textual Cohesion and the Chinese Speakers of English." *Language Learning and Communication* 3.1 (1984): 69–73.

Kaoshiyuan 考試院 [Ministry of Examination]. *Putong kaoshi shiti huikan ershiyi nian zhi ershisi nian* 普通考試試題彙刊二十一年至二十四年 [A Collection of Civil Service Examination Papers, 1932–35]. Nanjing, 1935.

Kaplan, Robert B. "The Teaching of Writing around the Pacific Basin." Ed. Robert B. Kaplan. Spec. issue of *Journal of Asian Pacific Communication* 6.1 (1995): 5–12.

Keenan, Barry C. *Imperial China's Last Classical Academies: Social Change in the Lower Yangzi, 1864–1911.* Berkeley: Institute of East Asian Studies, 1995.

Kirkpatrick, Andy. "China's First Systematic Account of Rhetoric: An Introduction to Chen Kui's *Wen Ze.*" *Rhetorica* 23.2 (2005): 103–52.

——. "Chinese Rhetoric: Methods of Argument." *Multilingua* 14 (1995): 271–95.

Kittredge, George L., and Sarah L. Arnold. *The Mother Tongue.* Vol. 2, *An Elementary English Grammar with Lessons in Composition.* Boston: Ginn, 1903.

Lamberton, Mary. *St. John's University, Shanghai, 1879–1951.* New York: United Board for Christian Colleges in China, 1955.

Lary, Diana. "Teaching English in China." *China Quarterly* 24 (1965): 1–14.

Leki, Ilona. "Material, Educational, and Ideological Challenges of Teaching EFL Writing at the Turn of the Century." *International Journal of English Studies* 1 (2001): 197–209.

Li, Xiaoju. "In Defence of the Communicative Approach." *ELT Journal* 28.1 (1984): 2–13.

——. 李筱菊. *Jiaoji yingyu jiaocheng* 交際英語教程 [Communicative English for Chinese Learners]. Shanghai: Shanghai waiyu jiaoyu chubanshe, 1987.

Liang Qichao 梁啟超. "Weishenme yao zhuzhong xushi wenzi" 為什麼要注重敍事文字 [Why We Should Pay More Attention to Narratives]. Liang, *Yinbingshi heji* 43: 81–87.

——. *Yinbingshi heji* 飲冰室合集 [The Yinbingshi Collection]. Beijing: Zhonghua shuju, 1989.

——. "Zuowen jiaoxue fa" 作文教學法 [Composition Pedagogy]. Liang, *Yinbingshi heji* 70: 1–41.

Li Dzeh-Djen. Letter to an unknown friend. 1923. Lindquist Papers.

Li Funing 李賦寧. *Li Funing lun yingyu xuexi he xifang wenxue* 李賦寧論英語學習和西方文學 [Li Funing on English Learning and Western Literature]. Beijing: Beijing daxue chubanshe, 1985.

——. "Reminiscences of My Early College Life: A Speech Delivered at Nanjing Normal University in the Fall of 1987." Chen Yilun 32–40.

——. "Tantan jingduke" 談談精讀課 [A Discussion of the Intensive Reading Course]. Li Funing, *Li Funing* 42–47.

——. "Tigao yingyu de bitou biaoda nengli" 提高英語的筆頭表達能力 [Improving Expressive Competence in Written English]. Li Funing, *Li Funing* 30–33.

Li Guanyi 李觀儀, and Xue Fankang 薛蕃康. *Xinbian yingyu jiaocheng* 新編英語教程 [New English Coursebook]. 4 vols. Shanghai: Shanghai waiyu jiaoyu chubanshe, 1986.

Li Hongli 李宏麗. Personal interview. 11 Sept. 2007.

Li Hwei-Siu. "My First Year at Ginling College." 1923. Lindquist Papers.

Li Liangyou 李良佑, and Liu Li 劉犁, eds. *Waiyu jiaoyu wangshi tan: Jiaoshoumen de huiyi* 外語教育往事談：教授們的回憶 [On the History of Foreign Language

Education in China: Some Professors' Recollections]. Shanghai: Shanghai waiyu jiaoyu chubanshe, 1988.

Li Liangyou 李良佑, Zhang Risheng 張日昇, and Liu Li 劉犁. *Zhongguo yingyu jiaoxue shi* 中國英語教學史 [A History of English Language Teaching in China]. Shanghai: Shanghai waiyu jiaoyu chubanshe, 1988.

Lindquist, Dorothy, Papers. 1923. RG Manuscript No. 8. Yale Divinity School Lib., New Haven, Conn.

Lingnan University. *Announcements for the Academic Year, 1929–1930*. Canton, 1929.

———. *Catalogue with Announcement*. Canton, 1926–34.

———. *Information and Curriculum, 1946–1948*. Canton, 1946.

Lin Qingfen 林清芬. *Kangzhan shiqi woguo liuxue jiaoyu shiliao, gesheng kaoxuan liuxuesheng* 抗戰時期我國留學教育史料, 各省考選留學生 [Archives of Overseas Education during the Anti-Japanese War Period, Examinations and Recruitments in Different Provinces]. Vols. 1–5. Taipei: Historica Sinica, 1994.

Lin Yutang 林語堂. *Kaiming di'er yingwen duben* 開明第二英文讀本 [Kaiming's Second English Book]. Shanghai: Kaiming shudian, 1933.

———. *Kaiming yingwen duben* 開明英文讀本 [Kaiming's English Book]. Shanghai: Kaiming shudian, 1929.

———. *Kaiming yingwen jiangyi* 開明英文講義 [Kaiming's English Textbook]. Vols. 1–4. Taipei: Taiwan kaiming shudian, 1957.

Liu, Yameng. "To Capture the Essence of Chinese Rhetoric: An Anatomy of a Paradigm in Comparative Rhetoric." *Rhetoric Review* 14.2 (1996): 318–35.

Liu, Yichun. *Translation in Second Language Writing: Exploration of the Cognitive Process of Translation*. Saarbrücken: VDM Verlag, 2009.

Liu Hsieh. *The Literary Mind and the Carving of Dragons*. Trans. Vincent Yu-chung Shih. New York: Columbia UP, 1959.

Liu Shaoqi. "How to Be a Good Communist." *Three Essays on Party Building*. Beijing: Foreign Language, 1980. 1–98.

Liu Tianyou 劉天佑, and Lin Jingyi 林靜怡. "Women zai shiyong xin yingyu jiaocheng zhong de yixie tihui" 我們在使用《新英語教程》中的一些體會 [Some Reflections on Our Use of *New Concept English*]. *Jichu yingyu jiaoxue lunwenji* 基礎英語教學論文集 [Collected Papers on Teaching English to Chinese Students: Approaches and Methods at the Foundation Stage]. Ed. Hu Wenzhong 胡文仲. Beijing: Waiyu jiaoxue yu yanjiu chubanshe, 1985. 181–84.

Liu Yunhua 劉耘華. *Quanshi de yuanhuan: Mingmo qingchu chuanjiaoshi dui rujia jingdian de jieshi jiqi bentu huiying* 詮釋的圓環: 明末清初傳教士對儒家經典的解釋及其本土回應 [The Circle of Exegesis: The Missionaries' Interpretations of Confucian Canons and the Chinese Responses in the Late Ming and the Early Qing Dynasties]. Beijing: Beijing daxue chubanshe, 2005.

Li Wenzhong 李文中. "Zhongguo yingyu yu zhongguo shi yingyu" 中國英語與中國式英語 [China English and Chinglish]. *Waiyu jiaoxue yu yanjiu* [Foreign Language Teaching and Research] 4 (1993): 18–24.

Li Xingbao 李杏保, and Gu Huangchu 顧黃初. *Zhongguo xiandai yuwen jiaoyu shi* 中國現代語文教育史 [A History of Modern Chinese Education]. Chengdu: Sichuan jiaoyu chubanshe, 2000.

Li Yinhua 李蔭華 et al., eds. *Daxue yingyu: jingdu* 大學英語 : 精讀 [College English: Intensive Reading]. Shanghai: Shanghai waiyu jiaoyu chubanshe, 1991.

Li Zhenlin 李振麟. "Guanyu jianli woguo waiyu jiaoxue fa kexue tixi de wenti" 關於建立我國外語教學法科學體系的問題 [On Establishing a Scientific System of Foreign Language Pedagogies in China]. *Waiyu jiaoxue yu fanyi* 外語教學與翻譯 [Foreign Language Teaching and Translation] 10 (1959): 11–19.

Lloyd, Keith. "Rethinking Rhetoric from an Indian Perspective: Implications in the *Nyaya Sutra*." *Rhetoric Review* 26.4 (2007): 365–84.

Long Baichun 龍伯純. *Wenzi fafan* 文字發凡 [An Introduction to Language]. Shanghai: Guangzhi shuju, 1905.

Lu, Min-Zhan. "An Essay on the Work of Composition: Composing English against the Order of Fast Capitalism." *College Composition and Communication* 56.1 (2004): 16–50.

Lu, Xing. *Rhetoric in Ancient China, Fifth to Third Century B.C.E.: A Comparison with Classical Greek Rhetoric*. Columbia: U of South Carolina P, 1998.

———. *Rhetoric of the Chinese Cultural Revolution: The Impact on Chinese Thought, Culture, and Communication*. Columbia: U of South Carolina P, 2004.

Lu Ce 呂策. *Zuixin xiongbian fa* 最新雄辯法 [The Principles of Argumentation]. Peking: Jicheng tushu gongsi, 1910.

Lu Deqing 路德慶, Shi Yaxi 施亞西, and Fan Peisong 範培松. *Xiezuo jiaocheng* 寫作教程 [Lectures on Writing]. Shanghai: Huadong shifan daxue chubanshe, 1982.

Ma Degao 毛德高, and Wen Zhifang 文治芳. "Daxue yingyu siji kaoshi linian quanzhen shiti toushi daokao (xiezuo)" 大學英語四級考試歷年全真試題: 透視導考 (寫作) [Authentic Papers of the College English Test Band-4: An Examination and a Guide (Writing)]. Xi'an: Shijie tushu chuban gongsi, 1999.

Man-Cheong, Iona D. *The Class of 1761: Examinations, State, and Elites in Eighteenth-Century China*. Stanford: Stanford UP, 2004.

Mao, LuMing. "Reflective Encounters: Illustrating Comparative Rhetoric." *Style* 37.4 (2003): 401–25.

———. "Rhetorical Borderlands: Chinese American Rhetoric in the Making." *College Composition and Communication* 56.3 (2005): 426–69.

Mao Zedong. "Combat Liberalism." Freemantle 197–99.

———. "Fandui dang bagu" 反對黨八股 [Against the Eight-Legged Style of Writing within the Party]. *Xiezuo luntang* 寫作論譚 [On Writing]. Ed. Liu Xiqing 劉錫慶, Zhu Jinshun 朱金順, Li Weiguo 李維國, and Wu Xuan 吳炫. Beijing: Zhongyang guangbo dianshi daxue chubanshe, 1983. 1–16.

———. *Mao Zedong waijiao wenxuan* 毛澤東外交文選 [Mao Zedong's Works on Diplomacy]. Beijing: Zhongyang wenxian chubanshe and shijie zhishi chubanshe, 1994.

———. "Talks at the Yenan Forum on Art and Literature." Freemantle 242–63.

———. "Talk with the American Correspondent Anna Louise Strong." Freemantle 176–79.

Mao Zhongming 毛忠明. "Daxue yingyu xiezuo jiaoxue de yizhong changshi" 大學英語寫作教學的一種嘗試 [A Trial in College English Writing Instruction]. *Waiyujie* 外語界 [Foreign Language World] 4 (1990): 28–31.

March, A. W. "The Place of English in Education in China." *Chinese Recorder* 46.2 (1915): 108–21.

Martin, W. A. P. *The Chinese: Their Education, Philosophy, and Letters*. New York: Harper & Brothers, 1881.

——. *A Cycle of Cathay; or, China, South and North, with Personal Reminiscences.* New York: Fleming H. Revell, 1896.

——. *Gewu rumen* 格物入門 [Elements of Natural Pilosophy and Chemistry]. Peking: University of Peking (Tong Wen Guan), 1868.

——. *Hanlin Papers: Essays on the History, Philosophy and Religion of the Chinese.* 2nd series. Shanghai: Kelly & Walsh, 1894.

——. *Report on the System of Public Instruction in China.* Washington, D.C.: GPO, 1877.

Matalene, Carolyn. "Contrastive Rhetoric: An American Writing Teacher in China." *College English* 47.8 (1985): 789–809.

Matsuda, Paul Kei. "Composition Studies and ESL Writing: A Disciplinary Division of Labor." *College Composition and Communication* 50.4 (1999): 699–721.

——. "Situating ESL Writing in a Cross-Disciplinary Context." *Written Communication* 15.1 (1998): 99–121.

Matsuda, Paul Kei, Christina Ortmeier-Hooper, and Xiaoye You, eds. *The Politics of Second Language Writing: In Search of the Promised Land.* West Lafayette, Ind.: Parlor, 2006.

Matsuura, Hiroko, Miho Fujieda, and Sean Mahoney. "The Officialization of English and ELT in Japan: 2000." *World Englishes* 23.3 (2004): 471–87.

Meisner, Maurice. *The Deng Xiaoping Era: An Inquiry into the Fate of Chinese Socialism, 1978–1994.* New York: Hill & Wang, 1996.

Meng Hua 孟華. "Yanguizi ciyuan chutan" "洋鬼子"詞源初探 [An Initial Exploration on the Etymology of "Foreign Devils"]. *Maixiang bijiao wenxue xin jieduan* 邁向比較文學新階段 [Toward a New Phase of Comparative Literature]. Ed. Cao Shunqing 曹順慶. Chengdu: Sichun renmin chubanshe, 2000. 371–88.

Miao Tingfu 繆廷輔. *Daxue yingyu zuowen* 大學英語作文 [New College Composition with Exercises]. Shanghai: Longmans, 1949.

Miller, Thomas. *The Formation of College English: Rhetoric and Belles Lettres in the British Cultural Provinces.* Pittsburgh: U of Pittsburgh P, 1997.

Muchiri, Mary, Nshindi Mulamba, Greg Myers, and Deoscorous Ndoloi. "Importing Composition: Teaching and Researching Academic Writing beyond North America." *College Composition and Communication* 46.2 (1995): 175–98.

Muehl, Lois, and Siegmar Muehl. *Trading Cultures in the Classroom: Two American Teachers in China.* Honolulu: U of Hawaii P, 1993.

Nanjing daxue waiyuxi sannianji yingyu jiaocai bianzhuan weiyuanhui 南京大學外語系三年級英語教材編撰委員會 [English Textbook Compiling Committee, Juniors of the Nanjing University Foreign Language Department]. *Daxue sannianji yingyu keben* 大學三年級英語課本 [English Textbook for Juniors]. Beijing: Shidai chubanshe, 1960.

Nanjing daxue waiyuxi yingyu zu ernianji shisheng 南京大學外語系英語組二年級師生 [Teachers and Sophomore Students of the Nanjing University Foreign Language Department]. "Yingyu jiaoxue zenyang duo kuai hao sheng" 英語教學怎樣多快好省 [How to Achieve Greater, Faster, Better, and More Economical Results in English Teaching and Learning]. *Xifang yuwen* 西方語文 [Western Languages and Literature] 3.1 (1959): 16–20.

Nesfield, John. C. *English Grammar, Past and Present.* London: Macmillan, 1889.

——. *Junior Course of English Composition.* London: Macmillan, 1901.

————. *Oral Exercises in English Composition.* London: Macmillan, 1905.

————. *Senior Course of English Composition.* London: Macmillan, 1903.

"Notes and Items." *Chinese Recorder* 27.11 (1896): 559–62.

Ouyang Huhua 歐陽護華. "Qianxi guowai eryu xiezuo lilun liupai he xiechangfa dingwei" 淺析國外二語寫作理論流派和寫長法定位 [A Brief Analysis of Overseas Second Language Writing Theories and the Location of the Length Approach]. *Yi xie cu xue: Yingyu xiechangfa de linian yu caozuo* 以寫促學：英語寫長法的理念與操作 [Improving English Learning through Writing: Theory and Practice of the Length Approach]. Ed. Zheng Chao 鄭超. Wuhan: Kexue Chubanshe, 2004. 18–21.

Palmer, Harold E. *The Principles of Language-Study.* Oxford: Oxford UP, 1921/1964.

Pan Chen 潘臣. "Cong guowen jiaoxue zhi zuoyou pai tan qi" 從國文教學之左右派談起 [Initiating the Conversation from the Left and the Right in Chinese Language Teaching]. *Xiezuo yu yuedu* 寫作與閱讀 [Writing and Reading] 1.6 (1937): 482–93.

Patry, William. "The Failure of the American Copyright System: Protecting the Idle Rich." *Notre Dame Law Review* 72.4 (1997): 907–33.

Peking University. *Announcement of Courses, 1923–1924.* Beijing, 1923.

————. *Announcement of the College of Arts and Sciences for Women, College of Arts and Sciences for Men, [and] School of Theology, 1920–1921.* Beijing: Bureau of Engraving and Printing, 1920.

————. *Colleges of Arts and Science, Announcement of Courses, 1925–1926.* Beijing, 1925.

————. *General Information, 1927–1928.* Beijing, 1927.

Pennycook, Alastair. *English and the Discourses of Colonialism.* New York: Routledge, 1998.

Perl, Sondra. "The Composing Processes of Unskilled College Writers." *Research in the Teaching of English* 13.4 (1979): 317–36.

Phillipson, Robert. *Linguistic Imperialism.* New York: Oxford UP, 1992.

Pi and Lu. "Our Factory—the Chemical Tile Factory." *Yingyu xuexi* 英語學習 [English Monthly] February 1958: 27–28.

Plato. *Phaedrus.* Trans. Robin Waterfield. New York: Oxford UP, 2003.

Pratt, Mary Louise. "Arts of the Contact Zone." *Profession* (1991): 33–40.

Prendergast, Catherine. *Buying into English: Language and Investment in the New Capitalist World.* Pittsburgh: U of Pittsburgh P, 2008.

Purver, G. L. *Yingyu jiaoke shu* 英語教科書 [English Language Textbook]. Trans. Shi Mingde 施明德. Beijing: Shangwu yinshuguan, 1959.

Quanguo daxue yingyu si liu ji kaoshi weiyuanhui 全國大學英語四、六級考試委員會 [College English Test Committee]. "Daxue yingyu kaoshi de sheji yuanze" 大學英語考試的設計原則 [The Principles in Designing the College English Tests]. 1999. 1 Sept. 2002 <http://www.sjtu.edu.cn/cet/>.

————. "Daxue yingyu si liu ji kaoshi huigu yu zhanwang" 大學英語四、六級考試回顧與展望 [The Past and the Future of the College English Tests]. Shanghai, 1996.

Rakhmanov, I. V. "Lun dangqian waiyu jiaoxuefa de renwu" 論當前外語教學法的任務 [On the Present Task of Foreign Language Pedagogies]. Trans. Tan Ziqiang. *Sulian yuwen jiaoxue de xin fangxiang* 蘇聯語文教學的新方向 [New Directions in Language Education in the Soviet Union]. Ed. Waiguoyu xuexiao waiyu jiaoxue congshu bianji weiyuanhui 外國語學校外語教學叢書編輯委員會 [Ed. The Editorial Committee for the Foreign Language Teaching Series for Foreign Language Schools]. Beijing: Wushi niandai chubanshe, 1953. 15–31.

Rawski, Evelyn Sakakida. *Education and Popular Literacy in Ch'ing China.* Ann Arbor: U of Michigan P, 1979.

Readings, Bill. *The University in Ruins.* Cambridge: Harvard UP, 1996.

Renmin jiaoyu chubanshe geming zaofan liandui 人民教育出版社革命造反聯隊. "Liu Deng fangeming xiuzheng zhuyi jituan Lu Dingyi Zhou Yang zhiliu zai zhongxiaoxue jiaocai bianshen gongzuo zhong fan dang fan shehui zhuyi fan Mao Zedong sixiang yanlun zhailu" 劉、鄧反革命修正主義集團陸定一、周揚之流在中小學教材編審工作中反黨反社會主義反毛澤東思想言論摘錄 [Quotes of Antiparty, Antisocialist, and anti–Mao Zedong Remarks Made by Lu Dingyi and Zhou Yang, Members of the Counterrevolutionary Revisionist Group Led by Liu Shaoqi and Deng Xiaoping, When Editing Elementary and Middle School Textbooks]. *Hongweibing ziliao* 紅衛兵資料 [Red Guard Publications]. Vol. 17. Reprinted by Center for Chinese Research Materials. Washington, D.C.: Assoc. of Research Libs., 1975. 5574–85.

Rickert, Thomas. *Acts of Enjoyment: Rhetoric, Zizek, and the Return of the Subject.* Pittsburgh: U of Pittsburgh P, 2007.

Rivers, Wilga M. *Teaching Foreign-Langauge Skills.* Chicago: U of Chicago P, 1968.

Royster, Jacqueline Jones, and Jean C. Williams. "History in the Spaces Left: African American Presence and Narratives of Composition Studies." *College Composition and Communication* 50.4 (1999): 563–84.

Santos, Terry. "On the Future of Second Language Writing: The ESL/EFL Split." *Journal of Second Language Writing* 9.1 (2000): 8–10.

———, et al. "On the Future of Second Language Writing: A Colloquium." *Journal of Second Language Writing* 9.1 (2000): 1–20.

Saussy, Haun. "'Ritual Separates, Music Unites': Why Musical Hermeneutics Matters." *Recarving the Dragon: Understanding Chinese Poetics.* Ed. Olga Lomova. Prague: Karolinum, 2003. 9–25.

Savignon, Sandra J. "Communicative Language Teaching: Language Theory and Classroom Practice." *Interpreting Communicative Language Teaching: Contexts and Concerns in Teacher Education.* New Haven: Yale UP, 2002. 1–27.

Schneider, Stephen. "Freedom Schooling: Stokely Carmichael and Critical Rhetorical Education." *College Composition and Communication* 58.1 (2006): 46–69.

Schultz, Lucille M. *The Young Composers: Composition's Beginnings in Nineteenth-Century Schools.* Carbondale: Southern Illinois UP, 1999.

Selber, Stuart. *Multiliteracies for a Digital Age.* Carbondale: Southern Illinois UP, 2004.

Shanghai College. *Catalogue and Announcements, 1922–1923.* Shanghai, 1922.

———. *Catalogue, 1924–1925; Announcements, 1925–1926.* Shanghai, 1924.

———. *Catalogue, 1929–1930.* Shanghai, 1929.

Shanghai waiguoyu xueyuan 上海外國語學院 [Shanghai Foreign Language Institute]. *Yingyu, diyice (shiyong ben)* 英語, 第一冊 (試用本) [English, Book 1 (trial ed.)]. Shanghai: Shanghai waiguoyu xueyuan, 1972.

Shang Yanliu 商衍鎏. *Qingdai keju kaoshi shulu* 清代科舉考試述錄 [A Brief Study of the Qing Examination System]. Beijing: Sanlian shudian, 1958.

Shaonian wenyi bianjibu《少年文藝》編輯部 [The Editorial Office for Youth Literature and Arts]. *Zhongxuesheng zuowen zhidao* 中學生作文指導 [A Guide to Middle-School Composition]. Shanghai: Shaonian ertong chubanshe, 1980.

Shimamura Hogetsu 島村抱月. *Shin bijigaku* 新美辭學 [New Rhetoric]. Totsuka-mura, Tokyofu: Waseda daigaku shuppanbu, 1916.

Silsby, J. A. "Teaching English in China." *Chinese Recorder* 34.1 (1903): 35–37.

Sinclair, T. L. "Teaching English: Does It Pay?" *Chinese Recorder* 55 (1924): 509–14.

Smith, Richard, ed. *Teaching English as a Foreign Language, 1912–1936: Pioneers of ELT*. Vol. 4. *Lawrence Faucett*. New York: Routledge, 2003.

Song Xuexia 宋學俠, and Tang Lianyi 唐連義, eds. *Gaokao yingyu shiti huibian: 1950–1980* 高考英語試題彙編: 1950–1980 [A Collection of College Entrance Exam Papers for the English Tests, 1950–1980]. Shenyang: Liaoning renmin chubanshe, 1980.

Soochow University. *Bulletin: Announcement of Courses, College of Arts and Sciences*. Suzhou, 1934.

———. *Courses and Announcements, 1919–1920*. Suzhou, 1919.

Speidel, William. "Learning and Labor at Tunghai." *Something to Write Home About: An Anthology of Shansi Rep Letters, 1951–1988*. Oberlin, Ohio: Oberlin Shansi Memorial Assoc., 2000. 30–33.

Spolsky, Bernard. *Measured Words*. Oxford: Oxford UP, 1995.

Stern, H. H. *Fundamental Concepts of Language Teaching*. New York: Oxford UP, 1983.

St. John's College. *Catalogue, 1907–1908*. Shanghai, 1907.

St. John's University. *Catalogue*. Shanghai, 1908–1940.

———. *St. John's University, 1879–1929*. Shanghai, 1929.

Stromberg, Ernest, ed. *American Indian Rhetorics of Survivance: Word Medicine, Word Magic*. Pittsburgh: U of Pittsburgh P, 2006.

Su Yurong 宿玉榮, Wang Fan 王帆, and Fan Yue 範悅. *Yingyu yanjiang bisai cansai zhinan* 英語演講比賽參賽指南 [A Guide to English Speaking Contests]. Beijing: Waiyu jiaoxue yu yanjiu chubanshe, 2006.

Takeshima Hogoromo 武島又次郎. *Shujigaku* 修辭學 [Rhetoric]. Tokyo: Hakubun-kan, 1908.

Tam, Kwok-kan. "English(es) in Global and Local Perspectives." *English and Globalization: Perspectives from Hong Kong and Mainland China*. Ed. Kwok-kan Tam and Timothy Weiss. Hong Kong: Chinese UP, 2004. xi–xxvii.

Tang Lixing 唐力行. *TEFL in China: Methods and Techniques*. Shanghai: Shanghai waiyu jiaoyu chubanshe, 1985.

Tang Xianzu 湯顯祖. "Wo wei jian hao ren zhe" 我未見好仁者 [I Have Never Yet Seen One Who Really Cared for Goodness]. Wang Kaifu 202–5.

Tappert, Esther. A Letter to Friends. 8 May 1939. RG Manuscript No. 21: Esther Tappert Mortensen Papers. Yale Divinity School Lib., New Haven, Conn.

Teng, Ssu-yu. "Chinese Influence on the Western Examination System: I. Introduction." *Harvard Journal of Asiatic Studies* 7.4 (1943): 267–312.

Tengchow College. *Catalogue*. Shanghai: American Presbyterian Mission, 1891.

Tian Dexin 田德新. "Jiaqiang yuedu jiaoxue tigao xuesheng yingyu xiezuo nengli" 加強閱讀教學提高學生英語寫作能力 [Strengthening Reading Instruction and Improving Students' English Writing Ability]. *Waiyujie* 外語界 [Foreign Language World] 3 (1993): 34–37.

Tien Tsui-Bao. "Autobiography." 1922. Lindquist Papers.

Tomasi, Massimiliano. *Rhetoric in Modern Japan: Western Influences on the Development of Narrative and Oratorical Style.* Honolulu: U Hawaii P, 2004.

Tong Wen Guan timing lu 同文館題名錄 [Calendar of Tongwen College]. Beijing, 1879.

"Triennial Examination at Peking." *Chinese Recorder* 20 (1889): 89–90.

Tsai Kwei. "My First Year in Ginling College." 1923. Lindquist Papers.

Tsu, Y. Y. "The New Literature of China." *St. John's Echo* 15.3 (1904): 13–15.

Tsu Do-Gia. "My First Year at Ginling." 1923. Lindquist Papers.

Tung Teh-Fu. "Intercollegiate English Debate Speeches (Won by Shanghai College at Shanghai, on December 14, 1922)." *University of Nanking Magazine* 12.3 (1923): 1–6.

United Board for Christian Higher Education in Asia. "Educational Programs Related to the People's Republic of China: General Statement." 1980. Archives of the United Board for Christian Higher Education in Asia. Yale Divinity School Lib., New Haven, Conn.

University of Nanking. *Catalogue.* Shanghai: American Presbyterian Mission, 1910–19.

———. *Catalogue, 1924–1925; Announcements, 1925–1926 and 1926–1927.* Shanghai, 1925.

———. *Catalogue, 1931–1932.* Shanghai, 1931.

———. "Condensed Schedule, College of Arts." Shanghai, 1947.

———. *Wenxue yuan gaikuan, 1936–1937* 文學院概況 1936–1937 [College of Arts, Catalogue, 1936–1937]. Shanghai, 1936.

Wang, James C. F. *Contemporary Chinese Politics: An Introduction.* 6th ed. Supper Saddle River, N.J.: Prentice, 1999.

Wang Chuming 王初明, Niu Ruiying 牛瑞英, and Zheng Xiaoxiang 鄭小湘. "Yi xie chu xue: Yixiang yingyu xiezuo jiaoxue gaige de shiyan" 以寫促學：一項英語寫作教學改革的試驗 [Improving English Learning through Writing: An Experiment in the Reform of English Writing Instruction]. *Waiyu jiaoxue yu yanjiu* 外語教學與研究 [Foreign Language Teaching and Research] 4 (2000): 43–49.

Wang Kaifu 王凱符, ed. *Baguwen gaishuo* 八股文概說 [An Introduction to Eight-Legged Essays]. Beijing: Zhonghua shuju, 2002.

Wang Lifei 王立非, and Zhang Zoucheng 張佐成, eds. *Yingyu xiezuo yanjiu: Zhongguo de shijiao yu shijian* 英語寫作研究：中國的視角與實踐 [EFL Writing Research: Chinese Perspectives and Practice]. Beijing: Waiyu jiaoxue yu yanjiu chubanshe, 2008.

Wang Peigen 王培根. "Shilun yingxiang dangqian daxue yingyu jiaoxue de fei zhengchang qingxiang" 試論影響當前大學英語教學的非正常傾向 [On the Abnormal Tendencies in the Current College English Teaching]. *Waiyu yu waiyu jiaoxue* 外語與外語教學 [Foreign Languages and Their Teaching] 5 (1998): 29–30.

Wang Rong 王蓉. "A Strategy of Saving the World." *2006 CCTV bei quanguo yingyu yanjiang dasai* 2006 CCTV 杯全國英語演講大賽 [2006 CCTV Cup English Speaking Contests]. Ed. Waiyu jiaoxue yu yanjiu chubanshe 外語教學與研究出版社. Beijing: Waiyu jiaoxue yu yanjiu chubanshe, 2007. 262.

Wang Wenyi, and Wen Qiufang. "L1 Use in the L2 Composing Process: An Exploratory Study of 16 Chinese EFL Writers." *Journal of Second Language Writing* 11 (2002): 225–46.

Wang Yi 王易. *Xiucixue* 修辭學 [Rhetoric]. Shanghai: Shangwu yinshuguan, 1926.

Wang Zhigan 王志剛. "Yingyu xiezuo lilun de xin fazhan" 英語寫作理論的新發展 [New Developments in English Writing Theories]. *Waiguoyu* 外國語 [Foreign Languages] 2 (1986): 73–77.

Wang Zongyan 王宗炎. "Liuge jiaoshi he yige yong di diaozi shuohua de ren" 六個教師和一個用低調子說話的人 [Six Teachers and One Who Spoke in a Low Tone]. Li and Liu 146–55.

Wang Zuoliang 王佐良. "Waiyu jiaoxue de juda chengjiu: Yige yingyu jiaoshi de tihui" 外語教學的巨大成就：一個英語教師的體會 [The Great Achievements of Foreign Language Teaching: An English Teacher's Perception]. *Waiyu jiaoxue yu yanjiu* 外語教學與研究 [Foreign Language Teaching and Research] 3.5 (1959): 257–66.

Ward, Charles H. *Theme-Building*. Chicago: Scott, Foresman, 1920.

Wei Yun, and Fei Jia. "Using English in China." *English Today* 19.4 (2003): 42–47.

West China Union University. *Catalogue*. Chengdu, 1915–37.

Widdowson, Henry G. *Teaching Language as Communication*. New York: Oxford UP, 1978.

Wong Kway-Sung. "The Great Chinese Garden in Shanghai." *St. John's Echo* 1.1 (1890): 3.

Woolf, Virginia. *A Room of One's Own*. Harcourt, Brace, 1929.

Woren 倭仁. "Da Tu Langxuan" 答塗朗軒 [Answering Tu Langxuan]. *Wo wenduan gong yishu* 倭文端公遺書 [The Bequeathed Works of Woren]. 2 vols. Taibei, 1968.

Wu Jinye 吳進業, and Qiao Xizhong 喬溪中. *Yingyu xiezuo jiaocheng* 英語寫作教程 [An English Writing Course]. Zhengzhou: Henan jiaoyu chubanshe, 1986.

Xiao Huiyun 蕭惠雲. "Zhua genben, jiu piancha: Jieshao CECL jiaocheng yu CECL jiaoxue" 抓根本，糾偏差：介紹CECL教程與CECL教學 [Grasping the Roots and Correcting Errors: Introducing CECL Textbook Series and the CECL Pedagogy]. *Xiandai waiyu* 現代外語 [Modern Foreign Languages] 3 (1987): 24–34.

Xiao Ji 驍驥. "Dui yingyu zhuanye gaonianji jingduke jiaoxue de yidian kanfa" 對英語專業高年級精讀課教學的一點看法 [Views on Teaching Intensive Reading to English Majors at the Advanced Stage]. *Waiyu jiaoxue yu yanjiu* 外語教學與研究 [Foreign Language Teaching and Research] 4 (1984): 59–63.

Xiao Xiaosui. "China Encounters Darwinism: A Case of Intercultural Rhetoric." *Quarterly Journal of Speech* 81 (1995): 83–99.

Xing Yongqing 邢永慶. *Gaokao chengbai zuowen bijiao yu pingxi* 高考成敗作文比較與評析 [A Comparative Analysis of Successful and Failed Compositions in College Entrance Exams]. Tianjing: Tianjing kexue jishu chubanshe, 2002.

Xu Daoxun 許道勳, and Xu Hongxing 徐洪興. *Zhongguo wenhua tongzhi (jingxue zhi)* 中國文化通志 (經學志) [A General Survey of Chinese Culture (Scholarship on the Classics)]. Shanghai: Shanghai renmin chubanshe, 1998.

Xu Guozhang 許國璋 et al. *Yingyu* 英語 [English]. Vols. 1–4. Beijing: Shangwu yinshuguan, 1982.

Xu Li 許莉, Wang Qi 王琦, and Yao Shuo'ang 姚朔昂. "Chengdu yi dasi nansheng yingyu siji wei guo tiaolou zisha" 成都一大四男生英語四級未過跳樓自殺 [A Senior College Student Committed Suicide by Jumping off a Building in Chengdu after Failing the College English Test Band-4]. 1 Mar. 2006. *Sichuan xinwen wang* 四川新聞網 [Sichun News Online]. 12 Mar. 2006 <http://scnews.newssc.org/system/2006/03/01/000059903.shtml>.

Xu Ming 許明, and Zheng Zhining 鄭志寧. *Yingyu xiezuo zhidao: Yufa yu xiuci* 英語寫作指導：語法與修辭 [A Guide to English Writing: Grammar and Rhetoric]. Changchun: Jilin jiaoyu chubanshe, 1986.

Xu Yanmou 徐燕謀 et al. *Yingyu* 英語 [English]. Vols. 7–8. Beijing: Shangwu yinshuguan, 1964.

Yan Binggang 顏炳罡. *Xin gui he chu: Rujia yu jidujiao zai jindai zhongguo* 心歸何處：儒家與基督教在近代中國 [Where Does the Soul Return?: Confucianism and Christianity in Modern China]. Jinan: Shandong renmin chubanshe, 2005.

Yang Huizhong 楊惠中, and C. Weir. *Daxue yingyu si liu ji kaoshi xiaodu yanjiu (xiezuo)* 大學英語四六級考試效度研究 (寫作) [Research on the Validity of College English Test Band-4 and 6 (the Writing Section)]. Shanghai: Shanghai waiyu jiaoyu chubanshe, 1998.

Yang Huizhong 楊惠中, Zheng Shutang 鄭樹棠, and Zhang Yanbin 張彥斌. *Daxue hexing yingyu: Duxie jiaocheng* 大學核心英語：讀寫教程 [College Core English: Reading and Writing]. Beijing: Gaodeng jiaoyu chubanshe, 1998.

Yang Xiahua 楊霞華. *Yingwen xiezuo yu xiuci* 英文寫作與修辭 [English Composition and Rhetoric]. Hefei: Anhui jiaoyu chubanshe, 1984.

Yang Xiaorong 楊曉榮. "Cong dajuan kan jiaoxue: TEM4–93 zuowen yuejuan shouji" 從答卷看教學：TEM4–93 作文閱卷手記 [A Discussion of Teaching from the Perspective of Examination: Notes on Grading the TEM-4 Writing Sections of 1993]. *Waiyu jiaoxue yu yanjiu* 外語教學與研究 [Foreign Language Teaching and Research] 4 (1993): 70–72.

Yao Enming 姚恩銘. "Xiaoxue zuowen jiaoshou fa" 小學作文教授法 [Composition Pedagogy for Primary School Students]. *Jiaoyu zazhi* 教育雜誌 [Chinese Educational Review] 7.6 (1915): 13–28.

Yeh, Wen-Hsin. *The Alienated Academy: Culture and Politics in Republican China, 1919–1937*. Cambridge, Mass.: Council on East Asian Studies and Harvard UP, 1990.

Ye Junjian 葉君健. "Xuexi waiyu he wo de wenxue chuangzuo" 學習外語和我的文學創作 [Foreign Language Learning and My Creative Writing]. Li and Liu 162–84.

Yenching University. *Announcement of Courses, 1936–1937*. Beijing, 1936.

———. *Announcement of Courses, 1947–1948*. Beijing, 1948.

———. *Faculty Directory, 1940–1941*. Beijing, 1940.

———, Students' Self-Government Association. *The Yanchinian, 1928–1929*. Beijing, 1928–29.

Ye Shaojun 葉紹君. *Zuowen lun* 作文論 [On Written Composition]. Shanghai: Shangwu yinshuguan, 1924.

Yetman, Michael. "China Days." Unpublished ms., 1982.

You, Xiaoye. "Globalization and the Politics of Teaching EFL Writing." Matsuda, Ortmeier-Hooper, and You 188–202.

———. "Ideology, Textbooks, and the Rhetoric of Production in China." *College Composition and Communication* 56.4 (2005): 632–53.

———. "New Directions in EFL Writing: A Report from China." *Journal of Second Language Writing* 13.4 (2004): 253–56.

Yuan Hui 袁輝, and Zong Tinghu 宗廷虎. *Hanyu xiucixue shi* 漢語修辭學史 [A History of Chinese Rhetorical Studies]. Taiyuan: Shanxi renmin chubanshe, 1995.

Yuan Shiyun. "Acquisition of a Better Writing Style (with Comparison and Contrast as Point of Departure)." *ELT in China: International Symposium on Teaching English in the Chinese Context (ISTEC), Guangzhou, China, 1985.* Ed. China English Language Educ. Assoc. Beijing: Foreign Language Teaching and Research, 1990. 344–55.

Yu Dayin 俞大絪 et al. *Yingyu* 英語 [English]. Vols. 5–6. Beijing: Shangwu yinshuguan, 1964.

Yu Jingxiang 于景祥. *Jinbang timing: Qingdai keju shuyao* 金榜題名：清代科舉述要 [Success in the Imperial Exams: Essentials of the Civil Service Exams in the Qing Dynasty]. Shenyang: Liaohai chubanshe, 1997.

Zamel, Vivian. "The Composing Processes of Advanced ESL Students: Six Case Studies." *TESOL Quarterly* 17 (1983): 165–87.

Zappen, James P. "Francis Bacon and the Historiography of Scientific Rhetoric." *Rhetoric Review* 8.1 (1989): 74–88.

———. "Scientific Rhetoric in the Nineteenth and Early Twentieth Centuries: Herbert Spencer, Thomas H. Huxley, and John Dewey." *Textual Dynamics of the Professions: Historical and Contemporary Studies of Writing in Professional Communities.* Ed. Charles Bazerman and James Paradis. Madison: U of Wisconsin P, 1991. 145–67.

Zavarzadeh, Mas'ud, and Donald Morton. *Theory as Resistance: Politics and Culture after (Post)structuralism.* New York: Guilford, 1994.

Zhang Yaoxue 張堯學. "Guanyu daxue benke gonggong yingyu jiaoxue gaige de zai sikao" 關於大學本科公共英語教學改革的再思考 [Reconsidering the Reform of College English Instruction]. 2003. 17 June, 2004 <http://www.edu.cn/20030804/3088972.shtml>.

Zhang Zhongzai 張中載. "Yong waiyu xiechu hao wenzhang" 用外語寫出好文章 [Writing Good Essays in a Foreign Language]. *Waiyu jiaoxue yu yanjiu* 外語教學與研究 [Foreign Language Teaching and Research] 2 (1981): 4–29.

Zhang Zuocheng 張佐成. "Zhongguo daxuesheng yingyu xiezuo xinli guocheng chutan" 中國大學生英語寫作心理過程初探 [An Initial Exploration on the Cognitive Aspect of Chinese College Students' Composing Process in English]. *Xiandai waiyu* 現代外語 [Modern Foreign Languages] 1 (1995): 27–31.

Zhao Yongqing 趙永青. "Cong yupian siwei moshi kan yingwen xiezuo jiaoxue" 從語篇思維模式看英文寫作教學 [A Discussion of English Writing Instruction in Light of Reasoning Patterns in Written Discourses]. *Xiandai waiyu* 現代外語 [Modern Foreign Languages] 2 (1995): 21–26.

Zhao Zhaoxiong 趙詔熊. "Dahao jichu buduan tigao" 打好基礎不斷提高 [Building a Solid Foundation and Making Constant Progress]. Chen Yilun 61–65.

Zheng Chao 鄭超. "Yi xie cu xue, rang xuesheng xie chu zixinxin he chengjiugan" 以寫促學，讓學生寫出自信心和成就感 [The Approach of Improving English Learning through Writing Fosters Students' Self-Confidence and Sense of Achievement]. *Guangdong waiyu waimao daxue xuebao* 廣東外語外貿大學學報 [Journal of Guangdong University of Foreign Studies] 13.4 (2002): 77–81.

———, ed. *Yi xie cu xue: Yingyu xiechangfa de linian yu caozuo* 以寫促學：英語"寫長法"的理念與操作 [Improving English Learning through Writing: Theory and Practice of the Length Approach]. Beijing: Kexue chubanshe, 2004.

Zheng Chao 鄭超 et al. *Yingyu xiezuo tongyong jiaocheng* 英語寫作通用教程 [A General Course of English Composition]. Beijing: Kexue chubanshe, 2008.

Zhonghua renmin gongheguo guojia tongjiju 中華人民共和國國家統計局 [National Bureau of Statistics of China]. *Quanguo renkou pucha gongbao* 全國人口普查公報 [National Census Reports]. 26 Sept. 2007 <http://www.stats.gov.cn/tjgb/rkpcgb/>.

Zhou Yulin 周玉林. "Guanyu wenti de sikao" 關於文體的思考 [Thoughts on the Modes]. *Jiangsu jiaoyu* 江蘇教育 [Jiangsu Education] 23 (2001): 22–25.

Zhu Binjie 褚斌傑. *Zhongguo gudai wenti gailun* 中國古代文體概論 [An Introduction to Genres in Ancient Chinese Writing]. Beijing: Beijing daxue chubanshe, 1984.

Zhu Dexi 朱德熙. *Zuowen zhidao* 作文指導 [Composition Guide]. Beijing: Kaiming chubanshe, 1951.

INDEX

accountability, 13, 117, 136, 138, 146, 171

aesthetics, 36, 50, 89, 130, 134

agency, 2, 18–19, 70, 90, 110–11, 179

Althusser, Louis, 6, 198n.6

Analects, 10–11, 18–20, 22, 25, 197n.2, 199n.7, 200n.14

Anderson, Elam J., 201n.17

Anglo-American teachers. *See under* teachers

antiquity, 17, 19–20, 26, 43, 56

appropriation, 2, 9, 21, 59, 62, 85, 166, 173

argumentation. *See* modes of discourse

Aristotle, 62, 89

arrangement. *See* organization

assessment, 75, 117, 138, 144–49, 162, 171; reliability, 147–48, 153; scoring, 147–48; standardized tests, 117, 138, 146; validity, 147–48, 153. *See also* exams

audience, 42, 52, 55, 59, 61–62, 64–65, 88, 91, 94, 99, 108, 121, 157, 160–61, 165, 172–73

Beijing Foreign Language Institute, 84, 94, 98–99, 107, 119

Beijing University, 30, 107–8, 123

Berlin, James, 36–37, 198n.4

Bhabha, Homi, 17, 160

Bizzell, Patricia, 173, 197n.1 (preface)

blending. *See* mixing

Britain, 5, 15, 39, 106, 120

British Council, 106–7

business, 7, 15, 29, 31, 73–74, 144, 154, 169, 177, 205n.6

Cai Jigang, 151–54

Campbell, George, 50, 52

Canagarajah, Suresh, 4, 176

Canton Christian College, 38, 60, 185

censorship, 17, 137, 156

Chen Lin, 84, 203n.7

Chen Wangdao, 52–53

Chinese Communist Party, 79, 89, 91–92, 105–6, 110, 132, 137, 161, 203n.2, 11, 205n.3, 206n.16; portrayed in student writings, 94–95, 114, 130, 140, 156

Chinese composition pedagogy. *See under* pedagogy

Chinese writing. *See under* writing

Christian College in China, 31, 185

Christian Educational Association of China, 202n.5

Christianity, 8, 16–17, 31, 38, 40, 56, 60, 66–69, 107–8, 173, 183

citation, 57–58, 121, 200n.11

classical Chinese rhetoric. *See under* rhetoric

College English Test. *See under* exams

colonialism, 1–6, 12, 15–16, 40, 45, 48, 68, 70–72, 88, 98, 101–2, 105, 107–8, 134–35, 144, 175–76

commenting, 25, 91, 120–21, 141, 164

communicative competence, 115–18, 135

Communicative English for Chinese Learners project, 126, 133, 163, 206n.15

communicative language teaching, 116, 125–27, 135

community, 8–9, 11, 19, 98, 118, 121, 166, 176, 178, 180

comparative rhetoric, 9–10

composing process, 55, 83, 162–63, 165

composition: advanced, 60, 74, 183, 189, 191–92; controlled, 74, 115, 147, 150; history, 11, 198n.4; oral, 35, 39, 76, 127, 183, 189; studies, xi–xii, 3–5, 11–13, 121, 162, 167, 175–80; transnational, xi–xii, 1–3, 5–9, 51, 61, 64, 72, 78, 82, 93, 97, 136–37, 154, 161, 175. *See also* writing

composition studies. *See under* composition

Xiaoye You is an assistant professor of English and Asian Studies at Penn State University, where he teaches courses in rhetoric, writing, and the teaching of writing. He is interested in comparative rhetoric and issues of multilingual writing. He has published articles in *College Composition and Communication, College English, Journal of Second Language Writing, Rhetoric Review, Rhetoric Society Quarterly,* and *World Englishes.* With Paul Kei Matsuda and Christina Ortmeier-Hooper, he coedited *The Politics of Second Language Writing: In Search of the Promised Land* (2006).